WILLIAM BLAKE

BY

ARTHUR SYMONS

COOPER SQUARE PUBLISHERS, INC.
NEW YORK
1970

TO

AUGUSTE RODIN

WHOSE WORK IS THE

MARRIAGE OF

HEAVEN AND HELL

Originally Published 1907
Published by Cooper Square Publishers, Inc.
59 Fourth Avenue, New York, N. Y. 10003
Standard Book Number 8154-0325-9
Library of Congress Catalog Card No. 79-115694

Printed in the United States of America

PREFACE

It was when Mr. Sampson's edition of Blake came into my hands in the winter of 1905 that the idea of writing a book on Blake first presented itself to me. From a boy he had been one of my favourite poets, and I had heard a great deal about him from Mr. Yeats as long ago as 1893, the year in which he and Mr. Ellis brought out their vast cyclopædia, *The Works of William Blake, Poetic, Symbolic, and Critical*. From that time to this Blake has never been out of my mind, but I have always hesitated to write down anything on a subject so great in itself, and already handled by great poets. Things have been written about Blake by Rossetti which no one will ever surpass; and in Mr. Swinburne's book Blake himself seems to speak again, as through the mouth of a herald. I read these, I read everything that had been written about him; gradually I got to know all his work, in all its kinds; and when I found, in Mr. Sampson's book, the rarest part of his genius, disentangled at last from the confusions of the commentators, I caught some impulse—was it from the careful enthusiasm of this editor, or perhaps straight from Blake?—and began to write down what now filled and overflowed my mind. Having begun on an impulse, I laid my plans as strictly as I could, and decided to make a book which would be, in its way, complete. There was to be, first, my own narrative, containing, as briefly as possible, every fact of importance, with my own interpretation of what I took to be Blake's achievements and intentions. But this was to be followed by a verbatim reprint of documents. These documents were the material of Gilchrist, but, even after Gilchrist's use of them, they remain of primary and undiminished im-

portance : they are the main evidence in
our case.

The documents which form the second
part of my book contain every personal
account of Blake which was printed during
his lifetime, and between the time of his
death and the publication of Gilchrist's *Life*
in 1863, together with the complete text
of every reference to Blake in the *Diary,
Letters, and Reminiscences* of Crabb Robinson, transcribed for the first time from the
original manuscripts. All these I have given
exactly as they stand, not correcting their
errors, for even errors have their value as
evidence. The only other document of the
period which exists was written by Frederick Tatham, within two years of the appearance of Cunningham's *Life*, and bound up
at the beginning of a coloured copy of Blake's
Jerusalem, now in the possession of Captain
Archibald Stirling. This manuscript was
consulted by Mr. Swinburne and afterwards
by Mr. Ellis and Mr. Yeats; but though
many extracts have been made from it, it

was printed for the first time by Mr. Archibald G. B. Russell in his edition of *The Letters of William Blake* (Methuen, 1906). This very important volume completes the task which I have here undertaken : the reprint of every record of Blake from contemporary sources.

The mere contact with Blake seems to awaken the natural generosity of those who have concerned themselves with him. To Mr. John Sampson, the editor of the only accurate edition of Blake's poems, I am indebted for more help and encouragement than I can hope to express in detail; and particularly for prompting me to a search among birth and marriage and death registers, by which I have been enabled to settle several disputed points of some interest. To Mr. A. G. B. Russell I owe constant personal help, and the very generous loan of the proofs of his edition of Blake's *Letters*, and of Tatham's *Life*, with free leave to use them in the narrative which I was writing at a time when his book had not yet appeared.

PREFACE

Through this favour I have been able to take such facts as Tatham is responsible for directly from Tatham, and not at second-hand. I am also indebted to Mr. Russell for reading my proofs and saving me from some errors of fact. I have to thank Mr. Buxton Forman for allowing me to read and describe the unpublished manuscript in Blake's handwriting in his possession. Finally, my particular thanks are due to the Librarian of Dr. Williams's Library, Mr. Francis H. Jones, for permission to copy and print the full text of all the references to Blake in the Crabb Robinson Manuscripts.

London, *April* 1907.

LIST OF BOOKS CONSULTED

1. *Life of William Blake.* By ALEXANDER GILCHRIST. Two volumes. Macmillan, 1863. New and enlarged edition, 1880.

2. *William Blake: A Critical Essay.* By ALGERNON CHARLES SWINBURNE. John Camden Hotten, 1868. New edition, Chatto & Windus, 1906.

3. *The Poetical Works of William Blake.* Edited by W. M. ROSSETTI. Aldine Edition. Bell & Sons, 1874.

4. *The Life and Letters of Samuel Palmer.* By A. H. Palmer. Seeley & Co., 1892.

5. *The Life of John Linnell.* By ALFRED T. STORY. Two volumes. Bentley, 1892.

6. *A Memoir of Edward Calvert.* By his third son [SAMUEL CALVERT]. S. Low & Co., 1893.

7. *The Works of William Blake: Poetic, Symbolic, and Critical.* Edited, with lithographs of the illustrated Prophetic Books, and a Memoir and Interpretation, by EDWIN JOHN ELLIS and WILLIAM

WILLIAM BLAKE

BUTLER YEATS. Three volumes. Quaritch,
1893.

8. *The Poems of William Blake.* Edited by W. B.
YEATS. 'The Muses' Library.' Lawrence &
Bullen, 1893.

9. *William Blake: his Life, Character, and Genius.*
By ALFRED T. STORY. Sonnenschein & Co.,
1893.

10. *William Blake: Painter and Poet.* By RICHARD
GARNETT. 'Portfolio,' 1895.

11. *Ideas of Good and Evil.* By W. B. YEATS.
(William Blake and the Imagination, William
Blake and his Illustrations to the Divine
Comedy.) A. H. Bullen, 1903.

12. *The Rossetti Papers* (1862 *to* 1870); a Compilation
by W. M. ROSSETTI. Sands & Co., 1903.

13. *The Prophetic Books of William Blake: Jerusalem.*
Edited by E. R. D. MACLAGAN and A. G. B.
RUSSELL. Bullen, 1904.

14. *The Poetical Works of William Blake.* Edited by
JOHN SAMPSON. Oxford, 1905.

15. *The Letters of William Blake;* together with a Life
by FREDERICK TATHAM. Edited by ARCHIBALD
G. B. RUSSELL. Methuen, 1906.

LIST OF BOOKS CONSULTED

16. *The Poetical Works of William Blake.* Edited and annotated by EDWIN J. ELLIS. Two volumes. Chatto & Windus, 1906. (The only edition containing the Prophetic Books.)

17. *William Blake.* Vol. I. Illustrations of the Book of Job, with a general Introduction by LAURENCE BINYON. Methuen, 1906.

18. *The Real Blake.* A Portrait Biography. By EDWIN J. ELLIS. Chatto & Windus, 1907.

CONTENTS

PART I

PART II

RECORDS FROM CONTEMPORARY SOURCES:

WILLIAM BLAKE

INTRODUCTION

I

WHEN Blake spoke the first word of the nineteenth century there was no one to hear it, and now that his message, the message of emancipation from reality through the 'shaping spirit of imagination,' has penetrated the world, and is slowly remaking it, few are conscious of the first utterer, in modern times, of the message with which all are familiar. Thought to-day, wherever it is most individual, owes either force or direction to Nietzsche, and thus we see, on our topmost towers, the Philistine armed and winged, and without the love or fear of God or man in his heart, doing battle in Nietzsche's name against the ideas of Nietzsche. No one can think, and escape Nietzsche; but Nietzsche has come after Blake, and will pass before Blake passes.

The Marriage of Heaven and Hell antici-

pates Nietzsche in his most significant para-
doxes, and, before his time, exalts energy
above reason, and Evil, 'the active springing
from energy' above Good, 'the passive that
obeys reason.' Did not Blake astonish
Crabb Robinson by declaring that 'there
was nothing in good and evil, the virtues
and vices'; that 'vices in the natural world
were the highest sublimities in the spiritual
world'? 'Man must become better and
wickeder,' says Nietzsche in *Zarathustra*;
and, elsewhere; 'Every man must find his
own virtue.' Sin, to Blake, is negation, is
nothing; 'everything is good in God's eyes';
it is the eating of the tree of the knowledge
of good and evil that has brought sin into
the world : education, that is, by which we
are taught to distinguish between things
that do not differ. When Nietzsche says :
'Let us rid the world of the notion of sin,
and banish with it the idea of punishment,'
he expresses one of Blake's central doctrines,
and he realises the corollary, which, however, he does not add. 'The Christian's
soul,' he says, 'which has freed itself from
sin is in most cases ruined by the hatred
against sin. Look at the faces of great

Christians. They are the faces of great
haters.' Blake sums up all Christianity as
forgiveness of sin :

'Mutual forgiveness of each vice,
Such are the gates of Paradise.'

The doctrine of the Atonement was to him
a 'horrible doctrine,' because it seemed to
make God a hard creditor, from whom pity
could be bought for a price. ' Doth Jehovah
forgive a debt only on condition that it shall
be paid? . . . That debt is not forgiven!'
he says in *Jerusalem.* To Nietzsche, far as
he goes on the same road, pity is 'a weakness, which increases the world's suffering';
but to Blake, in the spirit of the French
proverb, forgiveness is understanding. 'This
forgiveness,' says Mr. Yeats, 'was not the
forgiveness of the theologian who has
received a commandment from afar off,
but of the poet and artist, who believes
he has been taught, in a mystical vision,
"that the imagination is the man himself,"
and believes he has discovered in the
practice of his art that without a perfect
sympathy there is no perfect imagination,
and therefore no perfect life.' He trusted

the passions, because they were alive; and,
like Nietzsche, hated asceticism, because

'Abstinence sows sand all over
The ruddy limbs and flaming hair,
But desire gratified
Plants fruits of life and beauty there.'

'Put off holiness,' he said, 'and put on intellect.' And 'the fool shall not enter into
heaven, let him be ever so holy.' Is not
this a heaven after the heart of Nietzsche?
Nietzsche is a Spinoza à rebours. The
essence of the individual, says Spinoza, 'is
the effort by which it endeavours to persevere in its own being.' 'Will and understanding are one and the same.' 'By virtue
and power I understand the same thing.'
'The effort to understand is the first and
sole basis of virtue.' So far it might be
Nietzsche who is speaking. Only, in Spinoza,
this affirmation of will, persistent egoism,
power, hard understanding, leads to a conclusion which is far enough from the conclusion of Neitzsche. 'The absolute virtue
of the mind is to understand; its highest
virtue, therefore, to understand or know
God.' That, to Nietzsche, is one of 'the
beautiful words by which the conscience is

lulled to sleep.' 'Virtue is power,' Spinoza, leads us to think, because it is virtue; 'power is virtue,' affirms Nietzsche, because it is power. And in Spinoza's profound heroism of the mind, really a great humility, 'he who loves God does not desire that God should love him in return,' Nietzsche would find the material for a kind of desperate heroism, made up wholly of pride and defiance.

To Blake, 'God-intoxicated' more than Spinoza, 'God only acts and is, in existing beings and men,' as Spinoza might also have said; to him, as to Spinoza, all moral virtue is identical with understanding, and 'men are admitted into heaven, not because they have curbed and governed their passions, but because they have cultivated their understandings.' Yet to Blake Spinoza's mathematical approach to truth would have been a kind of negation. Even an argument from reason seemed to him atheistical : to one who had truth, as he was assured, within him, reason was only 'the bound or outward circumference of energy,' but 'energy is the only life,' and, as to Nietzsche, is 'eternal delight.'

Yet, to Nietzsche, with his strange, scientific distrust of the imagination, of those who so 'suspiciously' say 'We see what others do not see,' there comes distrust, hesitation, a kind of despair, precisely at the point where Blake enters into his liberty. 'The habits of our senses,' says Nietzsche, 'have plunged us into the lies and deceptions of feeling.' 'Whoever believes in nature,' says Blake, 'disbelieves in God; for nature is the work of the Devil.' 'These again,' Nietzsche goes on, 'are the foundations of all our judgments and "knowledge," there is no escape whatever, no back-way or by-way into the real world.' But the real world, to Blake, into which he can escape at every moment, is the world of imagination, from which messengers come to him, daily and nightly.

Blake said 'The tigers of wrath are wiser than the horses of instruction,' and it is partly in what they helped to destroy that Blake and Nietzsche are at one; but destruction, with Blake, was the gesture of a hand which brushes aside needless hindrances, while to Nietzsche it was 'an intellectual thing,' the outer militant part of 'the silent, self-sufficient man in the midst of a general enslavement, who practises self-defence against the outside world, and is constantly living in a state of supreme fortitude.' Blake rejoins Nietzsche as he had rejoined Spinoza, by a different road, having fewer devils to cast out, and no difficulty at all in maintaining his spiritual isolation, his mental liberty, under all circumstances. And to Blake, to be 'myself alone, shut up in myself,' was to be in no merely individual but in a universal world, that world of imagination whose gates seemed to him to be open to every human being. No less than Nietzsche he says to every man : Be yourself, nothing else matters or exists; but to be myself, to him, was to enter by the imagination into eternity.

The philosophy of Nietzsche was made out of his nerves and was suffering, but to Blake it entered like sunlight into the eyes. Nietzsche's mind is the most sleepless of minds; with him every sensation turns instantly into the stuff of thought; he is terribly alert, the more so because he never stops to systematise; he must be for ever apprehending. He darts out feelers in every direction, relentlessly touching the whole substance of the world. His apprehension is minute rather than broad; he is content to seize one thing at a time, and he is content if each separate thing remains separate; no theory ties together or limits his individual intuitions. What we call his philosophy is really no more than the aggregate of these intuitions coming to us through the medium of a remarkable personality. His personality stands to him in the place of a system. Speaking of Kant and Schopenhauer, he says : 'Their thoughts do not constitute a passionate history of the soul.' His thoughts are the passionate history of his soul. It is for this reason that he is an artist among philosophers rather than a pure philosopher. And remember that he is also not, in the absolute sense, the poet, but the artist. He saw and dreaded the weaknesses of the artist, his side-issues in the pursuit of truth. But in so doing he dreaded one of his own weaknesses.

Blake, on the other hand, receives nothing through his sensations, suffers nothing through his nerves. 'I know of no other

Christianity,' he says, 'and of no other
Gospel than the liberty both of body and
mind to exercise the divine arts of Imagination : Imagination, the real and eternal
world of which this vegetable universe is
but a faint shadow, and in which we shall
live in our eternal or imaginative bodies,
when these vegetable mortal bodies are no
more.' To Nietzsche the sense of a divine
haunting became too heavy a burden for
his somewhat inhuman solitude, the solitude
of Alpine regions, with their steadfast
glitter, their thin, high, intoxicating air.
'Is this obtrusiveness of heaven,' he cries,
'this inevitable superhuman neighbour, not
enough to drive one mad?' But Blake,
when he says, 'I am under the direction
of messengers from heaven, daily and
nightly,' speaks out of natural joy, which
is wholly humility, and it is only 'if we
fear to do the dictates of our angels, and
tremble at the tasks set before us,' it is only
then that he dreads, as the one punishment,
that 'every one in eternity will leave him.'

II

'THERE are three powers in man of conversing with Paradise,' said Blake, and he defined them as the three sons of Noah who survived the flood, and who are Poetry, Painting, and Music. Through all three powers, and to the last moments of his life on earth, Blake conversed with Paradise. We are told that he used to sing his own songs to his own music, and that, when he was dying, 'he composed and uttered songs to his Maker,' and 'burst out into singing of the things he saw in heaven.' And with almost the last strength of his hands he had made a sketch of his wife before he 'made the rafters ring,' as a bystander records, with the improvisation of his last breath.

Throughout life his desire had been, as he said, 'to converse with my friends in eternity, see visions, dream dreams, and prophesy and speak parables unobserved.' He says again :

'I rest not from my great task
To open the eternal worlds, to open the immortal
eyes

Of Man inwards into the worlds of thought, into
    eternity,
Ever expanding in the bosom of God, the human
    imagination.'

And, writing to the uncomprehending Hayley
(who had called him 'gentle, visionary Blake'),
he says again : ' I am really drunk with
intellectual vision whenever I take a pencil
or graver into my hand.' To the news-
papers of his time, on the one or two
occasions when they mentioned his name,
he was ' an unfortunate lunatic '; even to
Lamb, who looked upon him as ' one of the
most extraordinary persons of the age,' he
was a man ' flown, whither I know not—
to Hades or a madhouse.' To the first
editor of his collected poems there seemed
to be ' something in his mind not exactly
sane '; and the critics of to-day still discuss
his sanity as a man and as a poet.

It is true that Blake was abnormal ; but
what was abnormal in him was his sanity.
To one who believed that ' The ruins of
Time build mansions in eternity,' that
' imagination is eternity,' and that ' our
deceased friends are more really with us
than when they were apparent to our mortal

part,' there could be none of that confusion
at the edge of mystery which makes a man
mad because he is unconscious of the gulf.
No one was ever more conscious than Blake
was of the limits of that region which we
call reality and of that other region which
we call imagination. It pleased him to
reject the one and to dwell in the other,
and his choice was not the choice of most
men, but of some of those who have been
the greatest saints and the greatest artists.
And, like the most authentic among them,
he walked firmly among those realities to
which he cared to give no more than a side-
glance from time to time; he lived his own
life quietly and rationally, doing always
exactly what he wanted to do, and with so
fine a sense of the subtlety of mere worldly
manners, than when, at his one moment of
worldly success, in 1793, he refused the post
of drawing-master to the royal family, he
gave up all his other pupils at the same
time, lest the refusal should seem ungracious
on the part of one who had been the friend
of revolutionaries. He saw visions, but not
as the spiritualists and the magicians have
seen them. These desire to quicken mortal

sight until the soul limits itself again, takes body, and returns to reality ; but Blake, the inner mystic, desired only to quicken that imagination which he knew to be more real than the reality of nature. Why should he call up shadows when he could talk in the spirit with spiritual realities ? 'Then I asked,' he says in *The Marriage of Heaven and Hell*, 'does a firm persuasion that a thing is so, make it so ?' He replied, "All poets believe that it does."'

In the *Descriptive Catalogue* to his exhibition of pictures in 1809, Blake defines, more precisely than in any other place, what vision was to him. He is speaking of his pictures, but it is a plea for the raising of painting to the same 'sphere of invention and visionary conception' as that which poetry and music inhabit. 'The Prophets,' he says, 'describe what they saw in vision as real and existing men, whom they saw with their imaginative and immortal organs ; the Apostles the same ; the clearer the organ, the more distinct the object. A spirit and a vision are not, as the modern philosophy supposes, a cloudy vapour, or a nothing. They are organised and minutely

articulated beyond all that the mortal and
perishing nature can produce.   He who does
not imagine in stronger and better lineaments and in stronger and better light than
his perishing and mortal eye can see, does
not imagine at all.   The painter of this work
asserts that all his imaginations appear to
him infinitely more perfect and more minutely
organised than anything seen by his mortal
eye.'   'Inspiration and vision,' he says in
one of the marginal notes to Reynolds's *Discourses*, 'was then, and now is, and I hope
will always remain, my element, my eternal
dwelling-place.'   And 'God forbid,' he says
also, 'that Truth should be confined to
mathematical demonstration.   He who does
not know Truth at sight is not worthy of
her notice.'

The mind of Blake lay open to eternity as
a seed-plot lies open to the sower.   In 1802
he writes to Mr. Butts from Felpham : 'I am
not ashamed, afraid, or averse to tell you
what ought to be told—that I am under the
direction of messengers from heaven, daily
and nightly.'   'I have written this poem,'
he says of the *Jerusalem*, 'from immediate
dictation, twelve or sometimes twenty or

thirty lines at a time, without premeditation, and even against my will.' 'I may praise it,' he says in another letter, 'since I dare not pretend to be any other than the secretary; the authors are in eternity.' In these words, the most precise claim for direct inspiration which Blake ever made, there is nothing different in kind, only in degree, from what must be felt by every really creative artist and by every profoundly and simply religious person. There can hardly be a poet who is not conscious of how little his own highest powers are under his own control. The creation of beauty is the end of art, but the artist should rarely admit to himself that such is his purpose. A poem is not written by the man who says: I will sit down and write a poem; but rather by the man who, captured by rather than capturing an impulse, hears a tune which he does not recognise, or sees a sight which he does not remember, in some 'close corner of his brain,' and exerts the only energy at his disposal in recording it faithfully, in the medium of his particular art. And so in every creation of beauty, some obscure desire stirred in the soul, not realised by the mind for what it was, and, aiming at most other things in the world than pure beauty, produced it. Now, to the critic this is not more important to remember than it is for him to remember that the result, the end, must be judged, not by the impulse which brought it into being, nor by the purpose which it sought to serve, but by its success or failure in one thing : the creation of beauty. To the artist himself this precise consciousness of what he has done is not always given, any more than a precise consciousness of what he is doing. Only in the greatest do we find vision and the correction of vision equally powerful and equally constant.

To Blake, as to some artists and to most devout people, there was nothing in vision to correct, nothing even to modify. His language in all his letters and in much of his printed work is identical with the language used by the followers of Wesley and Whitefield at the time in which he was writing. In Wesley's journal you will find the same simple and immediate consciousness of the communion of the soul with the world of spiritual reality : not a vague longing, like

Shelley's, for a principle of intellectual beauty, nor an unattained desire after holiness, like that of the conventionally religious person, but a literal 'power of conversing with Paradise,' as Blake called it, and as many Methodists would have been equally content to call it. And in Blake, as in those whom the people of that age called 'enthusiasts' (that word of reproach in the eighteenth century and of honour in all other centuries), there was no confusion (except in brains where 'true superstition,' as Blake said, was 'ignorant honesty, and this is beloved of God and man') between the realities of daylight and these other realities from the other side of day. Messrs. Ellis and Yeats quote a mysterious note written in Blake's handwriting, with a reference to Spurzheim, page 154. I find that this means Spurzheim's *Observations on the Deranged Manifestations of the Mind, or Insanity* (1817), and the passage in the text is as follows: 'Religion is another fertile cause of insanity. Mr. Haslam, though he declares it sinful to consider religion as a cause of insanity, adds, however, that he would be ungrateful, did he not avow his

obligations to Methodism for its supply of
numerous cases.   Hence the primitive feelings of religion may be misled and produce
insanity ; that is what I would contend for,
and in that sense religion often leads to
insanity.'   Blake has written : 'Methodism,
etc., p. 154.   Cowper came to me and said :
"Oh! that I were insane, always.   I will
never rest.   Can not you make me truly
insane ?   I will never rest till I am so.
Oh ! that in the bosom of God I was hid.
You retain health and yet are mad as any of
us all—over us all—mad as a refuge from
unbelief—from Bacon, Newton, and Locke."'
What does this mean but that 'madness,'
the madness of belief in spiritual things,
must be complete if it is to be effectual, and
that, once complete, there is no disturbance
of bodily or mental health, as in the doubting and distracted Cowper, who was driven
mad, not by the wildness of his belief, but
by the hesitations of his doubt ?

Attempts have been made to claim Blake
for an adept of magic.   But whatever cab-
balistical terms he may have added to the
somewhat composite and fortuitous naming
of his mythology ('all but names of persons

and places,' he says, 'is invention, both in
poetry and painting'), his whole mental attitude was opposed to that of the practisers
of magic. We have no record of his ever
having evoked a vision, but only of his
accepting or enduring visions. Blake was,
above all, spontaneous : the practiser of
magic is a deliberate craftsman in the art
of the soul. I can no more imagine Blake
sitting down to juggle with symbols or to
gaze into a pool of ink than I can imagine
him searching out words that would make
the best effects in his lyrics, or fishing for
inspiration, pen in hand, in his own ink-pot.
A man does not beg at the gate of dreams
when he is the master for whose entrance
the gate stands open.

Of the definite reality of Blake's visions
there can be no question ; no question that,
as he once wrote, 'nothing can withstand
the fury of my course among the stars of
God, and in the abysses of the accuser.'
But imagination is not one, but manifold ;
and the metaphor, professing to be no more
than metaphor, of the poet, may be vision
as essential as the thing actually seen by
the visionary. The difference between im-

agination in Blake and in, say, Shakespeare, is that the one (himself a painter) has a visual imagination and sees an image or metaphor as a literal reality, while the other, seeing it not less vividly but in a more purely mental way, adds a 'like' or an 'as,' and the image or metaphor comes to you with its apology or attenuation, and takes you less by surprise. But to Blake it was the universe that was a metaphor.

WILLIAM BLAKE

I

THE origin of the family of William Blake has not yet been found ; and I can claim no more for the evidence that I have been able to gather than that it settles us more firmly in our ignorance. But the names of his brothers and sister, their dates and order of birth, and the date of his wife's birth, have never, so far as I know, been correctly given. Even the date of his own birth has been contested by Mr. Swinburne 'on good MS. authority,' which we know to be that of Frederick Tatham, who further asserts, wrongly, that James was younger than William, and that John was 'the eldest son.' Gilchrist makes no reference to John, but says, wrongly, that James was 'a year and a half William's senior,' and that William had a sister 'nearly seven years younger than himself'; of whom, says Mr. Yeats,

'we hear little, and among that little not
even her name.' Most of these problems
can be settled by the entries in parish registers, and I have begun with the registers
of the church of St. James, Westminster.

I find by these entries that James Blake,
the son of James and Catherine Blake, was
born July 10, and christened July 15,
1753; John Blake ('son of John and Catherine,' says the register, by what is probably
a slip of the pen) was born May 12, and
christened June 1, 1755; William Blake
was born November 28, and christened
December 11, 1757; another John Blake
was born March 20, and christened March
30, 1760; Richard Blake was born June
19, and christened July 11, 1762; and
Catherine Elizabeth Blake was born January
7, and christened January 28, 1764. Here,
where we find the daughter's name and the
due order of births, we find one perplexity
in the name of Richard, whose date of birth
fits the date given by Gilchrist and others
to Robert, William's favourite brother,
whose name he has engraved on a design
of his 'spiritual form' in *Milton*, whom he
calls Robert in a letter to Butts, and whom

J. T. Smith recalls not only as Robert, but as 'Bob, as he was familiarly called.' In the entry of 'John, son of John and Catherine Blake,' I can easily imagine the clerk repeating by accident the name of the son for the name of the father; and I am inclined to suppose that there was a John who died before the age of five, and that his name was given to the son next born. Precisely the same repetition of name is found in the case of Lamb's two sisters christened Elizabeth, and Shelley's two sisters christened Helen. 'My brother John, the evil one,' would therefore be younger than William; but Tatham, in saying that he was older, may have been misled by there having been two sons christened John.

There are two theories as to the origin of Blake's family; but neither of them has yet been confirmed by the slightest documentary evidence. Both of these theories were put forth in the same year, 1893, one by Mr. Alfred T. Story in his *William Blake*, the other by Messrs. Ellis and Yeats in their *Works of William Blake*. According to Mr. Story, Blake's family was connected with the Somerset family of the Admiral, through a Wiltshire family of Blakes; but for this theory he gives merely the report of 'two ladies, daughters of William John Blake, of Southampton, who claim to be second cousins of William Blake,' and in a private letter he tells me that he has not been able to procure any documentary evidence of the statement. According to Messrs. Ellis and Yeats, Blake's father was Irish, and was originally called O'Neil. His father, John O'Neil, is supposed to have changed his name, on marrying Ellen Blake, from O'Neil to Blake, and James O'Neil, his son by a previous union, to have taken the same name, and to have settled in London, while a younger son, the actual son of Ellen Blake, went to Malaga. This statement rests entirely on the assertion of Dr. Carter Blake, who claimed descent from the latter; and it has never been supported by documentary evidence. In answer to my inquiry, Mr. Martin J. Blake, the compiler of two volumes of *Blake Family Records* (first series, 1300-1600; second series, 1600-1700), writes : 'Although I have made a special study of the genealogies of the Blakes of Ireland, I have not come across any Ellen Blake who married John O'Neil who afterwards (as is said by Messrs. Ellis and Yeats) adopted the surname of Blake.'

Mr. Sampson points out that Blake's father was certainly a Protestant. He is sometimes described as a Swedenborgian, always as a Dissenter, and it is curious that about half of the Blakes recorded in the *Dictionary of National Biography* were also conspicuous as Puritans or Dissenters. Mr. Sampson further points out that Blake in one of his poems speaks of himself as 'English Blake.' It is true that he is contrasting himself with the German Klopstock; yet I scarcely think an Irishman would have used the expression even for contrast. Blake is nowhere referred to as having been in any way Irish, and the only apparent exception to this is one which I am obliged to set up with one hand and knock down with the other. In the index to Crabb Robinson's *Diary* one of the references to Blake shows us Mr. Sheil speaking at the Academical Society while 'Blake, his countryman, kept watching him to keep

him in order.' That this does not refer to
William Blake I have found by tracking
through the unpublished portions of the
Diary in the original manuscript the
numerous references to 'a Mr. Blake' who
was accustomed to speak at the meetings
of the Academical Society. He is described
as 'a Mr. Blake who spoke with good sense
on the Irish side, and argued from the Irish
History and the circumstances which attended the passing of the bills.' He afterwards speaks 'sharply and coarsely,' and
answers Mr. Robinson's hour-long contention that the House of Commons should, or
should not, 'possess the power of imprison-
ing for a breach of privilege,' by 'opposing
the facts of Lord Melville's prosecution, the
Reversion Bill, etc., etc., and Burke's Re-
form Bill'; returning, in short, 'my civility
by incivility.' This was not the learning, nor were these the manners, of William
Blake.

I would again appeal to the evidence of
the parish register. I find Blakes in the
parish of St. James, Westminster, from
the beginning of the eighteenth century, the
first being a William Blake, the son of

Richard and Elizabeth, who was born
March 19, 1700. Between the years 1750
and 1767 (the time exactly parallel with the
births of the family of James and Catherine
Blake) I find among the baptisms the names
of Frances, Daniel, Reuben, John Cartwright,
and William (another William) Blake; and
I find among the marriages, between 1728
and 1747, a Robert, a Thomas, a James, and
a Richard Blake. The wife of James, who
was married on April 15, 1738, is called
Elizabeth, a name which we have already
found as the name of a Mrs. Blake, and
which we find again as the second name of
Catherine Elizabeth Blake (the sister of
William Blake), who was born in 1764.
I find two Williams, two Richards, and a
John among the early entries, at the beginning of the eighteenth century. It is impossible to say positively that any of these
families, not less than nine in number, all
bearing the name of Blake, all living in the
same parish, within a space of less than
forty years, were related to one another;
but it is easier to suppose so than to suppose
that one only out of the number, and one
which had assumed the name, should have

found itself accidentally in the midst of all the others, to which the name may be supposed to have more definitely belonged.

All that we know with certainty of James Blake, the father, is that he was a hosier ('of respectable trade and easy habits,' says Tatham; 'of fifty years' standing,' says Cunningham, at the time of his death), that he was a Dissenter (a Swedenborgian, or inclined to Swedenborgianism), and that he died in 1784 and was buried on July 4 in Bunhill Fields. The burial register says : 'July 4, 1784. Mr. James Blake from Soho Square in a grave, 13/6.' Of his wife Catherine all that we know is that she died in 1792, and was also buried in Bunhill Fields. The register says : 'Sept. 9, 1792. Catherine Blake; age 70; brought from St. James, Westminster. Grave 9 feet; E. & W. 16; N. & S. 42-43. 19/-.' Tatham says that 'even when a child, his mother beat him for running and saying that he saw the prophet Ezekiel under a tree in the fields.' At eight or ten he comes home from Peckham Rye saying that he has seen a tree filled with angels; and his father is going to beat him for telling a lie; but his mother

intercedes. It was the father, Tatham
says, who, noticing to what great anger
he was moved by a blow, decided not to
send him to school.

The eldest son, James, Tatham tells us,
'having a saving, somniferous mind, lived a
yard and a half life, and pestered his brother
with timid sentences of bread and cheese
advice.' On his father's death in 1784 he
carried on the business, and it was at his
house that Blake held his one exhibition of
pictures in 1809. 'These paintings filled
several rooms of an ordinary dwelling-house,'
says Crabb Robinson in his *Reminiscences*;
and, telling how he had bought four copies
of the catalogue, 'giving 10/-, I bargained
that I should be at liberty to go again.
"Free! as long as you live!" said the
brother, astonished at such a liberality, which
he had never experienced before nor I dare
say did afterwards.' Crabb Robinson had
at first written 'as long as you like,' and this
he altered into 'as long as you live,' as if
fancying, so long afterwards as 1852, that
he remembered the exact word; but in the
entry in the *Diary*, in 1810, we read 'Oh!
as often as you please!' so that we may

doubt whether the 'honest, unpretending shopkeeper,' who was looked upon by his neighbours, we are told, as 'a bit mad,' because he would 'talk Swedenborg,' can be credited with all the enthusiasm of the later and more familiar reading. James and William no longer spoke to one another when, after retiring from business, James came to live in Cirencester Street, near Linnell. Tatham tells us that 'he got together a little annuity, upon which he supported his only sister, and vegetating to a moderate age, died about three years before his brother William.'

Of John we know only that he was something of a scapegrace and the favourite son of his parents. He was apprenticed, at some cost, to a candle-maker, but ran away, and, after some help from William, enlisted in the army, lived wildly, and died young. Robert, the favourite of William, also died young, at the age of twenty-five. He lived with William and Catherine from 1784 to the time of his death in 1787, at 27 Broad Street, helping in the print-shop of 'Parker and Blake,' and learning from his brother to draw and engrave. One of his original

sketches, a stiff drawing of long, rigid,
bearded figures staring in terror, quite in
his brother's manner, is in the Print Room
of the British Museum. A story is told of
him by Gilchrist which gives us the whole
man, indeed the whole household, in brief.
There had been a dispute between him and
Mrs. Blake. Blake suddenly interposed,
and said to his wife : 'Kneel down and beg
Robert's pardon directly, or you will never
see my face again.' She knelt down (thinking it, as she said afterwards, 'very hard,'
for she felt herself to be in the right) and
said : 'Robert, I beg your pardon ; I am in
the wrong.' 'Young woman, you lie,' said
Robert, 'I am in the wrong.'

Early in 1787 Robert fell ill, and during
the last fortnight William nursed him without taking rest by day or night, until, at
the moment of death, he saw his brother's
soul rise through the ceiling 'clapping its
hands for joy'; whereupon he went to
bed and slept for three days and nights.
Robert was buried in Bunhill Fields
on February 11. The register says :
"Feb. 11, 1787. Mr. Robert Blake from
Golden Square in a grave, 13/6.' But his

spiritual presence was never to leave the
mind of William Blake, whom in 1800 we
find writing to Hayley : 'Thirteen years ago
I lost a brother, and with his spirit I converse daily and hourly in the spirit, and see
him in remembrance, in the regions of my
imagination. I hear his advice, and even
now write from his dictate.' It was Robert
whom he saw in a dream, not long after his
death, telling him the method by which he
was to engrave his poems and designs. The
spiritual forms of William and of Robert, in
almost exact parallel, are engraved on separate pages of the Prophetic Book of *Milton*.

Of the sister, Catherine Elizabeth, we
know only that she lived with Blake and
his wife at Felpham. He refers to her in
several letters, and in the poem sent to
Butts on October 2, 1800, he speaks of her
as 'my sister and friend.' In another poem,
sent to Butts in a letter dated November
22, 1802, but written, he explains, 'above
a twelvemonth ago, while walking from
Felpham to Lavant to meet my sister,' he
asks strangely :

> 'Must my wife live in my sister's bane,
>   Or my sister survive on my Love's pain ? '

but from the context it is not clear whether this is meant literally or figuratively. When Tatham was writing his life of Blake, apparently in the year 1831, he refers to ' Miss Catherine' as still living, 'having survived nearly all her relations.' Mrs. Gilchrist, in a letter written to Mr. W. M. Rossetti in 1862, reports a rumour, for which she gives no evidence, that 'she and Mrs. Blake got on very ill together, and latterly never met at all,' and that she died in extreme penury.

II

OF the childhood and youth of Blake we
know little beyond what Malkin and Smith
have to tell us. From the age of ten to the
age of fourteen he studied at Pars' drawing-
school in the Strand, buying for himself
prints after Raphael, Dürer, and Michelangelo at tne sale-rooms; at fourteen he
was apprenticed to Basire, the engraver,
who lived at 31 Great Queen Street, and
in his shop Blake once saw Goldsmith.
'His love for art increasing,' says Tatham,
' and the time of life having arrived when
it was deemed necessary to place him under
some tutor, a painter of eminence was
proposed, and necessary applications were
made ; but from the huge premium required,
he requested, with his characteristic generosity, that his father would not on any
account spend so much money on him, as
he thought it would be an injustice to his

brothers and sisters. He therefore himself
proposed engraving as being less expensive,
and sufficiently eligible for his future avoca-
tions. Of Basire, therefore, for a premium
of fifty guineas, he learnt the art of engraving.' We are told that he was apprenticed,
at his own request, to Basire rather than to
the more famous Ryland, the engraver to
the king, because, on being taken by his
father to Ryland's studio, he said : 'I do
not like the man's face : it looks as if he
will live to be hanged.' Twelve years later
Ryland was hanged for forgery.

Blake was with Basire for seven years,
and for the last five years much of his time
was spent in making drawings of Gothic
monuments, chiefly in Westminster Abbey,
until he came, says Malkin, to be 'himself
almost a Gothic monument.' Tatham tells
us that the reason of his being 'sent out
drawing,' as he fortunately was, instead of
being kept at engraving, was 'for the circumstance of his having frequent quarrels
with his fellow - apprentices concerning
matters of intellectual argument.'

It was in the Abbey that he had a vision
of Christ and the Apostles, and in the

Abbey, too, that he flung an intrusive Westminster schoolboy from the scaffolding, 'in the impetuosity of his anger, worn out with interruption,' says Tatham, and then laid a complaint before the Dean which has caused, to this day, the exclusion of Westminster schoolboys from the precincts.

It was at this time that Blake must have written the larger part of the poems contained in the *Poetical Sketches*, printed (we cannot say published) in 1783, for in the 'Advertisement' at the beginning of the book we are told that the 'following Sketches were the production of untutored youth, commenced in his twelfth, and occasionally resumed by the author till his twentieth year,' that is to say, between the years 1768 and 1777. The earliest were written while Goldsmith and Gray were still living, the latest (if we may believe these dates) after Chatterton's death, but before his poems had been published. Ossian had appeared in 1760, Percy's *Reliques* in 1765. The *Reliques* probably had their influence on Blake, Ossian certainly, an influence which returns much later, curiously mingled with the influence of Milton, in the form taken by the Prophetic Books. It has been suggested that some of Blake's mystical names, and his 'fiend in a cloud,' came from Ossian ; and Ossian is very evident in the metrical prose of such pieces as 'Samson,' and even in some of the imagery ('Their helmed youth and aged warriors in dust together lie, and Desolation spreads his wings over the land of Palestine'). But the influence of Chatterton seems not less evident, an influence which could hardly have found its way to Blake before the year 1777. In the fifth chapter of the fantastic *Island in the Moon* (probably written about 1784) there is a long discussion on Chatterton, while in the seventh chapter he is again discussed in company with Homer, Shakespeare, and Milton. As late as 1826 Blake wrote on the margin of Wordsworth's preface to the *Lyrical Ballads* : 'I believe both Macpherson and Chatterton that what they say is ancient is so,' and on another page, 'I own myself an admirer of Ossian equally with any poet whatever, of Rowley and Chatterton also.' Whether it be influence or affinity, it is hard to say, but if the 'Mad Song' of Blake has the hint of any predecessor in our literature, it is to be found in the abrupt energy and stormy masculine splendour of the High Priest's song in 'Aella,' 'Ye who hie yn mokie ayre'; and if, between the time of the Elizabethans and the time of 'My silks and fine array' there had been any other song of similar technique and similar imaginative temper, it was certainly the Minstrel's song in 'Aella,' 'O! synge untoe mie roundelaie.'

Of the direct and very evident influence of the Elizabethans we are told by Malkin, with his quaint preciseness : 'Shakespeare's *Venus and Adonis, Tarquin and Lucrece*, and his *Sonnets* . . . poems, now little read, were favourite studies of Mr. Blake's early days. So were Jonson's *Underwoods* and his *Miscellanies.*' 'My silks and fine array' goes past Jonson, and reaches Fletcher, if not Shakespeare himself. And the blank verse of 'King Edward the Third' goes straight to Shakespeare for its cadence, and for something of its manner of speech. And there is other blank verse which, among much not even metrically correct, anticipates something of the richness of Keats.

Some rags of his time did indeed cling

about him, but only by the edges ; there is
even a reflected ghost of the pseudo-Gothic
of Walpole in 'Fair Elenor,' who comes
straight from the *Castle of Otranto*, as
'Gwin, King of Norway,' takes after the
Scandinavian fashion of the day, and may
have been inspired by ' The Fatal Sisters' or
' The Triumphs of Owen' of Gray. 'Blind-
man's Buff,' too, is a piece of eighteenth-
century burlesque realism.   But it is in
the ode ' To the Muses' that Blake for
once accepts, and in so doing clarifies, the
smooth convention of eighteenth - century
classicism, and, as he reproaches it in its
own speech, illuminates it suddenly with
the light it had rejected :

> ' How have you left the ancient love
>   That bards of old enjoyed in you !
> The languid strings do scarcely move,
>   The sound is forced, the notes are few ! '

In those lines the eighteenth century dies
to music, and from this time forward we
find in the rest of Blake's work only a proof
of his own assertion, that 'the ages are all
equal ; but genius is above the age.'

In 1778 Blake's apprenticeship to Basire

came to an end, and for a short time he
studied in the Antique School at the newly
founded Royal Academy under Moser, the
first keeper. In the Life of Reynolds which
prefaces the 1798 edition of the *Discourses*,
Moser is spoken of as one who 'might in
every sense be called the Father of the
present race of Artists.' Blake has written
against this in his copy : ' I was once looking over the prints from Raphael and
Michael Angelo in the Library of the Royal
Academy. Moser came to me and said,
"You should not study these old hard,
stiff, and dry unfinished works of art.
Stay a little, and I will show you what you
should study." He then went and took
down Le Brun's and Rubens' Galleries.
How did I secretly rage. I also spoke my
mind. I said to Moser, "These things that
you call finished are not even begun : how
can they then be finished ? The man
who does not know the beginning never
can know the end of art."' Malkin tells
us that Blake 'professed drawing from life
always to have been hateful to him ; and
speaks of it as looking more like death, or
smelling of mortality. Yet still he drew a

good deal from life, both at the Academy
and at home.' A water-colour drawing
dating from this time, 'The Penance of
Jane Shore,' was included by Blake in his
exhibition of 1809. It is the last number
in the catalogue, and has the note: 'This
Drawing was done above Thirty Years ago,
and proves to the Author, and he thinks
will prove to any discerning eye, that the
productions of our youth and of our maturer
age are equal in all essential respects.' He
also did engravings, during several years,
for the booksellers, Harrison, Johnson, and
others, some of them after Stothard, who
was then working for the *Novelist's Magazine*. Blake met Stothard in 1780, and
Stothard introduced him to Flaxman, with
whom he had himself just become acquainted. In the same year Blake met
Fuseli, who settled near him in Broad
Street, while Flaxman, on his marriage in
1781, came to live near by, at 27 Wardour
Street. Bartolozzi and John Varley were
both, then or later, living in Broad Street,
Angelica Kauffmann in Golden Square. In
1780 (the year of the Gordon Riots, when
Blake, carried along by the crowd, saw the

burning of Newgate) he had for the first time a picture in the Royal Academy, the water-colour of 'The Death of Earl Godwin.'

It was at this time, in his twenty-fourth year, that he fell in love with 'a lively little girl' called Polly Wood. Tatham calls her 'a young woman, who by his own account, and according to his own knowledge, was no trifler. He wanted to marry her, but she refused, and was as obstinate as she was unkind.' Gilchrist says that on his complaining to her that she had 'kept company' with others besides himself, she asked him if he was a fool. 'That cured me of jealousy,' he said afterwards, but the cure, according to Tatham, made him so ill that he was sent for change of air to 'Kew, near Richmond' (really to Battersea), to the house of 'a market-gardener whose name was Boutcher.' While there, says Tatham, 'he was relating to the daughter, a girl named Catherine, the lamentable story of Polly Wood, his implacable lass, upon which Catherine expressed her deep sympathy, it is supposed, in such a tender and affectionate manner, that it quite won him. He immediately said, with the suddenness peculiar to him, "Do you pity

me ? " " Yes, indeed I do," answered she.
" Then I love you," said he again. Such was
their courtship. He was impressed by her
tenderness of mind, and her answer indi-
cated her previous feeling for him : for she
has often said that upon her mother's asking
her who among her acquaintances she could
fancy for a husband, she replied that she
had not yet seen the man, and she has
further been heard to say that when she
first came into the room in which Blake sat,
she instantly recognised (like Britomart in
Merlin's wondrous glass) her future partner,
and was so near fainting that she left his
presence until she recovered.' Tatham tells
us that Blake 'returned to his lodgings and
worked incessantly' for a whole year, 'resolv-
ing that he would not see her until he had
succeeded' in making enough money to be
able to marry her. The marriage took place
at Battersea in August 1762. 1782

Gilchrist says that he has traced relatives
of Blake to have been living at Battersea at
the time of his marriage. Of this he gives
no evidence ; but I think I have found
traces, in Blake's own parish, of relatives of
the Catherine Boucher whom he married at

Battersea. Tatham, as we have seen, says that she was the daughter of a market-gardener at 'Kew, near Richmond,' called Boutcher, to whose house Blake was sent for a change of air. Allan Cunningham says that 'she lived near his father's house.' I think I have found the reason for Cunningham's mistake, and the probable occasion of Blake's visit to the Bouchers at Battersea. I find by the birth register in St. Mary's, Battersea, that Catherine Sophia, daughter of William and Ann Boucher, was born April 25, and christened May 16, 1762. Four years after this, another Catherine Boucher, daughter of Samuel and Betty, born March 28, 1766, was christened March 31, 1766, in the parish church of St. James, Westminster; and in the same register I find the birth of Gabriel, son of the same parents, born September 1, and christened September 20, 1767; and of Ann, daughter of Thomas and Ann Boucher, born June 12, and christened June 29, 1761. Is it not, therefore, probable that there were Bouchers, related to one another, living in both parishes, and that Blake's acquaintance with the family living near him led to his going to stay with the family living at Battersea ?

The entry of Blake's marriage, in the register of St. Mary's Battersea, gives the name as Butcher, and also describes Blake as ' of the parish of Battersea,' by a common enough error. It is as follows :—

1782.
Banns of Marriage.

No. 281 William Blake of the Parish of Battersea Batchelor and Catherine Butcher of the same Parish Spinster were Married in this Church by License this Eighteenth Day of August in the Year One Thousand Seven Hundred and Eighty two by me J. Gardnor Vicar. This Marriage was solemnized between Us

William Blake
The mark of X Catherine Butcher

In the presence of Thomas Monger Butcher
Jas. Blake
Robt. Munday Parish Clerk.

I imagine that Thomas Monger Butcher was probably Catherine's brother; there are other Mongers not far off in the register, as if the name were a family name. His handwriting is mean and untidy, James Blake's

vague but fluent ; Catherine makes her mark
somewhat faintly. As the register lies open
there are entries of seven marriages ; out of
these, no fewer than three of the brides have
signed by making their mark. The name
William Blake stands out from these 'blotted
and blurred' signatures ; the ink is very
black, as if he had pressed hard on the pen ;
and the name has a 'firm and determinate
outline.'

Gilchrist describes Catherine Boucher as
'a bright-eyed, dark-haired brunette, with
expressive features and a slim, graceful
form.' This seems to be merely a re-writ-
ing of Allan Cunningham's vague statement
that she 'was noticed by Blake for the
whiteness of her hand, the brightness of
her eyes, and a slim and handsome shape,
corresponding with his own notions of sylphs
and naiads.' But if a quaint and lovely
pencil sketch in the Rossetti MS., representing a man in bed and a woman sitting
on the side of the bed, beginning to dress,
is really, as it probably is, done from life,
and meant for Mrs. Blake, we see at once
the model for his invariable type of woman,
tall, slender, and with unusually long legs.

There is a drawing of her head by Blake in
the Rossetti MS. which, though apparently
somewhat conventionalised, shows a clear
aquiline profile and very large eyes; still to
be divined in the rather painful head drawn
by Tatham when she was an old woman, a
head in which there is still power and fixity.
Crabb Robinson, who met her in 1825, says
that she had 'a good expression in her countenance, and, with a dark eye, remains of
beauty in her youth.'

No man of genius ever had a better wife.
To the last she called him 'Mr. Blake,'
while he, we are told, frequently spoke of
her as 'his beloved.' The most beautiful
reference to her which I find in his letters
is one in a letter of September 16, 1800, to
Hayley, where he calls her 'my dear and
too careful and over-joyous woman,' and
says 'Eartham will be my first temple and
altar; my wife is like a flame of many
colours of precious jewels whenever she hears
it named.' He taught her to write, and the
copy-book titles to some of his water-colours
are probably hers; to draw, so that after
his death she finished some of his designs; and to help him in the printing and

colouring of his engravings. A story is told, on the authority of Samuel Palmer, that they would both look into the flames of burning coals, and draw grotesque figures which they saw there, hers quite unlike his. 'It is quite certain,' says Crabb Robinson, 'that she believed in all his visions'; and he shows her to us reminding her husband, 'You know, dear, the first time you saw God was when you were four years old, and he put his head to the window, and set you a-screaming.' She would walk with him into the country, whole summer days, says Tatham, and far into the night. And when he rose in the night, to write down what was 'dictated' to him, she would rise and sit by him, and hold his hand. 'She would get up in the night,' says the unnamed friend quoted by Gilchrist, 'when he was under his very fierce inspirations, which were as if they would tear him asunder, while he was yielding himself to the Muse, or whatever else it could be called, sketching and writing. And so terrible a task did this seem to be, that she had to sit motionless and silent; only to stay him mentally, without moving hand or foot ; this for hours,

and night after night.' ' His wife being to
him a very patient woman,' says Tatham,
who speaks of Mrs. Blake as ' an irradiated
saint,' ' he fancied that while she looked on
him as he worked, her sitting quite still by
his side, doing nothing, soothed his impetuous mind ; and he has many a time, when a
strong desire presented itself to overcome
any difficulty in his plates or drawings, in
the middle of the night, risen, and requested
her to get up with him, and sit by his
side, in which she as cheerfully acquiesced.'
' Rigid, punctual, firm, precise,' she has been
described ; a good housewife and a good
cook ; refusing to have a servant not only
because of the cost, but because no servant
could be scrupulous enough to satisfy her.
' Finding,' says Tatham ' (as Mrs. Blake declared, and as every one else knows), the
more service the more inconvenience, she
. . . did all the work herself, kept the house
clean and herself tidy, besides printing all
Blake's numerous engravings, which was a
task sufficient for any industrious woman.'
He tells us in another place : ' it is a fact
known to the writer, that Mrs. Blake's
frugality always kept a guinea or sovereign

for any emergency, of which Blake never knew, even to the day of his death.'

Tatham says of Blake at the time of his marriage: ' Although not handsome, he must have had a most noble countenance, full of expression and animation ; his hair was of a yellow brown, and curled with the utmost crispness and luxuriance ; his locks, instead of falling down, stood up like a curling flame, and looked at a distance like radiations, which with his fiery eye and expressive forehead, his dignified and cheerful physiognomy, must have made his appearance truly prepossessing.'   In another place he says : ' William Blake in stature was short [he was not quite five and a half feet in height], but well made, and very well proportioned ; so much so that West, the great history painter, admired much the form of his limbs ; he had a large head and wide shoulders.   Elasticity and promptitude of action were the characteristics of his contour.   His motions were rapid and energetic, betokening a mind filled with elevated enthusiasm; his forehead was very high and prominent over the frontals; his eye most unusually large and glassy, with which he appeared to look into some

other world.' His eyes were prominent,
'large, dark, and expressive,' says Allan
Cunningham ; the flashing of his eyes remained in the memory of an old man who
had seen him in court at Chichester in 1804.
His nose, though 'snubby,' as he himself
describes it, had 'a little clenched nostril,
a nostril that opened as far as it could, but
was tied down at the end.' The mouth was
large and sensitive ; the forehead, larger
below than above, as he himself noted, was
broad and high ; and the whole face, as one
sees it in what is probably the best likeness
we have, Linnell's miniature of 1827, was
full of irregular splendour, eager, eloquent,
ecstatic ; eyes and mouth and nostrils all
as if tense with a continual suction, drinking
up 'large draughts of intellectual day' with
impatient haste. 'Infinite impatience,' says
Swinburne, 'as of a great preacher or apostle
—intense tremulous vitality, as of a great
orator—seem to me to give his face the
look of one who can do all things but
hesitate.'

After his marriage in August 1782 (which
has been said to have displeased his father,
though Tatham says it was 'with the appro-

bation and consent of his parents '), Blake
took lodgings at 23 Green Street, Leicester
Fields (now pulled down), which was only
the square's length away from Sir Joshua
Reynolds. Flaxman had married in 1781,
and had taken a house at 27 Wardour Street
and it was probably he who, about this time,
introduced Blake to 'the accomplished Mrs.
Matthew,' whose drawing-room in Rathbone
Place was frequented by literary and artistic
people. Mr. Matthew, a clergyman of taste,
who is said to have ' read the church service
more beautifully than any other clergyman
in London,' had discovered Flaxman, when
a little boy, learning Latin behind the counter
in his father's shop. 'From this incident,'
says J. T. Smith in his notice of Flaxman,
' Mr. Matthew continued to notice him, and,
as he grew up, became his first and best
friend. Later on, he was introduced to
Mrs. Matthew, who was so kind as to read
Homer to him, whilst he made designs on
the same table with her at the time she was
reading.' It was apparently at the Matthews'
house that Smith heard Blake sing his own
songs to his own music, and it was through
Mrs. Matthew's good opinion of these songs

that she 'requested the Rev. Henry Matthew,
her husband, to join Mr. Flaxman in his
truly kind offer of defraying the expense
of printing them': to which we owe the
'*Poetical Sketches*, by W. B.'; printed in
1783, and given to Blake to dispose of as
he thought fit. There is no publisher's
name on the book, and there is no reason
to suppose that it was ever offered for
sale.

'With his usual urbanity,' Mr. Matthew
had written a foolish 'Advertisement' to
the book, saying that the author had 'been
deprived of the leisure requisite to such a
revisal of these sheets, as might have rendered
them less unfit to meet the public eye,' 'his
talents having been wholly directed to the
attainment of excellence in his profession.'
The book is by no means incorrectly printed,
and it is not probable that Blake would
under any circumstances have given his poems
more 'revisal' than he did. He did at this
time a good deal of engraving, often after
the designs of Stothard, whom he was afterwards to accuse of stealing his ideas; and
in 1784 he had two, and in 1785 four, water-
colour drawings at the Royal Academy.

Fuseli, Stothard, and Flaxman [1] seem to
have been his chief friends, and it is probable
that he also knew Cosway, who practised
magic, and Cosway may have told him about
Paracelsus, or lent him Law's translation of
Behmen, while Flaxman, who was a Swedenborgian, may have brought him still more
closely under the influence of Swedenborg.

In any case, he soon tired of the coterie
of the Matthews, and we are told that it
soon ceased to relish his 'manly firmness
of opinion.' What he really thought of
it we may know with some certainty from
the extravaganza, *An Island in the Moon*,
which seems to belong to 1784, and
which is a light-hearted and incoherent
satire, derived, no doubt, from Sterne, and

---

[1] Compare the lines written in 1800 :
' I bless thee, O Father of Heaven and Earth, that ever I saw
    Flaxman's face.
Angels stand round my spirit in Heaven, the blessed of
    Heaven are my friends upon Earth.
When Flaxman was taken to Italy, Fuseli was given to me
    for a season . . .
And my Angels have told me that seeing such visions, I
    could not subsist on the Earth,
But by my conjunction with Flaxman, who knows to forgive
    nervous fear.'

pointing, as Mr. Sampson justly says, to
Peacock. It is unfinished, and was not
worth finishing, but it contains the first
version of several of the *Songs of Innocence*,
as well as the lovely song of Phœbe and
Jellicoe. It has the further interest of showing us Blake's first, wholly irresponsible
attempt to create imaginary worlds, and
to invent grotesque and impossible names.
It shows us the first explosions of that
inflammable part of his nature, which was
to burst through the quiet surface of his
life at many intervals, in righteous angers
and irrational suspicions. It betrays his
deeply rooted dislike of science, and, here
and there, a literary preference, for Ossian
or for Chatterton. The original MS. is in
the Fitzwilliam Museum, Cambridge, and
in this year, 1907, Mr. Edwin J. Ellis has
done Blake the unkindness of printing it for
the first time in full, in the pages of his
Real Blake. Blake's satire is only occasionally good, though occasionally it is supremely
good ; his burlesque is almost always bad ;
and there is little probability that he ever
intended to publish any part of the prose
and verse which he threw off for the relief

of personal irritations and spiritual indignations.

In *An Island in the Moon* we see Blake casting off the dust of the drawing-rooms, finally, so far as any mental obstruction was concerned; but he does not seem to have broken wholly with the Matthews, who, no doubt, were people of genuinely good intentions; and it is through their help that we find him, in 1784, on the death of his father, setting up as a print-seller, with his former fellow-apprentice, James Parker, at No. 27 Broad Street, next door to the house and shop which had been his father's, and which were now taken on by his brother James. Smith says that he took a shop and a first-floor; and here his brother Robert came to live with him as his pupil, and remained with him till his death in February 1787.

III

AFTER Robert's death Blake gave up the
print-shop and moved out of Broad Street
to Poland Street, a street running between
it and Oxford Street.   He took No. 28, a
house only a few doors down from Oxford
Street, and lived there for five years.
Here, in 1789, he issued the *Songs of
Innocence*, the first of his books to be produced by the method of his invention
which he described as 'illuminated printing.'   According to Smith, it was Robert
who 'stood before him in one of his visionary imaginations, and directed him in the
way in which he ought to proceed.'   The
process is thus described by Mr. Sampson:
'The text and surrounding design were
written in reverse, in a medium impervious
to acid, upon small copper-plates, which
were then etched in a bath of aqua-fortis
until the work stood in relief as in a stereo-

type. From these plates, which to econo-
mise copper were in many cases engraved
upon both sides, impressions were printed,
in the ordinary manner, in tints made to
harmonise with the colour scheme afterwards applied in water-colours by the artist.'
Gilchrist tells an improbable story about
Mrs. Blake going out with the last half-
crown in the house, and spending 1s. 10d.
of it in the purchase of 'the simple materials
necessary.' But we know from a MS. note
of John Linnell, referring to a somewhat
later date: 'The copper-plates which Blake
engraved to illustrate Hayley's life of Cowper were, as he told me, printed entirely by
himself and his wife in his own press—a
very good one which cost him forty pounds.'
These plates were engraved in 1803, but it
is not likely that Blake was ever able to
buy more than one press.

The problem of 'illuminated printing,'
however definitely it may have been solved
by the dream in which Robert 'stood before
him and directed him,' was one which had
certainly occupied the mind of Blake for
some years. A passage, unfortunately in-
complete, in *An Island in the Moon*, reads as

follows : '. . ." Illuminating the Manuscript "
—" Ay," said she, " that would be excellent."
" Then," said he, " I would have all the writing engraved instead of printed, and at
every other leaf a high finished print, all in
three volumes folio, and sell them a hundred
pounds a piece. They would print off two
thousand." " Then," said she, " whoever will
not have them, will be ignorant fools and
will not deserve to live." ' This is evidently
a foreshadowing of the process which is
described and defended, with not less confident enthusiasm, in an engraved prospectus issued from Lambeth in 1793. I
give it in full :—

October 10, 1793.

TO THE PUBLIC.

The Labours of the Artist, the Poet, the
Musician, have been proverbially attended by
poverty and obscurity ; this was never the fault
of the Public, but was owing to a neglect of means
to propagate such works as have wholly absorbed
the Man of Genius. Even Milton and Shakespeare could not publish their own works.

This difficulty has been obviated by the Author
of the following productions now presented to the

Public; who has invented a method of Printing both Letter-press and Engraving in a style more ornamental, uniform, and grand, than any before discovered, while it produces works at less than one-fourth of the expense.

If a method of Printing which combines the Painter and the Poet is a phenomenon worthy of public attention, provided that it exceeds in elegance all former methods, the Author is sure of his reward.

Mr. Blake's powers of invention very early engaged the attention of many persons of eminence and fortune; by whose means he has been regularly enabled to bring before the public works (he is not afraid to say) of equal magnitude and consequence with the productions of any age or country : among which are two large highly finished engravings (and two more are nearly ready) which will commence a Series of subjects from the Bible, and another from the History of England.

The following are the Subjects of the several Works now published and on Sale at Mr. Blake's, No. 13 Hercules Buildings, Lambeth :—

1. Job, a Historical Engraving.   Size 1 ft. $7\frac{1}{2}$ in. by 1 ft. 2 in.   Price 12s.

2. Edward and Elinor, a Historical Engraving. Size 1 ft. $6\frac{1}{2}$ in. by 1 ft.   Price 10s. 6d.

3. America, a Prophecy, in Illuminated Printing. Folio, with 18 designs.   Price 10s. 6d.

4. Visions of the Daughters of Albion, in Illuminated Printing. Folio, with 8 designs. Price 7s. 6d.

5. The Book of Thel, a Poem in Illuminated Printing. Quarto, with 6 designs. Price 3s.

6. The Marriage of Heaven and Hell, in Illuminated Printing. Quarto, with fourteen designs. Price 7s. 6d.

7. Songs of Innocence, in Illuminated Printing. Octavo, with 25 designs. Price 5s.

8. Songs of Experience, in Illuminated Printing. Octavo, with 25 designs. Price 5s.

9. The History of England, a small book of Engravings. Price 3s.

10. The Gates of Paradise, a small book of Engravings. Price 3s.

The Illuminated Books are Printed in Colours, and on the most beautiful wove paper that could be procured.

No Subscriptions for the numerous great works now in hand are asked, for none are wanted ; but the Author will produce his works, and offer them to sale at a fair price.

By this invention (which it is absurd to consider, as some have considered it, a mere makeshift, to which he had been driven by the refusal of publishers to issue his poems and engravings according to the ordinary trade methods) Blake was the first, and remains the only, poet who has in the complete sense made his own books with his own hands: the words, the illustrations, the engraving, the printing, the colouring, the very inks and colours, and the stitching of the sheets into boards. With Blake, who was equally a poet and an artist, words and designs came together and were inseparable; and to the power of inventing words and designs was added the skill of engraving, and thus of interpreting them, without any mechanical interference from the outside. To do this must have been, at some time or another, the ideal of every poet who is a true artist, and who has a sense of the equal importance of every form of art, and of every detail in every form. Only Blake has produced a book of poems vital alike in inner and outer form, and, had it not been for his lack of a technical knowledge of music, had he but been able to write down his inventions in that art also, he would have left us the creation of something like an universal art. That universal art he did, during his own lifetime, create; for he sang his songs to his own music; and thus, while he lived, he was the complete realisation of the poet in all his faculties, and the only complete realisation that has ever been known.

To define the poetry of Blake one must find new definitions for poetry; but, these definitions once found, he will seem to be the only poet who is a poet in essence; the only poet who could, in his own words, 'enter into Noah's rainbow, and make a friend and companion of one of these images of wonder, which always entreat him to leave mortal things.' In this verse there is, if it is to be found in any verse, the 'lyrical cry'; and yet, what voice is it that cries in this disembodied ecstasy? The voice of desire is not in it, nor the voice of passion, nor the cry of the heart, nor the cry of the sinner to God, nor of the lover of nature to nature. It neither seeks nor aspires nor laments nor questions. It is like the voice of wisdom in a child, who has not yet forgotten the world out of which the soul came. It is as spontaneous as the note of a bird, it is an affirmation of life; in its song, which seems mere music, it is the mind which sings; it is lyric thought.

What is it that transfixes one in any couplet such as this :

> 'If the sun and moon should doubt
> They 'd immediately go out' ?

It is no more than a nursery statement, there is not even an image in it, and yet it sings to the brain, it cuts into the very flesh of the mind, as if there were a great weight behind it.   Is it that it is an arrow, and that it comes from so far, and with an impetus gathered from its speed out of the sky ?

The lyric poet, every lyric poet but Blake, sings of love ; but Blake sings of forgiveness :

> 'Mutual forgiveness of each vice,
> Such are the gates of Paradise.'

Poets sing of beauty, but Blake says :

> 'Soft deceit and idleness,
> These are Beauty's sweetest dress.'

They sing of the brotherhood of men, but Blake points to the 'divine image' :

> 'Cruelty has a human heart,
>   And Jealousy a human face ;
> Terror the human form divine,
>   And Secrecy the human dress.'

Their minds are touched by the sense of
tears in human things, but to Blake 'a tear
is an intellectual thing.' They sing of 'a
woman like a dewdrop,' but Blake of 'the
lineaments of gratified desire.' They shout
hymns to God over a field of battle or in
the arrogance of material empire ; but Blake
addresses the epilogue of his *Gates of Paradise* 'to the Accuser who is the God of this
world' :

> 'Truly, my Satan, thou art but a dunce,
>   And dost not know the garment from the man ;
> Every harlot was a virgin once,
>   Nor canst thou ever change Kate into Nan.
> Though thou art worshipped by the names divine
>   Of Jesus and Jehovah, thou art still
> The son of morn in weary night's decline,
>   The lost traveller's dream under the hill.'

Other poets find ecstasy in nature, but
Blake only in imagination. He addresses
the Prophetic Book of *The Ghost of Abel* 'to
Lord Byron in the wilderness,' and asks :
'What doest thou here, Elijah? Can a
poet doubt of the visions of Jehovah?
Nature has no outline, but Imagination has.
Nature has no time, but Imagination has.
Nature has no supernatural, and dissolves.

Imagination is eternity.' The poetry of Blake is a poetry of the mind, abstract in substance, concrete in form; its passion is the passion of the imagination, its emotion is the emotion of thought, its beauty is the beauty of idea. When it is simplest, its simplicity is that of some 'infant joy' too young to have a name, or of some 'infant sorrow' brought aged out of eternity into the 'dangerous world,' and there,

> 'Helpless, naked, piping loud,
> Like a fiend hid in a cloud.'

There are no men and women in the world of Blake's poetry, only primal instincts and the energies of the imagination.

His work begins in the garden of Eden, or of the childhood of the world, and there is something in it of the naïveté of beasts : the lines gambol awkwardly, like young lambs. His utterance of the state of innocence has in it something of the grotesqueness of babies, and enchants the grown man, as they do. Humour exists unconscious of itself, in a kind of awed and open-eyed solemnity. He stammers into a speech of angels, as if just awakening out of Paradise.

It is the primal instincts that speak first, before riper years have added wisdom to intuition. It is the supreme quality of this wisdom that it has never let go of intuition. It is as if intuition itself ripened. And so Blake goes through life with perfect mastery of the terms of existence, as they present themselves to him : 'perfectly happy, wanting nothing,' as he said, when he was old and poor ; and able in each stage of life to express in art the corresponding stage of his own development. He is the only poet who has written the songs of childhood, of youth, of mature years, and of old age ; and he died singing.

IV

BLAKE lived in Poland Street for five years, and issued from it the *Songs of Innocence* (1789), and, in the same year, *The Book of Thel, The Marriage of Heaven and Hell* in 1790, and, in 1791, the first book of *The French Revolution: a Poem in Seven Books*, which Gilchrist says was published anonymously, in ordinary type, and without illustrations, by the bookseller Johnson. No copy of this book is known to exist. At this time he was a fervent believer in the new age which was to be brought about by the French Revolution, and he was much in the company of revolutionaries and freethinkers, and the only one among them who dared wear the 'bonnet rouge' in the street. Some of these, Thomas Paine, Godwin, Holcroft, and others, he met at Johnson's shop in St. Paul's Churchyard, where Fuseli and Mary

Wollstonecraft also came. It was at Johnson's, in 1792, that Blake saved the life of
Paine, by hurrying him off to France, with
the warning, 'You must not go home, or
you are a dead man,' at the very moment
when a warrant had been issued for his
arrest. Johnson himself was in 1798 put
into gaol for his republican sympathies, and
continued to give his weekly literary dinners
in gaol.

Blake's back-windows at Poland Street
looked out on the yard of Astley's circus,
and Tatham tells a story of Blake's wonder,
indignation, and prompt action on seeing a
wretched youth chained by the foot to a
horse's hobble. The neighbour whom he regarded as 'hired to depress art,' Sir Joshua
Reynolds, died in 1792. A friend quoted
by Gilchrist tells us : 'When a very young
man he had called on Reynolds to show him
some designs, and had been recommended
to work with less extravagance and more
simplicity, and to correct his drawing.
This Blake seemed to regard as an affront
never to be forgotten. He was very indignant when he spoke of it.' There is
also a story of a meeting between Blake and

Reynolds, when each, to his own surprise, seems to have found the other very pleasant.

Blake's mother died in 1792, at the age of seventy, and was buried in Bunhill Fields on September 9. In the following year he moved to 13 Hercules Buildings, Lambeth,[1] where, during the next seven years, he did engraving, both of his own designs and of those of others, and published the engraved book of designs called *The Gates of Paradise* (1793), the poems and illustrations of the *Songs of Experience* (1794), and the greater part of the Prophetic Books, besides writing, apparently in 1797, the vast and never really finished MS. of *The Four Zoas.* This period was that of which

[1] Gilchrist (i. 98) gives a long account of the house which he took to be Blake's, and which he supposed to be on the west side of Hercules Road. But it has been ascertained beyond a doubt, on the authority of the Lambeth rate-books, confirmed by Norwood's map of London at the end of the eighteenth century, that Blake's house, then numbered 13 Hercules Buildings, was on the east side of the road, and is the house now numbered 23 Hercules Road. Before 1842 the whole road was renumbered, starting at the south end of the western side and returning by the eastern side, so that the house which Gilchrist saw in 1863 as 13 Hercules Buildings was what afterwards became 70 Hercules Road, and is now pulled down. The road was finally renumbered in 1890, and the house became 23 Hercules Road.

we have the largest and most varied result, in written and engraved work, together with a large number of designs, including five hundred and thirty-seven done on the margin of Young's *Night Thoughts*, and the earliest of the colour-prints. It was Blake's one period of something like prosperity, as we gather from several stories reported by Tatham, who says that during the absence of Blake and his wife on one of their long country walks, which would take up a whole day, thieves broke into the house, and 'carried away plate to the value of £60 and clothes to the amount of £40 more.' Another £40 was lent by Blake to 'a certain freethinking speculator, the author of many elaborate philosophical treatises,' who complained that 'his children had not a dinner.' A few days afterwards the Blakes went to see the destitute family, and the wife 'had the audacity to ask Mrs. Blake's opinion of a very gorgeous dress, purchased the day following Blake's compassionate gift.' Yet another story is of a young art-student who used to pass the house every day carrying a portfolio under his arm, and whom Blake pitied for his poverty and sickly looks, and taught for nothing and looked after till he died. Blake had other pupils too, among 'families of high rank,' but being 'aghast' at the prospect of 'an appointment to teach drawing to the Royal Family,' he gave up all his pupils, with his invariably exquisite sense of manners, on refusing the royal offer.

It was in 1799 that Blake found his first patron, and one of his best friends, in Thomas Butts, 'that remarkable man—that great patron of British genius,' as Samuel Palmer calls him, who, for nearly thirty years, with but few intervals, continued to buy whatever Blake liked to do for him, paying him a small but steady price, and taking at times a drawing a week. A story which, as Palmer says, had 'grown in the memory,' connects him with Blake at this time, and may be once more repeated, if only to be discredited. There was a back-garden at the house in Hercules Buildings, and there were vines in it, which Blake would never allow to be pruned, so that they grew luxuriant in leaf and small and harsh in fruit. Mr. Butts, according to Gilchrist, is supposed to have come one day into 'Blake's Arcadian

Arbour,' as Tatham calls it, and to have
found Blake and his wife sitting naked,
reading out Milton's *Paradise Lost* 'in
character,' and to have been greeted with :
' Come in, it is only Adam and Eve.' John
Linnell, in some notes written after reading
Gilchrist, and quoted in Story's *Life of
Linnell*, writes with reason : ' I do not think
it possible. Blake was very unreserved in
his narrations to me of all his thoughts and
actions, and I think if anything like this
story had been true, he would have told me
of it. I am sure he would have laughed
heartily at it if it had been told of him or of
anybody else, for he was a hearty laugher
at absurdities.' In such a matter, Linnell's
authority may well be final, if indeed any
authority is required, beyond a sense of
humour, and the knowledge that Blake possessed it.

Another legend of the period, which has
at least more significance, whether true or
not, is referred to by both Swinburne and
Mr. W. M. Rossetti, on what authority I
cannot discover, and is thus stated by
Messrs. Ellis and Yeats : ' It is said that
Blake wished to add a concubine to his

establishment in the Old Testament manner,
but gave up the project because it made
Mrs. Blake cry.' 'The element of fable,'
they add, 'lies in the implication that the
woman who was to have wrecked this household had a bodily existence. . . . There is a
possibility that he entertained mentally
some polygamous project, and justified it
on some patriarchal theory. A project and
theory are one thing, however, and a woman
is another; and though there is abundant
suggestion of the project and theory, there
is no evidence at all of the woman.' I have
found in the unpublished part of Crabb
Robinson's *Diary* and *Reminiscences* more
than a 'possibility' or even 'abundant suggestion' that Blake accepted the theory as
a theory. Crabb Robinson himself was so
frightened by it that he had to confide it
to his *Diary* in the disguise of German,
though, when he came to compile his *Reminiscences* many years later he ventured to
put it down in plain English which no editor
has yet ventured to print. Both passages
will be found in their place in the verbatim
reprint given later; but I will quote the
second here:

'13th June (1826).—I saw him again in June. He was as wild as ever, says my journal, but he was led to-day to make assertions more palpably mischievous and capable of influencing other minds, and immoral, supposing them to express the will of a responsible agent, than anything he had said before. As for instance, that he had learned from the Bible that wives should be in common. And when I objected that Marriage was a Divine institution he referred to the Bible, " that from the beginning it was not so." He affirmed that he had committed many murders, and repeated his doctrine, that reason is the only Sin, and that careless, gay people are better than those who think, etc., etc.'

This passage leaves no doubt as to Blake's theoretical view of marriage, but it brings us no nearer to any certainty as to his practical action in the matter. With Blake, as with all wise men, a mental decision in the abstract had no necessary influence on conduct. To have the courage of your opinions is one thing, and Blake always had this ; but he was of all people least impelled to go and do a thing because he considered

the thing a permissible one to do.   Throughout all his work Blake affirms freedom as
the first law of love; jealousy is to him the
great iniquity, the unforgivable selfishness.
He has the frank courage to praise in *The
Visions of the Daughters of Albion*

  ' Infancy, fearless, lustful, happy, nestling for delight
    In laps of pleasure ! Innocence, honest, open, seeking
    The vigorous joys of morning light';

and of woman he asks, ' Who taught thee
modesty, subtle modesty?' In the same
book, which is Blake's Book of Love, Oothoon
offers ' girls of mild silver or of furious
gold' to her lover; in the paradisal state of
Jerusalem ' every female delights to give
her maiden to her husband.'   All these
things are no doubt symbols, but they are
symbols which meet us on every page of
Blake, and I no not doubt that to him they
represented an absolute truth.   Therefore I
think it perfectly possible that some
' mentally polygamous project' was at one
time or another entertained by him, and
' justified on some patriarchal theory.' What
I am sure of, however, is that a tear of Mrs.
Blake ('for a tear is an intellectual thing')
was enough to wipe out project if not theory,

and that one to whom love was pity more than it was desire would have given no nearer cause for jealousy than some unmortal Oothoon.

It was in 1794 that Blake engraved the *Songs of Experience.* Four of the Prophetic Books had preceded it, but here Blake returns to the clear and simple form of the *Songs of Innocence,* deepening it with meaning and heightening it with ardour. Along with this fierier art the symbolic contents of what, in the *Songs of Innocence,* had been hardly more than a child's strayings in earthly or divine Edens, becomes angelic, and speaks with more deliberately hid or doubled meanings. Even ' The Tiger,' by which Lamb was to know that here was ' one of the most extraordinary persons of the age,' is not only a sublime song about a flame-like beast, but contains some hint that ' the tigers of wrath are wiser than the horses of instruction.' In this book, and in the poems which shortly followed it, in that MS. book whose contents have sometimes been labelled, after a rejected title of Blake's, *Ideas of Good and Evil,* we see Blake more wholly and more evenly him-

self than anywhere else in his work. From
these central poems we can distinguish the
complete type of Blake as a poet.

Blake is the only poet who sees all temporal things under the form of eternity.
To him reality is merely a symbol, and he
catches at its terms, hastily and faultily, as
he catches at the lines of the drawing-master,
to represent, as in a faint image, the clear
and shining outlines of what he sees with
the imagination; through the eye, not with
it, as he says. Where other poets use
reality as a spring-board into space, he
uses it as a foothold on his return from
flight. Even Wordsworth seemed to him
a kind of atheist, who mistook the changing
signs of ' vegetable nature ' for the unchang-
ing realities of the imagination. ' Natural
objects,' he wrote in a copy of Wordsworth,
' always did and now do weaken, deaden,
and obliterate imagination in me. Wordsworth must know that what he writes
valuable is not to be found in nature.'
And so his poetry is the most abstract of
all poetry, although in a sense the most
concrete. It is everywhere an affirmation,
the register of vision; never observation.

To him observation was one of the daughters
of memory, and he had no use for her among
his Muses, which were all eternal, and the
children of the imagination. 'Imagination,'
he said, 'has nothing to do with memory.'
For the most part he is just conscious that
what he sees as 'an old man grey' is no
more than a 'frowning thistle':

> 'For double the vision my eyes do see,
> And a double vision is always with me.
> With my inward eyes, 'tis an old man grey,
> With my outward, a thistle across my way.'

In being so far conscious, he is only recog-
nising the symbol, not admitting the reality.

In his earlier work, the symbol still
interests him, he accepts it without dispute; with, indeed, a kind of transfigur-
ing love. Thus he writes of the lamb
and the tiger, of the joy and sorrow of
infants, of the fly and the lily, as no poet
of mere observation has ever written of
them, going deeper into their essence than
Wordsworth ever went into the heart of
daffodils, or Shelley into the nerves of the
sensitive plant. He takes only the simplest
flowers or weeds, and the most innocent or
most destroying of animals, and he uses

them as illustrations of the divine attri-
butes. From the same flower and beast
he can read contrary lessons without change
of meaning, by the mere transposition of
qualities, as in the poem which now reads :

‘ The modest rose puts forth a thorn,
  The humble sheep a threatening horn :
  While the lily white shall in love delight,
  Nor a thorn, nor a threat, stain her beauty bright.’

Mr. Sampson tells us in his notes : ‘ Beginning by writing :

“The rose puts envious . . .”

he felt that “ envious ” did not express his
full meaning, and deleted the last three
words, writing above them “ lustful rose,”
and finishing the line with the words “ puts
forth a thorn.” He then went on :

“ The coward sheep a threatening horn ;
  While the lily white shall in love delight,
  And the lion increase freedom and peace ” ;

at which point he drew a line under the
poem to show that it was finished. On a
subsequent reading he deleted the last line,
substituting for it :

‘ “ The priest loves war, and the soldier peace ” ;

but here, perceiving that his rhyme had disappeared, he cancelled this line also, and gave the poem an entirely different turn by changing the word "lustful" to "modest," and "coward" to "humble," and completing the quatrain (as in the engraved version) by a fourth line simply explanatory of the first three.' This is not merely obeying the idle impulse of a rhyme, but rather a bringing of the mind's impulses into that land where 'contraries mutually exist.'

And when I say that he reads lessons, let it not be supposed that Blake was ever consciously didactic. Conduct does not concern him; not doing, but being. He held that education was the setting of a veil between light and the soul. 'There is no good in education,' he said. 'I hold it to be wrong. It is the great sin. It is eating of the tree of the knowledge of good and evil. This was the fault of Plato. He knew nothing but the virtues and vices, and good and evil. There is nothing in all that. Everything is good in God's eyes. And, as he says with his excellent courage : 'When I tell the truth, it is not for the sake of convincing those who do not know it, but for the sake of defending those who do'; and, again, with still more excellent and harder courage : 'When I am endeavouring to think rightly, I must not regard my own any more than other people's weaknesses'; so, in his poetry, there is no moral tendency, nothing that might not be poison as well as antidote; nothing indeed but the absolute affirmation of that energy which is eternal delight. He worshipped energy as the well-head or parent fire of life ; and to him there was no evil, only a weakness, a negation of energy, the ignominy of wings that droop and are contented in the dust.

And so, like Nietzsche, but with a deeper innocence, he finds himself 'beyond good and evil,' in a region where the soul is naked and its own master. Most of his art is the unclothing of the soul, and when at last it is naked and alone, in that 'thrilling' region where the souls of other men have at times penetrated, only to shudder back with terror from the brink of eternal loneliness, then only is this soul exultant with the supreme happiness.

V

IT is to the seven years at Lambeth that what may be called the first period of the Prophetic Books largely belongs, though it does not indeed begin there. The roots of it are strongly visible in *The Marriage of Heaven and Hell*, which was written at Poland Street, and they may be traced even further back. Everything else, until we come to the last or Felpham period, which has a new quality of its own, belongs to Lambeth.

In his earlier work Blake is satisfied with natural symbols, with nature as symbol; in his later work, in the final message of the Prophetic Books, he is no longer satisfied with what then seems to him the relative truth of the symbols of reality. Dropping the tools with which he has worked so well, he grasps with naked hands after an absolute truth of statement, which is like his attempt in his designs to render the outlines of vision literally, without translation into the forms of human sight. He invents names harsh as triangles, Enitharmon, Theotormon, Rintrah, for spiritual states and essences, and he employs them as Wagner employed his leading motives, as a kind of shorthand for the memory. His meaning is no longer apparent in the ordinary meaning of the words he uses; we have to read him with a key, and the key is not always in our hands; he forgets that he is talking to men on the earth in some language which he has learnt in heavenly places. He sees symbol within symbol, and as he tries to make one clear to us, he does but translate it into another, perhaps no easier, or more confusing. And it must be remembered, when even interpreters like Mr. Ellis and Mr. Yeats falter, and confess 'There is apparently some confusion among the symbols,' that after all we have only a portion of Blake's later work, and that probably a far larger portion was destroyed when the Peckham 'angel,' Mr. Tatham (copartner in foolish wickedness with Warburton's cook), sat down to burn the books which he did not understand. Blake's great system of wheels within wheels remains no better than a ruin, and can but at the best be pieced together tentatively by those who are able to trace the connection of some of its parts. It is no longer even possible to know how much consistency Blake was able to give to his symbols, and how far he failed to make them visible in terms of mortal understanding. As we have them, they evade us on every side, not because they are meaningless, but because the secret of their meaning is so closely kept. To Blake actual contemporary names meant even more than they meant to Walt Whitman. 'All truths wait in all things,' said Walt Whitman, and Blake has his own quite significant but perplexing meaning when he writes:

'The corner of Broad Street weeps; Poland Street
    languishes
To Great Queen Street and Lincoln's Inn: all is dis-
    tress and woe.'

He is concerned now only with his message, with the 'minutely particular' statement of it; and as he has ceased to accept any mortal medium, or to allow himself to be penetrated by the sunlight of earthly beauty, he has lost the means of making that message visible to us. It is a miscalculation of means, a contempt for possibilities; not, as people were once hasty enough to assume, the irresponsible rapture of madness. There is not even in these crabbed chronicles the wild beauty of the madman's scattering brain ; there is a concealed sanity, a precise kind of truth, which, as Blake said of all truth, ' can never be so told as to be understood, and not be believed.'

Blake's form, or apparent formlessness, in the Prophetic Books, was no natural accident, or unconsidered utterance of inspiration. Addressing the public on the first plate of *Jerusalem* he says : ' When this verse was first dictated to me, I considered a monotonous cadence like that used by Milton and Shakespeare and all writers of English blank verse, derived from the bondage of rhyming, to be a necessary and indispensable part of verse. But I soon found that in the mouth of a true orator such monotony was not only awkward, but as much a bondage as rhyme itself. I have therefore produced a variety in every line, both of cadences and number of syllables. Every word and every letter is studied and put into its fit place; the terrific numbers are reserved for the terrific parts, the mild and gentle for the mild and gentle parts, and the prosaic for inferior parts; all are necessary to each other.' This desire for variety at the expense of unity is illustrated in one of Blake's marginal notes to Reynolds' *Discourses.* 'Such harmony of colouring' (as that of Titian in the Bacchus and Ariadne) 'is destructive of Art. One species of equal hue over all is the cursed thing called harmony. It is the smile of a fool.' This is a carrying to its extreme limit of the principle that 'there is no such thing as softness in art, and that everything in art is definite and minute . . . because vision is determinate and perfect'; and that 'colouring does not depend on where the colours are put, but on where the lights and darks are put, and all depends on form or outline, on where that is put.' The whole aim of the Prophetic Books is to arrive at a style as 'determinate and perfect' as vision, unmodified by any of the deceiving beauties

of nature or of the distracting ornaments
of conventional form.   What is further interesting in Blake's statement is that he
aimed, in the Prophetic Books, at producing
the effect, not of poetry but of oratory, and
it is as oratory, the oratory of the prophets,
that the reader is doubtless meant to take
them.

'Poetry fettered,' he adds, 'fetters the
human race,' and I doubt not that he
imagined, as Walt Whitman and later
vers-libristes have imagined, that in casting
off the form he had unfettered the spirit
of poetry.   There seems never to have been
a time when Blake did not attempt to find
for himself a freer expression than he
thought verse could give him, for among
the least mature of the *Poetical Sketches*
are poems written in rhythmical prose, in
imitation partly of Ossian, partly of the
Bible.   An early MS. called *Tiriel*, probably of hardly later date, still exists,
written in a kind of metre of fourteen
syllables, only slightly irregular in beat,
but rarely fine in cadence.   It already hints,
in a cloudy way, at some obscure mythology,
into which there already come incoherent

names, of an Eastern colour, Ijim and
Mnetha. Tiriel appears again in *The Book
of Urizen* as Urizen's first-born, Thiriel, 'like
a man from a cloud born.' Har and Heva
reappear in *The Song of Los*. *The Book of
Thel*, engraved in 1789, the year of the
Songs of Innocence, is in the same metre of
fourteen syllables, but written with a faint
and lovely monotony of cadence, strangely
fluid and flexible in that age of strong
cæsuras, as in :

'Come forth, worm of the silent valley, to thy pensive
    queen.'

The sentiment is akin to that of the *Songs
of Innocence*, and hardly more than a
shadow of the mythology remains. It
sings or teaches the holiness and eternity
of life in all things, the equality of life in
the flower, the cloud, the worm, and the
maternal clay of the grave; and it ends
with the unanswered question of death to
life : why ? why ? In 1790 Blake engraved
in two forms, on six and ten infinitesimal
plates, a tractate which he called, *There
is no Natural Religion*. They contain, the
one commenting on the other, a clear and

concise statement of many of Blake's fundamental beliefs; such as : ' That the poetic
Genius is the true Man, and that the Body
or outward form of Man is derived from the
Poetic Genius.' ' As all men are alike in
outward form, so (and with the same infinite
variety) all are alike in the Poetic Genius.'
' Man's perceptions are not bounded by
organs of perception, he perceives more than
sense (though ever so acute) can discover.'
Yet, since ' Man's desires are limited by his
perceptions, none can desire what he has not
perceived.' ' Therefore God becomes as we
are, that we may become as he is.'

In the same year, probably, was engraved
The Marriage of Heaven and Hell, a prose
fantasy full of splendid masculine thought,
and of a diabolical or infernal humour, in
which Blake, with extraordinary boldness,
glorifies, parodies, and renounces at once
the gospel of his first master in mysticism,
' Swedenborg, strongest of men, the Samson
shorn by the Churches,' as he was to call
him long afterwards, in *Milton*. Blake's
attitude towards Christianity might be
roughly defined by calling him a heretic of
the heresy of Swedenborg. *The Marriage*

of Heaven and Hell begins : ' As a new
heaven is begun, and it is now thirty-three
years since its advent, the Eternal Hell
revives. And lo ! Swedenborg is the Angel
sitting on the tomb : his writings are the
linen clothes folded up.' Swedenborg himself, in a prophecy that Blake must have
heard in his childhood, had named 1757,
the year of Blake's birth, as the first of a
new dispensation, the dispensation of the
spirit, and Blake's acceptance of the prophecy marks the date of his escape from the
too close influence of one of whom he said,
as late as 1825, ' Swedenborg was a divine
teacher. Yet he was wrong in endeavouring
to explain to the rational faculty what
reason cannot comprehend.' And so we are
warned, in *The Marriage of Heaven and
Hell*, against the ' confident insolence
sprouting from systematic reasoning. Thus
Swedenborg boasts that what he writes is
new, though it is only the contents or index
of already published books.' And again :
' Any man of mechanical talents may
from the writings of Paracelsus or Jacob
Behmen produce ten thousand volumes of
equal value with Swedenborg's, and from

those of Dante or Shakespeare an infinite
number. But when he has done this, let
him not say that he knows better than his
master, for he only holds a candle in sunshine.' With Paracelsus it is doubtful if
Blake was ever more than slightly acquainted; the influence of Behmen, whom
he had certainly read in William Law's
translation, is difficult to define, and seems
to have been of the most accidental or
partial kind, but Swedenborg had been a
sort of second Bible to him from childhood,
and the influence even of his 'systematic
reasoning' remained with him as at least a
sort of groundwork, or despised model;
'foundations for grand things,' as he says in
the *Descriptive Catalogue.* When Swedenborg says, ' Hell is divided into societies in
the same manner as heaven, and also into as
many societies as heaven ; for every society
in heaven has a society opposite to it in
hell, and this for the sake of equilibrium,'
we see in this spirit of meek order a matter-
of-fact suggestion for Blake's 'enormous
wonders of the abysses,' in which heavens
and hells change names and alternate
through mutual annihilations.

The last note which Blake wrote on the margins of Swedenborg's *Wisdom of Angels* is this : ' Heaven and Hell are born together.' The edition which he annotated is that of 1788, and the marginalia, which are printed in Mr. Ellis's *Real Blake*, will show how attentive, as late as two years before the writing of the book which that note seems to anticipate, Blake had been to every shade of meaning in one whom he was to deny with such bitter mockery. But, even in these notes, Blake is attentive to one thing only, he is reaching after a confirmation of his own sense of a spiritual language in which man can converse with paradise and render the thoughts of angels. He comments on nothing else, he seems to read only to confirm his conviction ; he is equally indifferent to Swedenborg's theology and to his concern with material things ; his hells and heavens, ' uses,' and ' spiritual suns,' concern him only in so far as they help to make clearer and more precise his notion of the powers and activities of the spirit in man. To Blake, as he shows us in *Milton*, Swedenborg's worst error was not even that of ' systematic reasoning,' but that of

'Showing the Transgressors in Hell: the proud
    Warriors in Heaven:
    Heaven as a Punisher and Hell as one under
    Punishment.'

It is for this more than for any other error
that Swedenborg's 'memorable relations' are
tossed back to him as 'memorable fancies,'
in a solemn parody of his own manner; that
his mill and vault and cave are taken from
him and used against him; and that one
once conversant with his heaven, and now
weary of it, 'walks among the fires of hell,
delighted with the enjoyments of Genius,
which to Angels look like torments and
insanity.' Blake shows us the energy of
virtue breaking the Ten Commandments,
and declares: 'Jesus was all virtue, and
acted from impulse, not from rules.' Speaking through 'the voice of the Devil,' he
proclaims that 'Energy is eternal delight,'
and that 'Everything that lives is holy.'
And, in a last flaming paradox, still mocking
the manner of the analyst of heaven and
hell, he bids us: 'Note. This Angel, who is
now become a Devil, is my particular friend:
we often read the Bible together, in its
infernal or diabolical sense, which the world

shall have if they behave well. I have also
the Bible of Hell, which the world shall
have whether they will or no.' The Bible
of Hell is no doubt the Bible of Blake's new
gospel, in which contraries are equally true.
We may piece it together out of many
fragments, of which the first perhaps is the
sentence standing by itself at the bottom of
the page : ' One Law for the Lion and Ox is
Oppression.'

The Marriage of Heaven and Hell is loud
with ' the clangour of the Arrows of Intellect,' each of the ' Proverbs of Hell ' is a
jewel of concentrated wisdom, the whole
book is Blake's clearest and most vital statement of his new, his reawakened belief; it
contains, as I have intimated, all Nietzsche ;
yet something restless, disturbed, uncouth,
has come violently into this mind and art,
wrenching it beyond all known limits, or
setting alight in it an illuminating, devour-
ing, and unquenchable flame. In common
with Swedenborg, Blake is a mystic who
enters into no tradition, such as that tradition of the Catholic Church which has a
liturgy awaiting dreams. For Saint John
of the Cross and for Saint Teresa the words

of the vision are already there, perfectly translating ecstasy into familiar speech; they have but to look and to speak. But to Blake, as to Swedenborg, no tradition is sufficiently a matter of literal belief to be at hand with its forms; new forms have to be made, and something of the crudity of Swedenborg comes over him in his rejection of the compromise of mortal imagery.

The Marriage of Heaven and Hell may be called or not called a Prophetic Book, in the strict sense; with *The Visions of the Daughters of Albion*, engraved at Lambeth in 1793, the series perhaps more literally begins. Here the fine masculine prose of *The Marriage of Heaven and Hell* has given place to a metre vaguer than the metre of *The Book of Thel*, and to a substance from which the savour has not yet gone of the *Songs of Innocence*, in such lines as :

‘ The new washed lamb tinged with the village smoke,
    and the bright swan
By the red earth of our immortal river.’

It is Blake’s book of love, and it defends the honesty of the natural passions with un-slackening ardour. There is no mythology

in it, beyond a name or two, easily explicable.
Oothoon, the virgin joy, oppressed by laws
and cruelties of restraint and jealousy, vindi-
cates her right to the freedom of innocence
and to the instincts of infancy.

' And trees and birds and beasts and men behold their
eternal joy.
Arise, you little glancing wings, and sing your infant
joy :
Arise, and drink your bliss, for everything that lives
is holy ! '

It is the gospel of *The Marriage of Heaven
and Hell*, and, as that proclaimed liberty for
the mind, so this, with abundant rhetoric,
but with vehement conviction, proclaims
liberty for the body. In form it is still clear,
its eloquence and imagery are partly biblical,
and have little suggestion of the manner of
the later Prophetic Books.

America, written in the same year, in the
same measure as the *Visions of the Daughters
of Albion*, is the most vehement, wild, and
whirling of all Blake's prophecies. It is a
prophecy of revolution, and it takes the
revolt of America against England both
literally and symbolically, with names of
' Washington, Franklin, Paine and Warren,

Gates, Hancock and Green,' side by side with
Orc and the Angel of Albion ; it preaches
every form of bodily and spiritual liberty in
the terms of contemporary events, Boston's
Angel, London's Guardian, and the like, in
the midst of cataclysms of all nature, fires
and thunders temporal and eternal. The
world for a time is given into the power of
Orc, unrestrained desire, which is to bring
freedom through revolution and the destroying of the bonds of good and evil. He is
called 'Antichrist, Hater of Dignities, lover
of wild rebellion, and transgressor of God's
Law.' He is the Satan of *The Marriage of
Heaven and Hell*, and he also proclaims :

'For everything that lives is holy, life delights in
    life ;
Because the soul of sweet delight can never be
    defil'd.'

As, in that book, Blake had seen ' the fiery
limbs, the flaming hair ' of the son of fire
' spurning the clouds written with curses,
stamping the stony law to dust ' ; so, here,
he hears the voice of Orc proclaiming :

' The fierce joy, that Urizen perverted to ten commands,
  What night he led the starry hosts through the wild
      wilderness ;

That stony law I stamp to dust : and scatter religion
    abroad
To the four winds as a torn book, and none shall
    gather the leaves.'

Liberty comes in like a flood bursting all
barriers :

' The doors of marriage are open, and the Priests in
    rustling scales
    Rush into reptile coverts, hiding from the fires of
        Orc,
    That play around the golden roofs in wreaths of fierce
        desire,
    Leaving the females naked and glowing with the lusts
        of youth.
    For the female spirits of the dead pining in bonds of
        religion
    Run from their fetters reddening, and in long-drawn
        arches sitting,
    They feel the nerves of youth renew, and desires of
        ancient times,
    Over their pale limbs as a vine when the tender grape
        appears.'

The world, in this regeneration through
revolution (which seemed to Blake, no doubt,
a thing close at hand, in those days when
France and America seemed to be breaking
down the old tyrannies), is to be no longer

a world laid out by convention for the un-
trustworthy ; and he asks :

'Who commanded this? what God ? what Angel?
  To keep the generous from experience till the un-
      generous
  Are unrestrained performers of the energies of
      nature,
  Till pity is become a trade, and generosity a science
  That men get rich by.'

For twelve years, from the American to the
French revolution, 'Angels and weak men'
are to govern the strong, and then Europe
is to be overwhelmed by the fire that had
broken out in the West, though the ancient
guardians of the five senses 'slow advance
to shut the five gates of their law-built
houses.'

'But the gates were consumed, and their bolts and
      hinges melted,
  And the fierce flames burnt round the heavens, and
      round the abode of men.'

Here the myth, though it is present
throughout, is an undercurrent, and the
crying of the message is what is chiefly
heard. In *Europe* (1794), which is written
in lines broken up into frequent but not

very significant irregularities, short lines
alternating with long ones, in the manner
of an irregular ode, the mythology is like
a net or spider's web over the whole text.
Names not used elsewhere, or not in the
same form, are found : Manatha-Varcyon,
Thiralatha, who in *Europe* is Diralada. The
whole poem is an allegory of the sleep of
Nature during the eighteen hundred years
of the Christian era, under bonds of narrow
religions and barren moralities and tyrannous
laws, and of the awakening to forgotten joy,
when ' Nature felt through all her pores the
enormous revelry,' and the fiery spirit of
Orc, beholding the morning in the east, shot
to the earth,

' And in the vineyards of red France appear'd the light
    of his fury.'

It is another hymn of revolution, but this
time an awakening more wholly mental,
with only occasional contemporary allusions
like that of the judge in Westminster whose
wig grows to his scalp, and who is seen
' grovelling along Great George Street
through the Park gate.'   ' Howlings and
hissings, shrieks and groans, and voices of

despair,' are heard throughout ; we see
thought change the infinite to a serpent :

' Then was the serpent temple formed, image of infinite
  Shut up in finite revolutions, and man become an
        angel ;
  Heaven a mighty circle turning ; God a tyrant crown'd.'

The serpent temple shadows the whole
island :

' Enitharmon laugh'd in her sleep to see (O woman's
        triumph)
  Every house a den, every man bound : the shadows
        are filled
  With spectres, and the windows wove over with curses
        of iron :
  Over the doors Thou shalt not : and over the chimneys
        Fear is written :
  With bands of iron round their necks fasten'd into the
        walls
  The citizens : in leaden gyves the inhabitants of
        suburbs
  Walk heavy : soft and bent are the bones of villagers.'

The whole book is a lament and protest, and
it ends with a call to spiritual battle.   In a
gay and naïve prologue, written by Blake
in a copy of *Europe* in the possession of Mr.
Linnell, and quoted by Ellis and Yeats,
Blake tells us that he caught a fairy on a
streaked tulip, and brought him home :

'As we went along
Wild flowers I gathered, and he show'd me each eternal
flower.
He laughed aloud to see them whimper because they
were pluck'd,
Then hover'd round me like a cloud of incense. When
I came
Into my parlour and sat down and took my pen to
write,
My fairy sat upon the table and dictated *Europe.*'

The First Book of Urizen (1794) is a myth, shadowed in dark symbols, of the creation of mortal life and its severing from eternity ; the birth of Time out of the void and ' self-contemplating shadow ' of unimaginative Reason ; the creation of the senses, each a limiting of eternity, and the closing of the tent of heavenly knowledge, so that Time and the creatures of Time behold eternity no more. We see the birth of Pity and of Desire, woman the shadow and desire the child of man. Reason despairs as it realises that life lives upon death, and the cold pity of its despair forms into a chill shadow, which follows it like a spider's web, and freezes into the net of religion, or the restraint of the activities. Under this net the senses shrink inwards, and that creation which is ' the body of our death' and our stationing in time and space is finished :

> ' Six days they shrank up from existence,
> And on the seventh they rested
> And they bless'd the seventh day, in sick hope,
> And forgot their eternal life.'

Then the children of reason, now ' sons and daughters of sorrow,'

> ' Wept and built
> Tombs in the desolate places,
> And form'd laws of prudence and call'd them
> The eternal laws of God.'

But Fuzon, the spirit of fire, forsook the ' pendulous earth' with those children of Urizen who would still follow him.

Here, crystallised in the form of a myth, we see many of Blake's fundamental ideas. Some of them we have seen under other forms, as statement rather than as image, in *The Marriage of Heaven and Hell* and *There is no Natural Religion*. We shall see them again, developed, elaborated, branching out into infinite side-issues, multiplying upon themselves, in the later Prophetic Books, partly as myth, partly as statement ; we shall see them in many of the lyrical poems, transformed into song, but still never varying in their message; and we shall see them, in the polemical prose of all the remaining fragments, and in the private letters, and in the annotations of Swedenborg, and in Crabb Robinson's records of conversations. The *Book of Urizen* is a sort of nucleus, the germ of a system.

Next to the *Book of Urizen*, if we may judge from the manner of its engraving, came *The Song of Los* (1795), written in a manner of vivid declamation, the lines now lengthening, now shrinking, without fixed beat or measure. It is the song of Time, 'the Eternal Prophet,' and tells the course of inspiration as it passes from east to west, 'abstract philosophy' in Brahma, 'forms of dark delusion' to Moses on Mount Sinai, the mount of law; 'a gospel from wretched Theotormon' (distressed human love and pity) to Jesus, 'a man of sorrows'; the 'loose Bible' of Mahomet, setting free the senses; Odin's 'code of war.'

'These were the Churches, Hospitals, Castles, Palaces,
    Like nets and gins and traps to catch the joys of
        Eternity,
And all the rest a desart :
Till like a dream Eternity was obliterated and erased.'

'The vast of Nature' shrinks up before the 'shrunken eyes' of men, till it is finally enclosed in the 'philosophy of the five senses,' the philosophy of Newton and Locke. 'The Kings of Asia,' the cruelties of the heathen, the ancient powers of evil, call on 'famine from the heath, pestilence from the fen,'

> 'To turn man from his path,
> To restrain the child from the womb,
> To cut off the bread from the city,
> That the remnant may learn to obey,
> That the pride of the heart may fail,
> That the lust of the eyes may be quench'd,
> That the delicate ear in its infancy
> May be dull'd, and the nostrils clos'd up:
> To teach mortal worms the path
> That leads from the gates of the grave.'

But, in the darkness of their 'ancient woven dens,' they are startled by 'the thick-flaming, thought-creating fires of Orc'; and at their cry Urizen comes forth to meet and challenge the liberating spirit; he thunders against the pillar of fire that rises out of the darkness of Europe; and at the clash of their mutual onset 'the Grave shrieks aloud.' But 'Urizen wept,' the cold pity of reason which, as we have seen in the book named after him, freezes into nets of religion, ' twisted like to the human brain.'

The Book of Los (also dated 1795) is written in the short lines of *Urizen* and *Ahania*, a metre following a fixed, insistent beat, as of Los's hammer on his anvil. It begins with the lament of ' Eno, aged Mother,' over the liberty of old times :

> ' O Times remote !
> When Love and Joy were adoration,
> And none impure were deem'd.
> Not Eyeless Covet,
> Nor Thin-lip'd Envy,
> Nor Bristled Wrath,
> Nor Curled Wantonness ' ;

none of these, that is, yet turned to evil, but still unfallen energies. At this, flames of desire break out, ' living, intelligent,' and Los, the spirit of Inspiration, divides the flames, freezes them into solid darkness, and is imprisoned by them, and escapes, only in terror, and falls through ages into the void (' Truth has bounds, Error none '), until he has organised the void and brought into it a light which makes visible the form of the void. He sees it as the backbone of Urizen, the bony outlines of reason, and then begins, for the first time in the Prophetic Books, that building of furnaces, and wielding of hammer and anvil of which we are to hear so much in *Jerusalem*. He forges the sun, and chains cold intellect to vital heat, from whose torments

'a twin
Was completed, a Human Illusion
In darkness and deep clouds involved.'

In *The Book of Los* almost all relationship to poetry has vanished ; the myth is cloudier and more abstract. Scarcely less so is *The Book of Ahania* (1795), written in the same short lines, but in a manner occasionally more concrete and realisable. Like *Urizen*, it is almost all myth. It follows Fuzon, 'son of Urizen's silent burnings,' in his fiery revolt against

'This cloudy God seated on waters,
Now seen, now obscured, king of Sorrows.'

From the stricken and divided Urizen is born Ahania ('so name his parted soul'), who is 'his invisible lust,' whom he loves, hides, and calls Sin.

'She fell down, a faint shadow wandering,
In chaos, and circling dark Urizen,

As the moon anguished circles the earth,
Hopeless, abhorred, a death shadow,
Unseen, unbodied, unknown,
The mother of Pestilence.'

But Urizen, recovering his strength, seizes
the bright son of fire, his energy or passion,
and nails him to the dark 'religious' 'Tree
of Mystery,' from under whose shade comes
the voice of Ahania, 'weeping upon the
void,' lamenting her lost joys of love, and
the days when

'Swelled with ripeness and fat with fatness,
Bursting on winds my odours,
My ripe figs and rich pomegranates,
In infant joy at my feet,
O Urizen, sported and sang.'

In *The Four Zoas* Ahania is called 'the
feminine indolent bliss, the indulgent self of
weariness.' 'One final glimpse,' says Mr.
Swinburne, 'we may take of Ahania after
her division—the love of God, as it were,
parted from God, impotent therefore and
a shadow, if not rather a plague and blight;
mercy severed from justice, and thus made
a worse thing than useless.' And her
lament ends in this despair :

'But now alone over rocks, mountains,
Cast out from thy lovely bosom
Cruel jealousy, selfish fear,
Self-destroying; how can delight
Renew in these chains of darkness
Where bones of beasts are strown
On the bleak and snowy mountains,
Where bones from the birth are buried
Before they see the light.'

The mythology, of which parts are developed in each of these books, is thrown together, in something more approaching a whole, but without apparent cohesion or consistency, in *The Four Zoas*, which probably dates from 1797 and which exists in seventy sheets of manuscript, of uncertain order, almost certainly in an unfinished state, perhaps never intended for publication, but rather as a storehouse of ideas. This manuscript, much altered, arranged in a conjectural order, and printed with extreme incorrectness, was published by Messrs. Ellis and Yeats in the third volume of their book on Blake, under the first, rejected, title of *Vala*.[1] They describe it as being in itself a sort of compound of all

[1] The text of *Vala*, with corrections and additional errors, is now accessible in the second volume of Mr. Ellis' edition of Blake's *Poetical Works*.

Blake's other books, except *Milton* and *Jerusalem*, which are enriched by scraps taken from *Vala*, but are not summarised in it.   In the uncertain state in which we have it, it is impossible to take it as a wholly authentic text; but it is both full of incidental beauty and of considerable assistance in unravelling many of the mysteries in *Milton* and *Jerusalem*, the books written at Felpham, both dated 1804, in which we find the final development of the myth, or as much of that final development as has come to us in the absence of the manuscripts destroyed or disposed of by Tatham.   Those two books indeed seem to presuppose in their readers an acquaintance with many matters told or explained in this, from which passages are taken bodily, but with little apparent method.   As it stands, *Vala* is much more of a poem than either *Milton* or *Jerusalem*; the cipher comes in at times, but between there are broad spaces of cloudy but not wholly unlighted imagery.   Blake still remembers that he is writing a poem, earthly beauty is still divine beauty to him, and the message is not yet so stringent as to forbid all lingering by the way.

In some parts of the poem the manner is frankly biblical, and suggests the book of Proverbs, as thus :

' What is the price of experience ?   Do men buy it for
    a song,
  Or wisdom for a dance in the street ?   No, it is bought
    with the price
  Of all that a man hath—his wife, his house, his
    children.
  Wisdom is sold in the desolate market where none
    comes to buy,
  And in the withered fields where the farmer ploughs
    for bread in vain.'

Nature is still an image accepted as an adequate symbol, and we get reminiscences here and there of the simpler, early work of *Thel*, for instance, in such lines as :

' And as the little seed waits eagerly watching for its
    flower and fruit,
  Anxious its little soul looks out into the clear
    expanse
  To see if hungry winds are abroad with their invisible
    array ;
  So man looks out in tree and herb, and fish and bird
    and beast,
  Collecting up the scattered portions of his immortal
    body
  Into the elemental forms of everything that grows.'

There are descriptions of feasts, of flames, of last judgments, of the new Eden, which are full of colour and splendour, passing without warning into the 'material sublime' of Fuseli, as in the picture of Urizen 'stonied upon his throne' in the eighth 'Night.' In the passages which we possess in the earlier and later version we see the myth of Blake gradually crystallising, the transposition of every intelligible symbol into the secret cipher. Thus we find 'Mount Gilead' changed into 'Mount Snowdon,' 'Beth Peor' into 'Cosway Vale,' and a plain image such as this :

'The Mountain called out to the Mountain, Awake, oh brother Mountain,'

is translated backwards into :

'Ephraim called out to Tiriel, Awake, oh brother Mountain.'

Images everywhere are seen freezing into types; they stop half-way, and have not yet abandoned the obscure poetry of the earlier Prophetic Books for the harder algebra of *Milton* and *Jerusalem*.

VI

THE first statement by Blake of his aims
and principles in art is to be found in some
letters to George Cumberland and to Dr.
Trusler, contained in the Cumberland Papers
in the British Museum. These letters were
first printed by Dr. Garnett in the *Hampstead Annual* of 1903, but with many mis-
takes and omissions.[1] I have recopied from
the originals the text of such letters as I
quote. It appears that in the year 1799
Blake undertook, at the suggestion of Cumberland, to do some drawings for a book by
Dr. Trusler, a sort of quack writer and
publisher, who may be perhaps sufficiently
defined by the quotation of the title of one
of his books, which is *The Way to be Rich
and Respectable.* On August 16, Blake
writes to say : ' I find more and more that
my Style of Designing is a Species by
itself, and in this which I send you have

[1] They are now to be read in Mr. Russell's edition of *The
Letters of William Blake.*

been compelled by my Genius or Angel to
follow where he led ; if I were to act otherwise it would not fulfil the purpose for
which alone I live, which is in conjunction
with such men as my friend Cumberland to
renew the lost Art of the Greeks.' He tells
him that he has attempted to 'follow his
Dictate' every morning for a fortnight, but
'it was out of my power!' He then
describes what he has done, and says : 'If
you approve of my manner, and it is agreeable to you, I would rather Paint Pictures
in oil of the same dimensions than make
Drawings, and on the same terms. By this
means you will have a number of Cabinet
pictures, which I flatter myself will not be
unworthy of a Scholar of Rembrant and
Teniers, whom I have Studied no less than
Rafael and Michaelangelo.' The next letter,
which I will give in full, for it is a document of great importance, is dated a week
later, and the nature of the reply which it
answers can be gathered from Blake's comment on the matter to Cumberland, three
days later still. 'I have made him,' he says,
'a Drawing in my best manner : he has
sent it back with a Letter full of Criticisms,

in which he says It accords not with his
Intentions, which are, to Reject all Fancy
from his Work. How far he expects to
please, I cannot tell. But as I cannot paint
Dirty rags and old Shoes where I ought to
place Naked Beauty or simple ornament, I
despair of ever pleasing one Class of Men.'
'I could not help smiling,' he says later,
'at the difference between the doctrines of
Dr. Trusler and those of Christ.' Here, then,
is the letter in which Blake accounts for
himself to the quack doctor (who has
docketed it: 'Blake, Dimd with superstition'), as if to posterity :—

REVD. SIR,

   I really am sorry that you are falln out with
the Spiritual World, Especially if I should have
to answer for it. I feel very sorry that your
Ideas and Mine on Moral Painting differ so
much as to have made you angry with my method
of study. If I am wrong I am wrong in good
company. I had hoped your plan comprehended
All Species of this Art, and Especially that you
would not regret that Species which gives Existence to Every other, namely, Visions of Eternity.
You say that I want somebody to Elucidate my
Ideas. But you ought to know that what is

Grand is necessarily obscure to Weak men. That which can be made Explicit to the Ideot is not worth my care. The wisest of the Ancients considerd what is not too Explicit as the fittest for Instruction, because it rouzes the faculties to act. I name Moses, Solomon, Esop, Homer, Plato.

But as you have favord me with your remarks on my Design, permit me in return to defend it against a mistaken one, which is, That I have supposed Malevolence without a Cause. Is not Merit in one a Cause of Envy in another, and Serenity and Happiness and Beauty a Cause of Malevolence? But Want of Money and the Distress of a Thief can never be alledged as the Cause of his Thievery, for many honest people endure greater hardships with Fortitude. We must therefore seek the Cause elsewhere than in the want of Money, for that is the Miser's passion, not the Thief's.

I have therefore proved your Reasonings Ill proportiond, which you can never prove my figures to be. They are those of Michael Angelo, Rafael and the Antique, and of the best living Models. I perceive that your Eye is perverted by Caricature Prints, which ought not to abound so much as they do. Fun I love, but too much Fun is of all things the most loathsome. Mirth is better than Fun, and Happiness is better than Mirth. I feel that a Man may be happy in This World, and I know that This World is a World of Imagination and Vision. I see Everything I paint In This World: but

Every body does not see alike. To the Eyes of a Miser a Guinea is more beautiful than the Sun, and a bag worn with the use of Money has more beautiful proportions than a Vine filled with Grapes. The tree which moves some to tears of joy is in the Eyes of others only a Green thing that stands in the way. Some see Nature all Ridicule and Deformity, and by these I shall not regulate my proportions; and some scarce see Nature at all. But to the Eyes of the Man of Imagination, Nature is Imagination itself. As a Man is, so he sees. As the Eye is formed, such are its Powers. You certainly Mistake when you say that the Visions of Fancy are not to be found in This World. To Me This World is all One continued Vision of Fancy or Imagination, and I feel Flattered when I am told so. What is it sets Homer, Virgil, and Milton in so high a rank of Art? Why is the Bible more Entertaining and Instructive than any other book? Is it not because they are addressed to the Imagination, which is Spiritual Sensation, and but mediately to the Understanding or Reason? Such is True Painting, and such was alone valued by the Greeks and the best modern Artists. Consider what Lord Bacon says—'Sense sends over to Imagination before Reason have judged, and Reason sends over to Imagination before the Decree can be acted.' See *Advancement of Learning*, Part 2, P. 47, of first Edition.

But I am happy to find a Great Majority of

Fellow Mortals who can Elucidate My Visions, and Particularly they have been Elucidated by Children, who have taken a greater delight in contemplating my Pictures than I even hoped. Neither Youth nor Childhood is Folly or Incapacity. Some Children are Fools, and so are some old Men. But There is a vast Majority on the side of Imagination or Spiritual Sensation.

To Engrave after another Painter is infinitely more laborious than to Engrave one's own Inventions. And of the size you require my price has been Thirty Guineas, and I cannot afford to do it for less. I had Twelve for the Head I sent you as a Specimen ; but after my own designs I could do at least Six times the quantity of labour in the same time, which will account for the difference in price, as also that Chalk Engraving is at least Six times as laborious as Aqua tinta. I have no objection to Engraving after another Artist. Engraving is the profession I was apprenticed to, and I should never have attempted to live by any thing else If orders had not come in for my Designs and Paintings, which I have the pleasure to tell you are Increasing Every Day. Thus If I am a Painter it is not to be attributed to Seeking after. But I am contented whether I live by Painting or Engraving.

I am, Revd. Sir, your very obedient Servant,
WILLIAM BLAKE.

13 HERCULES BUILDINGS, LAMBETH,
August 23, 1799.

Blake tells Cumberland the whole story quite cheerfully, and ends with these significant words, full of patience, courtesy, and sad humour : 'As to Myself, about whom you are so kindly Interested, I live by Miracle. I am Painting small Pictures from the Bible. For as to Engraving, in which art I cannot reproach myself with any neglect, yet I am laid by in a corner as if I did not exist, and since my Young's Night Thoughts have been published, even Johnson and Fuseli have discarded my Graver. But as I know that He who works and has his health cannot starve, I laugh at Fortune and Go on and on. I think I foresee better Things than I have ever seen. My Work pleases my employer, and I have an order for Fifty small Pictures at One Guinea each, which is something better than mere copying after another artist. But above all I feel myself happy and contented, let what will come. Having passed now near twenty years in ups and downs, I am used to them, and perhaps a little practice in them may turn out to benefit. It is now exactly Twenty years since I was upon the ocean of business, and tho I laugh at Fortune,

I am persuaded that She Alone is the Governor of Worldly Riches, and when it is Fit She will call on me. Till then I wait with Patience, in hopes that She is busied among my Friends.'

The employer is, no doubt, Mr. Butts, for whom Blake had already begun to work: we know some of the 'frescoes' and colour-prints which belong to this time; among them, or only just after, the incomparable 'Crucifixion,' in which the soldiers cast lots in the foreground and the crosses are seen from the back, against a stormy sky and lances like Tintoretto's. But it was also the time of all but the latest Prophetic Books (or of all but the latest of those left to us), and we may pause here for a moment to consider some of the qualities that Blake was by this time fully displaying in his linear and coloured inventions and 'Visions of Eternity.'

It is by his energy and nobility of creation that Blake takes rank among great artists, in a place apart from those who have been content to study, to observe, and to copy. His invention of living form is like nature's, unintermittent, but without the

measure and order of nature, and without
complete command over the material out of
which it creates. In his youth he had
sought after prints of such inventive work
as especially appealed to him, Michelangelo,
Raphael, Dürer; it is possible that, having
had 'very early in life the ordinary opportunities,' as Dr. Malkin puts it, ' of seeing
pictures in the houses of noblemen and
gentlemen, and in the king's palaces,' he
had seen either pictures, or prints after
pictures, of the Italian Primitives, whose
attitudes and composition he at times suggests; and, to the end, he worked with
Dürer's ' Melancholia' on his work-table and
Michelangelo's designs on his walls. It
not unfrequently happened that a memory
of form created by one of these great
draughtsmen presented itself as a sort of
short cut to the statement of the form
which he was seeing or creating in his
own imagination. A Devil's Advocate has
pointed out 'plagiarisms' in Blake's design,
and would dismiss in consequence his reputation for originality. Blake had not
sufficient mastery of technique to be always
wholly original in design ; and it is to his

dependence on a technique not as flexible
as his imagination was intense that we must
attribute what is unsatisfying in such remarkable inventions as 'The House of
Death' (Milton's lazar-house) in the Print
Room of the British Museum. Its appeal
to the imagination is partly in spite of what
is 'organised and minutely articulated beyond all that the mortal and perishing
nature can produce.' Death is a version
of the Ancient of Days and of Urizen, only
his eyes are turned to blind terror and his
beard to forked flame; Despair, a statue of
greenish bronze, is the Scofield of *Jerusalem*; the limbs and faces rigid with agony
are types of strength and symbols of pain.
Yet even here there is creation, there is the
energy of life, there is a spiritual awe.
And wherever Blake works freely, as in the
regions of the Prophetic Books, wholly outside time and space, appropriate form multi-
plies under his creating hand, as it weaves
a new creation of worlds and of spirits,
monstrous and angelical.

Blake distinguished, as all great imaginative artists have distinguished, between
allegory, which is but realism's excuse for

existence, and symbol, which is none of the
'daughters of Memory,' but itself vision or
inspiration. He wrote in the MS. book:
'Vision or imagination is a representation
of what actually exists, really and unchange-
ably. Fable or allegory is formed by the
daughters of Memory.' And thus in the
designs which accompany the text of his
Prophetic Books there is rarely the mere
illustration of those pages. He does not
copy in line what he has said in words, or
explain in words what he has rendered in
line; a creation probably contemporary is
going on, and words and lines render between them, the one to the eyes, the other
to the mind, the same image of spiritual
things, apprehended by different organs of
perception.

And so in his pictures, what he gives us
is not a picture after a mental idea; it is
the literal delineation of an imaginative
vision, of a conception of the imagination.
He wrote : 'If you have not nature before
you for every touch, you cannot paint portrait; and if you have nature before you at
all, you cannot paint history.' There is a
water-colour of Christ in the carpenter's

shop : Christ, a child, sets to the floor that
compass which Blake saw more often in the
hands of God the Father, stooping out of
heaven ; his mother and Joseph stand on
each side of him, leaning towards him with
the stiff elegance of guardian angels on a
tomb. That is how Blake sees it, and not
with the minute detail and the aim at local
colour with which the Pre-Raphaelites have
seen it ; it is not Holman Hunt's ' Bethle-
hem ' nor the little Italian town of Giotto ;
it is rendered carefully after the visual
imagination which the verses of the Bible
awakened in his brain. In one of those
variations which he did on the ' Flight into
Egypt ' (the ' Riposo,' as he called it), we
have a lovely and surprising invention of
landscape, minute and impossible, with a
tree built up like a huge vegetable, and
flowers growing out of the bare rock, and a
red and flattened sun going down behind
the hills ; Joseph stands under the tree,
nearly of the same height, but grave and
kindly, and the Mother and Child are mild
eighteenth-century types of innocence ; the
browsing donkey has an engaging rough
homeliness of hide and aspect. It is all as

unreal as you like, made up of elements not
combined into any faultless pattern ; art has
gone back further than Giotto, and is careless of human individuality; but it is seen
as it were with faith, and it conveys to you
precisely what the painter meant to convey.
So, in a lovely water-colour of the creation
of Eve, this blue-haired doll of obviously
rounded flesh has in her something which is
more as well as less than the appeal of bodily
beauty, some suggestion to the imagination
which the actual technical skill of Blake has
put there. With less delicacy of colour, and
with drawing in parts actually misleading,
there is a strange intensity of appeal, of
realisation not so much to the eyes as
through them to the imagination, in another
water-colour of the raising of Lazarus, where
the corpse swathed in grave-clothes floats
sidelong upward from the grave, the weight
of mortality as if taken off, and an unearthly
lightness in its disemprisoned limbs, that
have forgotten the laws of mortal gravity.

Yet, even in these renderings of what is
certainly not meant for reality, how abun-
dantly nature comes into the design : mere
bright parrot-like birds in the branches of

the tree of knowledge of good and evil, the
donkey of the 'Riposo,' the sheep's heads
woven into the almost decorative border.
Blake was constantly on his guard against
the deceits of nature, the temptation of a
'facsimile representation of merely mortal
and perishing substances.' His dread of
nature was partly the recoil of his love ; he
feared to be entangled in the 'veils of Vala,'
the seductive sights of the world of the
senses ; and his love of natural things is
evident on every page of even the latest
of the Prophetic Books. It is the natural
world, the idols of Satan, that creep in at
every corner and border, setting flowers to
grow, and birds to fly, and snakes to glide
harmlessly around the edges of these hard
and impenetrable pages. The minute life
of this 'vegetable world' is awake and in
subtle motion in the midst of these cold
abstractions. 'The Vegetable World opens
like a flower from the Earth's centre, in which
is Eternity,' and it is this outward flower-
ing of eternity in the delicate living forms of
time that goes on incessantly, as if by the
mere accident of the creative impulse, as
Blake or Los builds Golgonooza or the City

of God out of the 'abstract void' and the 'indefiniteness of unimaginative existence.' It is, on every page, the visible outer part of what, in the words, can but speak a language not even meant to be the language of the 'natural man.'

In these symbolic notations of nature, or double language of words and signs, these little figures of men and beasts that so strangely and incalculably decorate so many of Blake's pages, there is something Egyptian, which reminds me of those lovely riddles on papyri and funeral tablets, where the images of real things are used so decoratively, in the midst of a language itself all pictures, with colours never seen in the things themselves, but given to them for ornament. *The Marriage of Heaven and Hell* is filled with what seem like the hieroglyphics on an Egyptian tomb or obelisk, little images which might well mean things as definite as the images of Egyptian writing. They are still visible, sometimes mere curves or twines, in the latest of the engraved work, and might exist equally for some symbolic life which they contain, or for that decorative life of design which makes them as expressive mosaics of pattern as the hieroglyphics.   I cannot but think that it was partly from what he had seen, in actual basalt, or in engravings after ancient monuments which must have been about him at Basire the engraver's, that Blake found the suggestion of his picture-writing in the Prophetic Books.   He believed that all Greek art was but a pale copy of a lost art of Egypt, 'the greater works of the Asiatic Patriarchs,' 'Apotheoses of Persian, Hindu, and Egyptian antiquity.'   In such pictures as 'The Spiritual Form of Pitt guiding Behemoth,' he professed to be but 'applying to modern heroes, on a smaller scale,' what he had seen in vision of these ' stupendous originals now lost, or perhaps buried till some happier age.'   Is it not likely therefore that in his attempt to create the religious books of a new religion, 'the Everlasting Gospel' of 'the Poetic Genius, which is the Lord,' he should have turned to the then unintelligible forms in which the oldest of the religions had written itself down in a visible pictorial message ?

But, whatever suggestions may have come

to him from elsewhere, Blake's genius was
essentially Gothic, and took form, I doubt
not, during those six years of youth when
he drew the monuments in Westminster
Abbey, and in the old churches about London. He might have learned much from the
tombs in the Abbey, and from the brasses,
and from the carved angels in the chapels,
and from the naïve groups on the screen in
the chapel of Edward the Confessor, and
from the draped figures round the sarco-
phagus of Aymer de Valence. There is
often, in Blake's figures, something of the
monumental stiffness of Gothic stone, as
there is in the minute yet formal character-
isation of the faces. His rendering of terrible and evil things, the animal beings who
typify the passions and fierce distortions of
the soul, have the same childlike detail,
content to be ludicrous if it can only be
faithful to a distinct conception, of the
carvers of gargoyles and of Last Judgments.
Blake has, too, the same love of pattern for
its own sake, the same exuberance of ornament, always living and organic, growing
out of the structure of the design or out of
the form of the page, not added to it from

without. Gothic art taught him his hatred of vacant space, his love of twining and trailing foliage and flame and water; and his invention of ornament is as unlimited as theirs. A page of one of his illuminated books is like the carving on a Gothic capital. Lines uncoil from a hidden centre and spread like branches or burst into vast vegetation, emanating from leaf to limb, and growing upward into images of human and celestial existence. The snake is in all his designs; whether, in *Jerusalem*, rolled into chariot-wheels and into the harness of a chariot drawn by hoofed lions, and into the curled horns of the lions, and into the pointing fingers of the horns; or, in *The Marriage of Heaven and Hell*, a leviathan of the sea with open jaws, eyed and scaled with poisonous jewels of purple and blood-red and corroded gold, swelling visibly out of a dark sea that foams aside from its passage; or, curved above the limbs and wound about the head of a falling figure in lovely diminishing coils like a corkscrew which is a note of interrogation; or, in mere unterrifying beauty, trailed like a branch of a bending tree across the tops of pages; or, bitted and bridled and a thing of blithe gaiety, ridden by little, naked, long-legged girls and boys in the new paradise of an America of the future. The Gothic carvers loved snakes, but hardly with the strange passion of Blake. They carved the flames of hell and of earthly punishment with delight in the beauty of their soaring and twisting lines; but no one has ever made of fire such a plaything and ecstasy as Blake has made of it. In his paintings he invents new colours to show forth the very soul of fire, a soul angrier and more variable than opals; and in his drawings he shows us lines and nooses of fire rushing upward out of the ground, and fire drifting across the air like vapour, and fire consuming the world in the last chaos. And everywhere there are gentle and caressing tongues and trails of fire, hardly to be distinguished from branches of trees and blades of grass and stems and petals of flowers. Water, which the Gothic carvers represented in curving lines, as the Japanese do, is in Blake a not less frequent method of decoration; wrapping frail human figures in wet caverns under the depths of the sea, and destroying and creating worlds.

Blake's colour is unearthly, and is used for
the most part rather as a symbol of emotion
than as a representation of fact.   It is at
one time prismatic, and radiates in broad
bands of pure colour; at another, and more
often, is as inextricable as the veins in
mineral, and seems more like a natural
growth of the earth than the creation of a
painter.   In the smaller Book of Designs in
the Print Room of the British Museum the
colours have mouldered away, and blotted
themselves together in a sort of putrefac-
tion which seems to carry the suggestions of
poisonous decay further than Blake carried
them.   This will be seen by a comparison
of the minutely drawn leviathan of *The
Marriage of Heaven and Hell*, with the
coloured print in the Book of Designs, in
which the outline of the folds melts and
crumbles into a mere chaos of horror.
Colour in Blake is never shaded, or, as
he would have said, blotted and blurred;
it is always pure energy.   In the faint
colouring of the *Book of Thel* there is the
very essence of gentleness; the colour is
a faultless interpretation of the faint and
lovely monotony of the verse, and of its

exquisite detail. Several of the plates recur
in the Book of Designs, coloured at a different and, no doubt, much later time; and
while every line is the same the whole atmosphere and mood of the designs is changed.
Bright rich colour is built up in all the
vacant spaces; and with the colour there
comes a new intensity; each design is seen
over again, in a new way. Here, the mood
is a wholly different mood, and this seeing
by contraries is easier to understand than
when, as in the splendid design on the
fourth page of *The Book of Urizen*, repeated in the Book of Designs, we see a
parallel, yet different, vision, a new, yet
not contrary, aspect. In the one, the
colours of the open book are like corroded
iron or rusty minerals; in the other, sharp
blues, like the wings of strange butterflies,
glitter stormily under the red flashes of a
sunset. The vision is the same, but every
colour of the thing seen is different.

To Blake, colour is the soul rather than
the body of his figures, and seems to clothe
them like an emanation. What Behmen says
of the world itself might be said of Blake's
rendering of the aspects of the world and

men. 'The whole outward visible World,' he tells us, 'with all its Being is a Signature, or Figure of the inward spiritual World; whatever is internally, and however its Operation is, so likewise it has its Character externally; like as the Spirit of each Creature sets forth and manifests the internal Form of its Birth, by its Body, so does the Eternal Being also.' Just as he gives us a naked Apollo for the 'spiritual form of Pitt' in the picture in the National Gallery, where Pitt is seen guiding Behemoth, or the hosts of evil, in a hell of glowing and obscure tumult, so he sees the soul of a thing or being with no relation to its normal earthly colour. The colours of fire and of blood, an extra-lunar gold, putrescent vegetable colours, and the stains in rocks and sunsets, he sees everywhere, and renders with an ecstasy that no painter to whom colour was valuable for its own sake has ever attained. It is difficult not to believe that he does not often use colour with a definitely musical sense of its harmonies, and that colour did not literally sing to him, as it seems, at least in a permissible figure, to sing to us out of his pages.

VII

AT the end of September 1800 Blake left
Lambeth, and took a cottage at Felpham,
near Bognor, at the suggestion of William
Hayley, the feeblest poet of his period, who
imagined, with foolish kindness, that he
could become the patron of one whom he
called 'my gentle visionary Blake.' Hayley
was a rich man, and, as the author of *The
Triumphs of Temper*, was looked upon as a
person of literary importance. He did his
best to give Blake opportunities of making
money, by doing engraving and by painting
miniatures of the neighbours. He read Greek
with him and Klopstock. 'Blake is just
become a Grecian, and literally learning the
language,' he says in one letter, and in
another : 'Read Klopstock into English to
Blake.' The effect of Klopstock on Blake
is to be seen in a poem of ribald magnificence,
which no one has yet ventured to print in
full. The effect of Blake on Hayley, and of

Hayley on Blake, can be realised from a few
passages in the letters.   At first we read :
' Mr. Hayley acts like a prince.'   Then : ' I
find on all hands great objections to my doing
anything but the mere drudgery of business,
and intimations that, if I do not confine
myself to this, I shall not live.'   Last : ' Mr.
H. is as much averse to my poetry as he is
to a chapter in the Bible.   He knows that
I have writ it, for I have shown it to him '
(this is apparently the *Milton* or the *Jerusalem*), ' and he has read part by his own
desire, and has looked with sufficient contempt to enhance my opinion of it. . . . But
Mr. H. approves of my designs as little as
he does of my poems, and I have been forced
to insist on his leaving me, in both, to my
own self-will ; for I am determined to be no
longer pestered with his genteel ignorance
and polite disapprobation.   I know myself
both poet and painter, and it is not his
affected contempt that can move to anything
but a more assiduous pursuit of both arts.
Indeed, by my late firmness I have brought
down his affected loftiness, and he begins to
think that I have some genius : as if genius
and assurance were the same thing !   But

his imbecile attempts to depress me only
deserve laughter.' What laughter they produced, while Blake was still suffering under
them, can be seen by any one who turns to
the epigrams on H. in the note-book. But
the letter goes on, with indignant serious-
ness: 'But I was commanded by my spiritual
friends to bear all and be silent, and to go
through all without murmuring, and, in fine,
hope till my three years shall be accomplished; at which time I was set at liberty
to remonstrate against former conduct, and
to demand justice and truth; which I have
done in so effectual a manner that my anta-
gonist is silenced completely, and I have
compelled what should have been of freedom
—my just right as an artist and as a man.'

In Blake's behaviour towards Hayley,
which has been criticised, we can test his
sincerity to himself under all circumstances:
his impeccable outward courtesy, his con-
cessions, 'bearing insulting benevolence'
meekly, his careful kindness towards Hayley
and hard labour on his behalf, until the
conviction was forced upon him from within
that 'corporeal friends were spiritual enemies,' and that Hayley must be given up.

' Remembering the verses that Hayley sung
  When my heart knocked against the roof of my tongue,'

Blake wrote down bitter epigrams, which
were written down for mere relief of mind,
and certainly never intended for publication ;
and I can see no contradiction between these
inner revolts and an outer politeness which
had in it its due measure of gratitude. Both
were strictly true, and only in a weak and
foolish nature can the consciousness of kindness received distract or blot out the consciousness of the intellectual imbecility which
may lurk behind it.   Blake said :

    ' I never made friends but by spiritual gifts,
  By severe contentions òf friendship and the burning
    fire of thought.'

What least ' contention of friendship' would
not have been too much for the ' triumphs
of temper' of ' Felpham's eldest son ' ? what
' fire of thought' could ever have enlightened
his comfortable darkness?   And is it surprising that Blake should have written in
final desperation :

  ' Thy friendship oft has made my heart to ache :
    Do be my enemy—for friendship's sake ' ?

He quarrelled with many of his friends, with those whom he had cared for most, like Stothard and Flaxman; but the cause was always some moral indignation, which, just or unjust, was believed, and which, being believed, could not have been acted upon. With Blake belief and action were simultaneous. 'Thought is Act,' as he wrote on the margin of Bacon's essays.

I am inclined to attribute to this period the writing down of a mysterious manuscript in the possession of Mr. Buxton Forman, which has never been printed, but which, by his kind permission, I have been allowed to read. This manuscript is headed in large lettering: 'The Seven Days of the Created World,' above which is written, as if by an afterthought, in smaller lettering: 'Genesis.' It is written at the beginning of a blue-covered copy-book, of which the paper is water-marked 1797. It consists of some two hundred lines of blank verse, numbered by tens in the margin up to one hundred and fifty, then follow over fifty more lines without numberings, ending without a full stop or any apparent reason for coming to an end. The handwriting is unmistakably Blake's;

on the first page or two it is large and
careful ; gradually it gets smaller and seems
more hurried or fatigued, as if it had all been
written at a single sitting. The earlier part
goes on without a break, but in the later
part there are corrections ; single words are
altered, sometimes as much as a line and a
half is crossed out and rewritten, the lines
are sometimes corrected in the course of
writing. If it were not for these signs of
correction I should find it difficult to believe
that Blake had actually composed anything
so tamely regular in metre or so destitute
of imagination or symbol. It is an argument or statement, written in the formal
eighteenth-century manner, with pious in-
vocations, God being addressed as ' Sire,'
and ' Wisdom Supreme ' as his daughter,
epithets are inverted that they may fit the
better into a line, and geographical names
heaped up in a scarcely Miltonic manner,
while Ixion strangely neighbours the 'press'd
African.' Nowhere is there any characteristic felicity, or any recognisable sign of
Blake.

When I saw first the manuscript it
occurred to me that it might have been a

fragment of translation from Klopstock, done at Felpham under the immediate dictation of Hayley. 'Read Klopstock into English to Blake' we have seen Hayley noting down. But I can find no original for it in Klopstock. That Blake could have written it out of his own head at any date after 1797 is incredible, even as an experiment in that 'monotonous cadence like that used by Milton and Shakespeare and all writers of English blank verse, derived from the modern bondage of rhyming,' which he tells us in the preface to *Jerusalem* he considered 'to be a necessary and indispensable part of verse,' at the time 'when this verse was first dictated to me.' The only resemblance which we find to it in Blake's published work is in an occasional early fragment like that known as 'The Passions,' and where it is so different from this or any of the early attempts at blank verse is in the absolute regularity of the metre. All I can suggest is that Blake may have written it at a very early age, and preserved a rough draft, which Hayley may have induced him to make a clean copy of, and that in the process of copying he may have touched up the metre

without altering the main substance. If
this is so, I think he stopped so abruptly
because he would not, even to oblige Hayley, go on any longer with so uncongenial a
task.

Blake's three years at Felpham (September
1800 to September 1803) were described by
him as 'my three years' slumber on the
banks of ocean,' and there is no doubt that,
in spite of the neighbourhood and kindly
antagonism of Hayley, that 'slumber' was,
for Blake, in a sense an awakening. It was
the only period of his life lived out of London,
and with Felpham, as he said in a letter to
Flaxman, ' begins a new life, because another
covering of earth is shaken off.' The cottage
at Felpham is only a little way in from a
seashore which is one of the loveliest and
most changing shores of the English coast.
Whistler has painted it, and it is always
as full of faint and wandering colour as a
Whistler. It was on this coast that Rossetti
first learned to care for the sea. To Blake
it must have been the realisation of much
that he had already divined in his imagination. There, as he wrote to Flaxman,
' heaven opens on all sides her golden gates ;

her windows are not obstructed by vapours ;
voices of celestial inhabitants are more distinctly heard and their forms more distinctly
seen ; and my cottage is also a shadow of
their houses.' He drew the cottage on one
of the pages of *Milton*, with a naked image
of himself walking in the garden, and the
image of an angel about to alight on a tree.
The cottage is still, as he found it, 'a perfect
model for cottages, and I think for palaces
of magnificence, only enlarging, not altering
its proportions, and adding ornaments and
not principles' ; and no man of imagination
could live there, under that thatched roof
and with that marvellous sea before him,
and not find himself spiritually naked and
within arm's reach of the angels.

The sea has the properties of sleep and of
awakening, and there can be no doubt that
the sea had both those influences on Blake,
surrounding him for once with an atmosphere like that of his own dreams. 'O
lovely Felpham,' he writes, after he had left
it, 'to thee I am eternally indebted for my
three years' rest from perturbation and the
strength I now enjoy.' Felpham represents
a vivid pause, in which he had leisure to

return upon himself; and in one of his
letters he says : 'One thing of real consequence I have accomplished by coming
into the country, which is to me consolation enough, namely, I have recollected all
my scattered thoughts on art, and resumed
my primitive and original ways of execution
in both painting and engraving, which in
the confusion of London I had very much
obliterated from my mind,' It is to this
period, no doubt (a period mentally overcome in the quiet of Felpham, but awaiting,
as we shall see, the electric spark of that
visit to the Truchsessian Gallery in London),
that Blake refers in the *Descriptive Catalogue*, when he speaks of the 'experiment
pictures' which 'were the result of temptations and perturbations, labouring to destroy
imaginative power, by means of that infernal machine, called Chiaro Oscuro, in the
hands of Venetian and Flemish demons,'
such as the 'outrageous demon,' Rubens,
the 'soft and effeminate and cruel demon,'
Correggio, and, above all, Titian. 'The
spirit of Titian,' we are told, in what is
really a confession of Blake's consciousness
of the power of those painters whose in-

fluence he dreaded, ' was particularly active in raising doubts concerning the possibility of executing without a model; and, when once he had raised the doubt, it became easy for him to snatch away the vision time after time; for when the artist took his pencil, to execute his ideas, his power of imagination weakened so much, and darkened, that memory of nature and of pictures of the various schools possessed his mind, instead of appropriate execution, resulting from the inventions.' It was thus at Felpham that he returned to himself in art, and it was at Felpham also that he had what seems to have been the culminating outburst of ' prophetic ' inspiration, writing from immediate dictation, he said, ' and even against my will.' Visions came readily to him out of the sea, and he saw them walk on the shore, ' majestic shadows, grey but luminous, and superior to the common height of men.'

It was at Felpham that Blake wrote the two last of the Prophetic Books which remain to us, *Milton* and *Jerusalem*. Both bear the date of 1804 on the title-page, and this, no doubt, indicates that the engraving

was begun in that year. Yet it is not
certain that the engraved text of *Jerusalem*,
at any rate, was formally published till after
1809. Pages were certainly inserted between those two dates. On p. 38 Blake
says :

'I heard in Lambeth's shades:
In Felpham I heard and saw the Visions of Albion:
I write in South Molton Street, what I both see and
    hear,
In regions of Humanity, in London's opening streets.'

That the main part was writen in Felpham
is evident from more than one letter to
Butts. In a letter dated April 25, 1803,
Blake says: 'But none can know the
spiritual acts of my three years' slumber
on the banks of ocean, unless he has seen
them in the spirit, or unless he should read
my long poem descriptive of those acts; for
I have in these years composed an immense
number of verses on one grand theme,
similar to Homer's *Iliad* or Milton's *Paradise Lost*; the persons and machinery
entirely new to the inhabitants of earth
(some of the persons excepted). I have
written the poems from immediate dictation,
twelve or sometimes twenty or thirty lines

at a time, without premeditation, and even against my will. The time it has taken in writing was thus rendered non-existent, and an immense poem exists which seems to be the labour of a long life, all produced without labour or study. I mention this to show you what I think the grand reason of my being brought down here.' The poem is evidently *Jerusalem*, for the address ' To the Public' on the first page begins : ' After my three years' slumber on the banks of the Ocean, I again display my Giant forms to the Public.' In the next letter, dated July 6, Blake again refers to the poem : 'Thus I hope that all our three years' trouble ends in good-luck at last, and shall be forgot by my affections, and only remembered by my understanding, to be a memento in time to come, and to speak to future generations by a sublime allegory, which is now perfectly completed into a grand poem. I may praise it, since I dare not pretend to be any other than the secretary ; the authors are in eternity. I consider it as the grandest poem that this world contains. Allegory addressed to the intellectual powers, while it is altogether hidden from the corporeal understanding, is my definition of the most sublime poetry. It is somewhat in the same manner defined by Plato. This poem shall, by divine assistance, be progressively printed and ornamented with prints, and given to the public.'

This I take to mean that before Blake's return to London in 1803 the letterpress of *Jerusalem* was, as he imagined, completely finished, but that the printing and illustration were not yet begun. The fact of this delay, and the fact that pages written after 1803 were inserted here and there, must not lead us to think, as many writers on Blake have thought, that there could be any allusion in *Jerusalem* to the attacks of the *Examiner* of 1808 and 1809, or that ' Hand,' one of the wicked sons of Albion, could possibly be, as Rossetti desperately conjectured, ' a hieroglyph for Leigh Hunt.' The sons of Albion are referred to on quite a third of the pages of *Jerusalem*, from the earliest to the latest, and must have been part of the whole texture of the poem from the beginning. In a passage of the ' Public Address,' contained in the Rossetti MS.,

Blake says : 'The manner in which my
character has been blasted these thirty
years, both as an artist and as a man, may
be seen particularly in a Sunday paper
called the *Examiner*, published in Beaufort's
Buildings ; the manner in which I have
rooted out the nest of villains will be seen
in a poem concerning my three years'
Herculean labours at Felpham, which I
shall soon publish.' Even if this is meant
for *Jerusalem*, as it may well be, Blake is
far from saying that he has referred in the
poem to these particular attacks : 'the nest
of villains' has undoubtedly a much broader
meaning, and groups together all the attacks
of thirty years, public or private, of which
the *Examiner* is but quoted as a recent
example.

The chief reason for supposing that *Jerusalem* may not have been published till after
the exhibition of 1809, is to be found in a
passage in the *Descriptive Catalogue* which
seems to summarise the main subject of the
poem, though it is quite possible that it
may refer to some MS. now lost. The
picture of the Ancient Britons, says Blake,
represents three men who 'were originally

one man who was fourfold. He was self-
divided, and his real humanity slain on the
stems of generation, and the form of the
fourth was like the Son of God. How he
became divided is a subject of great sublimity and pathos. The Artist has written
it, under inspiration, and will, if God please,
publish it. It is voluminous, and contains
the ancient history of Britain, and the world
of Satan and Adam.' ' All these things,' he
has just said, ' are written in Eden.' And
he says further: 'The British Antiquities
are now in the Artist's hands; all his
visionary contemplations relating to his
own country and its ancient glory, when it
was, as it again shall be, the source of
learning and inspiration.' 'Adam was a
Druid, and Noah.' In the description of
his picture of the 'Last Judgment' Blake
indicates ' Albion, our ancestor, patriarch of
the Atlantic Continent, whose history preceded that of the Hebrews, and in whose
sleep, or chaos, creation began. The good
woman is Britannia, the wife of Albion.
Jerusalem is their daughter.'

We see here the symbols, partly Jewish
and partly British, into which Blake had

gradually resolved his mythology. 'The persons and machinery,' he said, were 'entirely new to the inhabitants of earth (some of the persons excepted).' This has been usually, but needlessly, supposed to mean that real people are introduced under disguises. Does it not rather mean, what would be strictly true, that the 'machinery' is here of a kind wholly new to the Prophetic Books, while of the 'persons' some have already been met with, others are now seen for the first time? It is all, in his own words, 'allegory addressed to the intellectual powers, while it is altogether hidden from the corporeal understanding,' and the allegory becomes harder to read as it becomes more and more naked, concentrated, and unexplained. *Milton* seems to have arisen out of a symbol which came visibly before Blake's eyes on his first waking in the cottage at Felpham. 'Work will go on here with Godspeed,' he writes to Butts. 'A roller and two harrows lie before my window. I met a plough on my first going out at my gate the first morning after my arrival, and the ploughboy said to the ploughman, "Father, the gate is

open."' At the beginning of his poem
Blake writes :

'The Plow goes forth in tempests and lightnings and
the Harrow cruel
In blights of the east; the heavy Roller follows in
howlings';

and the imagery returns at intervals, in the
vision of 'the Last Vintage,' the 'Great
Harvest and Vintage of the Nations.' The
personal element comes in the continual
references to the cottage at Felpham;

'He set me down in Felpham's Vale and prepared a
beautiful
Cottage for me that in three years I might write all
these Visions
To display Nature's cruel holiness: the deceits of
Natural Religion';

and it is in the cottage near the sea that he
sees the vision of Milton, when he

'Descended down a Paved work of all kinds of precious
stones
Out from the eastern sky; descending down into my
Cottage
Garden; clothed in black, severe and silent he
descended.'

He awakes from the vision to find his wife
by his side :

'My bones trembled. I fell outstretched upon the
    path
A moment, and my Soul returned into its mortal state
To Resurrection and Judgment in the Vegetable Body,
And my sweet Shadow of delight stood trembling by
    my side.'

In the prayer to be saved from his friends
('Corporeal Friends are Spiritual Enemies'),
in the defence of wrath ('Go to thy labours
at the Mills and leave me to my wrath'), in
the outburst :

'The idiot Reasoner laughs at the Man of Imagination
    And from laughter proceeds to murder by under-
        valuing calumny,'

it is difficult not to see some trace or transposition of the kind, evil counsellor Hayley,
a 'Satan' of mild falsehood in the sight of
Blake. But the main aim of the book is
the assertion of the supremacy of the
imagination :

'The Imagination is not a State: it is the Human
    Existence itself,'

and the putting off of the 'filthy garments,'
of 'Rational Demonstration,' of 'Memory,'
of 'Bacon, Locke, and Newton,' the clothing
of oneself in imagination,

'To cast aside from Poetry, all that is not Inspira-
      tion,
That it shall no longer dare to mock with the asper-
      sion of Madness
Cast on the Inspired by the tame high finisher of
      paltry Blots,
Indefinite or paltry Rhymes ; or paltry harmonies.'

It is because ' Everything in Eternity shines
by its own Internal light,' and that jealousy
and cruelty and hypocrisy are all darkenings
of that light, that Blake declares his purpose of

                    ' Opening to every eye
These wonders of Satan's holiness showing to the
      Earth
The Idol Virtues of the Natural Heart, and Satan's
      Seat
Explore in all its Selfish Natural Virtue, and put off
In Self-annihilation all that is not of God alone.'

Such meanings as these flare out from time
to time with individual splendours of phrase,
like ' Time is the mercy of Eternity,' and
the great poetic epigram, ' O Swedenborg !
strongest of men, the Samson shorn by the
Churches ' (where, for a moment, a line falls
into the regular rhythm of poetry), and
around them are deserts and jungles, frag-

ments of myth broken off and flung before
us after this fashion :

> ‘ But Rahab and Tirzah pervert
> Their mild influences, therefore the Seven Eyes of
>   God walk round
> The Three Heavens of Ulro, where Tirzah and her
>   Sisters
> Weave the black Woof of Death upon Entuthon
>   Benython
> In the Vale of Surrey where Horeb terminates in
>   Rephaim.’

In *Jerusalem*, which was to have been
‘ the grandest poem which the world contains,’ there is less of the exquisite lyrical
work which still decorates many corners of
Milton, but it is Blake’s most serious
attempt to set his myth in order, and it
contains much of his deepest wisdom, with
astonishing flashes of beauty. In *Milton*
there was still a certain approximation to
verse, most of the lines had at least a beginning and an end, but in *Jerusalem*, although
he tells us that ‘ every word and every letter
is studied and put into its place,’ I am by
no means sure that Blake ever intended the
lines, as he wrote them, to be taken as
metrical lines, or read very differently from

the prose of the English Bible, with its
pause in the sense at the end of each verse.
A vague line, hesitating between six and
seven beats, does indeed seem from time
to time to emerge from chaos, and inversions
are brought in at times to accentuate a
cadence certainly intended, as here :

' Why should Punishment Weave the Veil with Iron
Wheels of War,
When Forgiveness might it Weave with Wings of
Cherubim ? '

But read the whole book as if it were prose,
following the sense for its own sake, and
you will find that the prose, when it is not
a mere catalogue, has generally a fine biblical
roll and swing in it, a rhythm of fine oratory;
while if you read each line as if it were
meant to be a metrical unit you will come
upon such difficulties as this :

' Such is the Forgiveness of the Gods, the Moral Virtues of the '

That is one line, and the next adds 'Heathen.'
There may seem to be small reason for such
an arrangement of the lines if we read
Jerusalem in the useful printed text of

Mr. Russell and Mr. Maclagan; but the
reason will be seen if we turn to the original
engraved page, where we shall see that
Blake had set down in the margin a lovely
little bird with outstretched wings, and that
the tip of the bird's wing almost touches the
last letter of the 'the' and leaves no room
for another word. That such a line was
meant to be metrical is unthinkable, as
unthinkable as that

' Los stood and stamped the earth, then he threw down
       his hammer in rage &
   In fury '

has any reason for existing in this form
beyond the mere chance of a hand that
writes until all the space of a given line is
filled. Working as he did within those
limits of his hand's space, he would accustom
himself to write for the most part, and
and especially when his imagination was
most vitally awake, in lines that came
roughly within those limits. Thus it will
often happen that the most beautiful passages will have the nearest resemblance to
a regular metrical scheme, as in such lines
as these :

In vain : he is hurried afar into an unknown Night.
He' bleeds in torrents of blood, as he rolls thro'
  heaven above,
He chokes up the paths of the sky : the Moon is
  leprous as snow :
Trembling and descending down, seeking to rest on
  high Mona :
Scattering her leprous snow in flakes of disease over
  Albion.
The Stars flee remote : the heaven is iron, the earth
  is sulphur,
And all the mountains and hills shrink up like a
  withering gourd.'

Here the prophet is no longer speaking with
the voice of the orator, but with the old,
almost forgotten voice of the poet, and with
something of the despised 'Monotonous
Cadence.'

Blake lived for twenty-three years after
the date on the title-page of *Jerusalem*, but,
with the exception of the two plates called
The Ghost of Abel, engraved in 1822, this
vast and obscure encyclopædia of unknown
regions remains his last gospel. He thought
it his most direct message. Throughout the
Prophetic Books Blake has to be translated
out of the unfamiliar language into which
he has tried to translate spiritual realities,

literally, as he apprehended them. Just as, in the designs which his hand drew as best it could, according to its limited and partly false knowledge, from the visions which his imagination saw with perfect clearness, he was often unable to translate that vision into its real equivalent in design, so in his attempts to put these other mental visions into words he was hampered by an equally false method, and often by reminiscences of what passed for 'picturesque' writing in the work of his contemporaries. He was, after all, of his time, though he was above it, and just as he only knew Michelangelo through bad reproductions, and could never get his own design wholly free, malleable, and virgin to his 'shaping spirit of imagination,' so, in spite of all his marvellous lyrical discoveries, made when his mind was less burdened by the weight of a controlling message, he found himself, when he attempted to make an intelligible system out of the 'improvisations of the spirit,' and to express that system with literal accuracy, the half-helpless captive of formal words, conventional rhythms, a language not drawn direct from its source. Thus we find,

in the Prophetic Books, neither achieved
poems nor an achieved philosophy. The
philosophy has reached us only in splendid
fragments (the glimmering of stars out of
separate corners of a dark sky), and we shall
never know to what extent these fragments
were once parts of a whole. Had they been
ever really fused, this would have been the
only system of philosophy made entirely out
of the raw material of poetry. As it has
come to us unachieved, the world has still
to wait for a philosophy untouched by the
materialism of the prose intelligence.

In the Prophetic Books Blake labours at
the creation of a myth, which may be figured
as the representation in space of a vast
spiritual tragedy. It is the tragedy of Man,
a tragedy in which the first act is creation.
Milton was content to begin with 'Man's
first disobedience,' but Blake would track
the human soul back into chaos, and beyond.
He knows, like Krishna, in the *Bhagavad
Gita*, that 'above this visible nature there
exists another, unseen and eternal, which,
when all created things perish, does not
perish'; and he sees the soul's birth in
that 'inward spiritual world,' from which it

falls to mortal life and the body, as into a death. He sees its new, temporal life, hung round with fears and ambushes, out of which, by a new death, the death of that mortal self which separates it from eternity, it may reawaken, even in this life, into the eternal life of imagination. The persons of the drama are the powers and passions of Man, and the spiritual forces which surround him, and are the 'states' through which he passes. Man is seen, as Blake saw all things, fourfold: Man's Humanity, his Spectre, who is Reason, his Emanation, who is Imagination, his Shadow, who is Desire. And the states through which Man passes, friendly or hostile, energies of good or of evil, are also four: the Four Zoas, who are the Four Living Creatures of Ezekiel, and are called Urizen, Luvah, Tharmas, and Urthona (or, to mortals, Los). Each Zoa has his Emanation: Ahania, who is the emanation of Intellect, and is named 'eternal delight'; Vala, the emanation of Emotion, who is lovely deceit, and the visible beauty of Nature; Enion, who is the emanation of the Senses, and typifies the maternal instinct; Enitharmon, who is

the emanation of Intuition, and personifies
spiritual beauty. The drama is the division,
death, and resurrection, in an eternal circle,
of the powers of man and of the powers in
whose midst he fights and struggles. Of
this incommensurable action we are told
only in broken hints, as of a chorus crying
outside doors where deeds are being done in
darkness. Images pass before us, make
their gesture, and are gone; the words
spoken are ambiguous, and seem to have
an under meaning which it is essential for
us to apprehend. We see motions of building and of destruction, higher than the topmost towers of the world, and deeper than
the abyss of the sea; souls pass through
furnaces, and are remade by Time's hammer
on the anvil of space; there are obscure
crucifixions, and Last Judgments return and
are re-enacted.

To Blake, the Prophetic Books were to be
the new religious books of a religion which
was not indeed new, for it was the 'Everlasting Gospel' of Jesus, but, because it
had been seen anew by Swedenborg and by
Wesley and by 'the gentle souls who guide
the great wine-press of Love,' among whom

was Teresa, seemed to require a new interpretation to the imagination.   Blake wrote
when the eighteenth century was coming to
an end ; he announced the new dispensation
which was to come, Swedenborg had said,
with the year (which was the year of Blake's
birth) 1757.   He looked forward steadfastly
to the time when 'Sexes must vanish and
cease to be,' when 'all their crimes, their
punishments, their accusations of sin, all
their jealousies, revenges, murders, hidings
of cruelty in deceit, appear only on the outward spheres of visionary Space and Time,
in the shadows of possibility by mutual forgiveness for evermore, and in the vision and
the prophecy, that we may foresee and
avoid the terrors of Creation and Redemp-
tion and Judgment.'   He spoke to literalists,
rationalists, materialists ; to an age whose
very infidels doubted only facts, and whose
deists affirmed no more than that man was
naturally religious.   The rationalist's denial
of everything beyond the evidence of his
senses seemed to him a criminal blindness ;
and he has engraved a separate sheet with
images and statements of the affirmation :
'There is no Natural Religion.'   To Blake

the literal meaning of things seemed to be of less than no importance. To worship the 'Goddess Nature' was to worship the 'God of this World,' and so to be an atheist, as even Wordsworth seemed to him to be. Religion was asleep, with Art and Literature in its arms : Blake's was the voice of the awakening angel. What he cried was that only eternal and invisible things were true, and that visible temporal things were a veil and a delusion. In this he knew himself to be on the side of Wesley and Whitefield, and that Voltaire and Rousseau, the voices of the passing age, were against him. He called them 'frozen sons of the feminine Tabernacle of Bacon, Newton, and Locke.' Wesley and Whitefield he calls the 'two servants' of God, his 'two witnesses.'

But it seemed to him that he could go deeper into the Bible than they, in their practical eagerness, had gone. 'What are the treasures of Heaven,' he asked, 'that we are to lay up for ourselves—are they any other than Mental Studies and Perform-ances?' 'Is the Holy Ghost,' he asked, 'any other than an intellectual Fountain?' It seemed to him that he could harmonise many things once held to be discordant, and adjust the many varying interpretations of the Bible and the other books of ancient religions by a universal application of what had been taken in too personal a way. Hence many of the puzzling 'correspondences' of English cities and the tribe of Judah, of 'the Poetic Genius, which is the Lord.'

There is an outcry in *Jerusalem* :

'No individual ought to appropriate to Himself
  Or to his Emanation, any of the Universal Character-
    istics
  Of David or of Eve, of the Woman, of the Lord,
  Of Reuben or of Benjamin, of Joseph or Judah or
    Levi.
  Those who dare appropriate to themselves Universal
    Attributes
  Are the Blasphemous Selfhoods and must be broken
    asunder.
  A Vegetable Christ and a Virgin Eve, are the Herma-
    phroditic
  Blasphemy : by his Maternal Birth he put off that
    Evil One,
  And his Maternal Humanity must be put off Eter-
    nally,
  Lest the Sexual Generation swallow up Regenera-
    tion :
  Come, Lord Jesus, take on Thee the Satanic Body of
    Holiness !'

Exactly what is meant here will be seen more clearly if we compare it with a much earlier statement of the same doctrine, in the poem 'To Tirzah' in the *Songs of Experience*, and the comparison will show us all the difference between the art of Blake in 1794, and what seemed to him the needful manner of his message ten years later. 'Tirzah' is Blake's name for Natural Religion.

> 'Whatever is Born of Mortal Birth
> Must be consumed with the Earth,
> To rise from Generation free:
> Then what have I to do with thee?
>
> The Sexes sprung from Shame and Pride
> Blow'd in the morn; in evening died;
> But Mercy changed Death into Sleep;
> The Sexes rose to work and weep.
>
> Thou Mother of my Mortal part
> With cruelty didst mould my Heart,
> And with false, self-deceiving Tears
> Didst bind my Nostrils, Eyes, and Ears;
>
> Didst close my Tongue in senseless clay,
> And me to Mortal Life betray:
> The Death of Jesus set me free:
> Then what have I to do with thee?'

Here is expressed briefly and exquisitely a

large part of the foundation of Blake's
philosophy : that birth into the world,
Christ's or ours, is a fall from eternal realities
into the material affections of the senses,
which are deceptions, and bind us under the
bondage of nature, our ' Mother,' who is the
Law ; and that true life is to be regained
only by the death of that self which cuts us
off from our part in eternity, which we enter
through the eternal reality of the imagination. In the poem, the death of Jesus
symbolises that deliverance ; in the passage
from *Jerusalem* the Church's narrow conception of the mortal life of Jesus is
rebuked, and its universal significance in-
dicated, but in how different, how obscure,
how distorted a manner. What has brought
about this new manner of saying the same
thing ?

I think it is an endeavour to do without
what had come to seem to Blake the deceiving imageries of nature, to express the truth
of contraries at one and the same time, and
to render spiritual realities in a literal translation. What he had been writing was
poetry ; now what he wrote was to be prophecy ; or, as he says in *Milton* :

> 'In fury of Poetic Inspiration,
> To build the Universe Stupendous, Mental Forms
> Creating.'

And, seeking always the 'Minute Particulars,' he would make no compromise with earthly things, use no types of humanity, no analogies from nature; for it was against all literal acceptance of nature or the Bible or reason, of any apparent reality, that he was appealing. Hence

> 'All Human Forms identified, even Tree, Metal, Earth, and Stone, all
> Human Forms identified, living, going forth, and returning wearied
> Into the planetary lives of Years, Months, Days, and Hours.'

Hence the affirmation:

> 'For all are Men in Eternity, Rivers, Mountains, Cities, Villages';

and the voice of London saying:

> 'My Streets are my Ideas of Imagination.'

Hence the parallels and correspondences, the names too well known to have any ready-made meaning to the emotions (London or Bath), the names so wholly unknown

that they also could mean nothing to the
emotions or to the memory (Bowlahoola,
Golgonooza), the whole unhuman mythology,
abstractions of frigid fire. In *Jerusalem*
Blake interrupts himself to say :

> ' I call them by their English names; English, the
> rough basement.
> Los built the stubborn structure of the Language,
> acting against
> Albion's melancholy, who must else have been a
> Dumb despair.'

In the Prophetic Books we see Blake
labouring upon a 'rough basement' of
'stubborn' English; is it, after all this
'consolidated and extended work,' this
'energetic exertion of his talent,' a building
set up in vain, the attempt to express what
must else have been, and must now for ever
remain, 'a dumb despair' ?

I think we must take the Prophetic Books
not quite as Blake would have had us take
them. He was not a systematic thinker,
and he was not content to be a lyric poet.
Nor indeed did he ever profess to offer us
a system, built on logic and propped by
reasoning, but a myth, which is a poetical
creation. He said in *Jerusalem* :

'I must Create a System, or be enslaved by another
  Man's.
I will not Reason or Compare : my business is to
  Create.'

To Blake each new aspect of truth came as
a divine gift, and between all his affirma-
tions of truth there is no contradiction, or
no other than that vital contradiction of
opposites equally true. The difficulty lies
in co-ordinating them into so minutely
articulated a myth, and the difficulty is
increased when we possess, instead of the
whole body of the myth, only fragments of
it. Of the myth itself it must be said that,
whether from defects inherent in it or from
the fragmentary state in which it comes to
us, it can never mean anything wholly
definite or satisfying even to those minds
best prepared to receive mystical doctrine.
We cannot read the Prophetic Books either
for their thought only or for their beauty
only. Yet we shall find in them both
inspired thought and unearthly beauty.
With these two things, not always found
together, we must be content.

The Prophetic Books bear witness, in
their own way, to that great gospel of

imagination which Blake taught and ex-
emplified. In *Jerusalem* it is stated in a
single sentence: ' I know of no other
Christianity and of no other Gospel than
the liberty both of body and mind to exercise the Divine Arts of Imagination: Imagination, the real and eternal World of
which this Vegetable Universe is but a faint
shadow, and in which we shall live in our
Eternal or Imaginative Bodies, when these
Vegetable Mortal Bodies are no more.' ' O
Human Imagination, O Divine Body I
have Crucified!' he cries; and he sees
continually

' Abstract Philosophy warring in enmity against
    Imagination,
  Which is the Divine Body of the Lord Jesus, blessed
    for ever.'

He finds the England of his time ' generalis-
ing Art and Science till Art and Science is
lost,' making

' A pretence of Art, to destroy Art, a pretence of
    Liberty
  To destroy Liberty, a pretence of Religion to destroy
    Religion.'

He sees that

'The Visions of Eternity, by reason of narrowed per-
    ceptions,
  Are become weak visions of Time and Space, fix'd
    into furrows of death.'

He sees everywhere 'the indefinite Spectre,
who is the Rational Power,' crying out :

'I am God, O Sons of Men! I am your Rational
    Power !
  Am I not Bacon and Newton and Locke who teach
    Humility to Man ?
  Who teach Doubt and Experiment : and my two
    kings, Voltaire, Rousseau.'

He sees this threefold spirit of doubt and
negation overspreading the earth, 'brooding
Abstract Philosophy,' destroying Imagination ; and, as he looked about him,

'Every Universal Form was become barren mountains
    of Moral
  Virtue : and every Minute Particular harden'd into
    grains of sand :
  And all the tenderness of the soul cast forth as filth
    and mire.'

It is against this spiritual deadness that
he brings his protest, which is to awaken
Albion out of the sleep of death, 'his long
and cold repose.' 'Therefore Los,' the spirit
of prophecy, and thus Blake, who 'kept the

Divine Vision in time of trouble,' stands in
London building Golgonooza, 'the spiritual
fourfold London,' the divine City of God.
Of the real or earthly London he says in
Jerusalem :

> 'I see London blind and age bent begging thro' the
>   Streets
> Of Babylon, led by a child, his tears run down his
>   beard !'

Babylon, in Blake, means 'Rational Mor-
ality.' In the *Songs of Innocence* we shall
see the picture, at the head of the poem
called 'London.' In that poem Blake numbers the cries which go up in 'London's
chartered streets,' the cry of the chimney-
sweeper, of the soldier, of the harlot; and
he says :

> 'In every cry of every man,
> In every infant's cry of fear,
> In every voice, in every ban,
> The mind-forged manacles I hear.'

Into these lines he condenses much of his
gospel. What Blake most hated on earth
were 'mind-forged manacles.' Reason seemed
to him to have laid its freezing and fetter-
ing hand on every warm joy, on every

natural freedom, of body and soul; all his
wrath went out against the forgers and the
binders of these fetters. In his earlier
poems he sings the instinctive joys of
innocence; in his later, the wise joys of
experience; and all the Prophetic Books are
so many songs of mental liberty and invec-
tives against every form of mental oppression. 'And Jerusalem is called Liberty
among the Children of Albion.' One of the
Prophetic Books, *Ahania*, can be condensed
into a single sentence, one of its lines : 'Truth
has bounds ; Error has none.' Yet this must
be understood to mean that error is the
'indefinite void' and truth a thing minutely
organised ; not that truth can endure bondage or limitation from without. He typifies
Moral Law by Rahab, the harlot of the
Bible, a being of hidden, hypocritic cruelty.
Chastity is no more in itself than a lure of
the harlot, typifying unwilling restraint, a
negation, and no personal form of energy.

'No individual can keep the Laws, for they are death
  To every energy of man, and forbid the springs
    of life.'

It is energy that is virtue, and, above all,

mental energy. 'The treasures of heaven are not negations of passion, but realities of intellect, from which all the passions emanate, uncurbed in their eternal glory.' 'It was the tree of the knowledge of good and evil that brought sin into the world by creating distinctions, by calling this good and that evil.' Blake says in *Jerusalem* :

'And in this manner of the Sons of Albion in their
    strength ;
They take the Two Contraries which are called Quali-
    ties, with which
Every Substance is clothed, they name them Good and
    Evil,
From them they make an Abstract, which is a Negation
Not only of the Substance from which it is derived,
A murderer of its own Body : but also a murderer
Of every Divine Member : it is the Reasoning Power,
An Abstract objecting power, that Negatives every-
    thing.
This is the Spectre of Man : the Holy Reasoning
    Power,
And in its Holiness is closed the Abomination of
    Desolation.'

The active form of sin is judgment, intellectual cruelty, unforgivingness, punishment. 'In Hell is all self-righteousness ; there is no such thing as forgiveness of sins.' In

his picture of the 'Last Judgment' he represents the Furies by men, not women ; and
for this reason : ' The spectator may suppose
them clergymen in the pulpit, scourging sin
instead of forgiving it.' In *Jerusalem* he
says :

> ' And the appearance of a Man was seen in the
>   Furnaces,
>   Saving those who have sinned from the punishment
>   of the Law
>   (In pity of the punisher whose state is eternal
>   death),
>   And keeping them from Sin by the mild counsels of
>   his love.'

And in his greatest paradox and deepest
passion of truth, he affirms :

> ' I care not whether a Man is Good or Evil; all that I
>   care
>   Is whether he is a Wise Man or a Fool. Go, put off
>   Holiness
>   And put on Intellect.'

That holiness may be added to wisdom
Blake asks only that continual forgiveness
of sins which to him meant understanding,
and thus intellectual sympathy; and he sees
in the death of Jesus the supreme symbol of
this highest mental state.

' And if God dieth not for Man and giveth not himself
    Eternally for Man, Man could not exist, for Man is love,
    As God is Love : every kindness to another is a little
        Death
    In the Divine Image, nor can Man exist but by
        Brotherhood.'

Of Blake it may be said as he says of
Albion : ' He felt that Love and Pity are
the same,' and to Love and Pity he gave
the ultimate jurisdiction over humanity.

Blake's gospel of forgiveness rests on a
very elaborate structure, which he has built
up in his doctrine of 'States.' At the head
of the address to the Deists in the third
chapter of *Jerusalem*, he has written : ' The
Spiritual States of the Soul are all Eternal.
Distinguish between the Man and his present State.' Much of his subtlest casuistry
is expended on this distinction, and, as he
makes it, it is profoundly suggestive. Erin
says, in *Jerusalem* :

' Learn therefore, O Sisters, to distinguish the Eternal
        Human
    That walks about among the stones of fire, in bliss
        and woe
    Alternate, from those States or Worlds in which the
        Spirit travels :
    This is the only means to Forgiveness of Enemies.'

The same image is used again :

'As the Pilgrim passes while the Country permanent remains,
So Men pass on; but States remain permanent for ever';

and, again, in almost the same words, in the prose fragment on the picture of the 'Last Judgment': 'Man passes on, but states remain for ever; he passes through them like a traveller, who may as well suppose that the places he has passed through exist no more, as a man may suppose that the states he has passed through exist no more: everything is eternal.' By states Blake means very much what we mean by moods, which, in common with many mystics, he conceives as permanent spiritual forces, through which what is transitory in man passes, while man imagines that they, more transitory than himself, are passing through him. It is from this conception of man as a traveller, and of good and evil, the passions and virtues and sensations and ideas of man, as spiritual countries, eternally remaining, through which he passes, that Blake draws his inference: condemn, if you

will, the state which you call sin, but do
not condemn the individual whose passage
through it may be a necessity of his journey.
And his litany is :

'Descend, O Lamb of God, and take away the imputa-
tion of Sin
By the creation of States and the deliverance of
Individuals evermore. Amen. . . .
Come then, O Lamb of God, and take away the
remembrance of Sin.'

VIII

BLAKE had already decided to leave Felpham, 'with the full approbation of Mr. Hayley,' as early as April 1803. 'But alas !' he writes to Butts, 'now I may say to you—what perhaps I should not dare to say to any one else—that I can alone carry on my visionary studies in London unannoyed, and that I may converse with my friends in eternity, see visions, dream dreams, and prophesy, and speak parables unobserved, and at liberty from the doubts of other mortals.' 'There is no medium or middle state,' he adds, 'and if a man is the enemy of my spiritual life while he pretends to be the friend of my corporeal, he is a real enemy.' Hayley, once fully realised, had to be shaken off, and we find Blake taking rooms on the first-floor at 17 South Molton Street, and preparing to move to London, when an incident occurs which leaves him,

as he put it in a letter to Butts, 'in a bustle
to defend myself against a very unwarrant-
able warrant from a justice of the peace in
Chichester, which was taken out against me
by a private in Captain Leathes' troop of
1st or Royal Dragoon Guards, for an assault
and seditious words.' This was a soldier
whom Blake had turned out of his garden,
'perhaps foolishly and perhaps not,' as he
said, but with unquestionable vigour. 'It
is certain,' he commented, 'that a too passive manner, inconsistent with my active
physiognomy, had done me much mischief.'
The 'contemptible business' was tried at
Chichester on January 11, 1804, at the
Quarter Sessions, and Blake was acquitted
of the charge of high treason; 'which so
gratified the auditory,' says the *Sussex
Advertiser* of the date, 'that the court was,
in defiance of all decency, thrown into an
uproar by their noisy exultations.'

London, on his return to it, seemed to
Blake as desirable as Felpham had seemed
after London; and he writes to Hayley:
'The shops in London improve; everything
is elegant, clean, and neat; the streets are
widened where they were narrow; even

Snow Hill is become almost level and is a
very handsome street, and the narrow part
of the Strand near St. Clement's is widened
and become very elegant.'   But there were
other reasons for satisfaction.   In a letter
written before he left Felpham, Blake said :
' What is very pleasant, every one who hears
of my going to London applauds it as the
only course for the interest of all concerned
in my works ; observing that I ought not
to be away from the opportunities London
affords of seeing fine pictures, and the
various improvements in works of art going
on in London.'   In October 1804 he writes
to Hayley, in the most ecstatic of his
letters, recording the miracle or crisis that
has suddenly opened his eyes, vitalising the
meditations of Felpham.   ' Suddenly,' says
the famous letter, ' on the day after visiting
the Truchsessian Gallery of pictures, I was
again enlightened with the light I enjoyed
in my youth, and which has for exactly
twenty years been closed from me as by
a door and by window-shutters. . . . Dear
Sir, excuse my enthusiasm, or rather madness, for I am really drunk with intellectual
vision whenever I take a pencil or graver

into my hand, even as I used to be in my
youth, and as I have not been for twenty
dark, but very profitable years.'   Some of
this new radiance may be seen in the water-
colour of ' The River of Life,' which has
been assigned by Mr. Russell to this year ;
and in those ' Inventions ' in illustration of
Blair's *Grave*, by which Blake was to make
his one appeal to the public of his time.

That appeal he made through the treacherous services of a sharper named Cromek, an engraver and publisher of prints,
who bought the twelve drawings for the price
of twenty pounds, on the understanding that
they were to be engraved by their designer ;
and thereupon handed them over to the
fashionable Schiavonetti, telling Blake 'your
drawings have had the good fortune to be
engraved by one of the first artists in
Europe.'   He further caused a difference
between Blake and Stothard which destroyed
a friendship of nearly thirty years, never
made up in the lifetime of either, though
Blake made two efforts to be reconciled.
The story of the double commission given by
Cromek for a picture of Chaucer's *Canterbury Pilgrims*, and of the twofold accusation

of plagiarism, is told clearly enough in the narrative of J. T. Smith (p. 368 below), while Cunningham does his best to confuse the facts in the interests of Cromek. It has been finally summed up by Mr. Swinburne, who comes to this reasonable conclusion : ' It is probable that Stothard believed himself to be not in the wrong ; it is certain that Blake was in the right.' As for Cromek, he has written himself down for all time in his true character, naked and not ashamed, in a letter to Blake of May 1807, where the false bargainer asserts : ' Herein I have been gratified ; for I was determined to bring you food as well as reputation, though, from your late conduct, I have some reason to embrace your wild opinion, that to manage genius, and to cause it to produce good things, it is absolutely necessary to starve it ; indeed, the opinion is considerably heightened by the recollection that your best work, the illustrations of *The Grave*, was produced when you and Mrs. Blake were reduced so low as to be obliged to live on half a guinea a week.' Cromek published the book by subscription in August 1808, with an ' advertisement ' invoking the approval of

the drawings as 'a high and original effort
of genius' by eleven Royal Academicians,
including Benjamin West, Flaxman, Lawrence, and Stothard. 'To the elegant and
classical taste of Mr. Fuseli,' he tells us
further, 'he is indebted for the excellent
remarks on the moral worth and picturesque
dignity of the Designs that accompany
this Poem.' Fuseli praises pompously the
'genuine and unaffected attitudes,' the
'simple graces which nature and the heart
alone can dictate, and only an eye inspired
by both, discover,' though finding the artist
'playing on the very verge of legitimate
invention.'

It is by the designs to Blair's *Grave* that
Blake is still perhaps chiefly known, outside
his own public; nor was he ever so clear,
or, in a literal way, so convincing in his
rendering of imaginative reality. Something formal tempers and makes the ecstasy
explicit; the drawing is inflexibly elegant;
all the Gothic secrets that had been learnt
among the tombs in Westminster Abbey
find their way into these stony and yet
strangely living death-beds and monuments
of death. No more vehement movement

was ever perpetrated than that leap together
of the soul and body meeting as the grave
opens. If ever the soul was made credible
to the mind through the eyes, it is in these
designs carved out of abstract form, and
planned according to a logic which is partly
literal faith in imagination and partly the
curtailment of scholastic drawing.

The book contains the names of more than
five hundred subscribers, but only one contemporary notice has been found, a notice of
two columns, mere drivel and mere raving,
signed by the happily undiscovered initials
R. H., in the thirty-second number of Leigh
Hunt's paper, *The Examiner* (August 7,
1808, pp. 509, 510). It is under the
heading 'Fine Arts,' and is called 'Blake's
edition of Blair's *Grave*.' The notice is
rendered specially grotesque by its serious
air of arguing with what it takes to be
absurdity coupled with 'an appearance of
libidinousness' which 'intrudes itself upon
the holiness of our thoughts and counteracts
their impression.' Like most moralists of
the press, this critic's meaning is hard to
get at. Here, however, is a specimen:
'But a more serious censure attaches to

two of these most heterogeneous and serio-fantastic designs. At the awful day of judgment, before the throne of God himself, a male and female figure are described in most indecent attitudes. It is the same with the salutation of a man and his wife meeting in the pure mansions of Heaven.' Thus sanctified a voice was it that first croaked at Blake out of the 'nest of villains' which he imagined that he was afterwards to 'root out' of *The Examiner*.

A quite different view of him is to be found in a book which was published before the *Grave* actually came out, though it contains a reference to the designs and to the 'ardent and encomiastic applause' of 'some of the first artists in the country.' The book, which contained an emblematic frontispiece designed by Blake and engraved by Cromek, was *A Father's Memoirs of his Child*, written by Benjamin Heath Malkin, then headmaster of Bury Grammar School, in which the father gives a minute and ingenuous account of his child, a prodigy of precocious intellect, who died at the age of nearly seven years. The child was accustomed to do little drawings, some of which are reproduced in the book in facsimile, and the father, after giving his own opinion of them, adds : ' Yet, as my panegyric on such a subject can carry with it no recommendation, I subjoin the testimony of Mr. Blake to this instance of peculiar ingenuity, who has given me his opinion of these various performances in the following terms :—

' " They are all firm, determinate outlines, or identical form. Had the hand which executed these little ideas been that of a plagiary, who works only from the memory, we should have seen blots, called masses ; blots without form, and therefore without meaning. These blots of light and dark, as being the result of labour, are always clumsy and indefinite ; the effect of rubbing out and putting in, like the progress of a blind man, or of one in the dark, who feels his way, but does not see it. These are not so. Even the copy of Raphael's cartoon of St. Paul preaching is a firm, determinate outline, struck at once, as Protogenes struck his line, when he meant to make himself known to Apelles. The map of Allestone has the same character of the firm and determinate. All his efforts prove this

little boy to have had that greatest of all
blessings, a strong imagination, a clear idea,
and a determinate vision of things in his
own mind.' It is in the lengthy dedication
of the book to Thomas Johnes, the translator of Froissart, that Dr. Malkin gives the
very interesting personal account of Blake
which is reprinted on p. 307 below.

It is not certain whether Blake had ever
known little Thomas Malkin, and it would
be interesting to know whether it was
through any actual influence of his that the
child had come to his curious invention of
an imaginary country. He drew the map
of this country, peopled with names (Nob-
blede and Bobblobb, Punchpeach and
Closetha) scarcely more preposterous than
the names which Blake was just then discovering for his own spiritual regions, wrote
its chronicles, and even made music for it.
The child was born in 1795 and died in
1802, and Blake had been at Felpham since
September 1800; but, if they had met
before that date, there was quite time for
Blake's influence to have shown itself. In
1799 the astonishing child 'could read,
without hesitation, any English book. He

could spell any words. . . . He knew the Greek alphabet'; and on his fourth birthday, in that year, he writes to his mother saying that he has got a Latin grammar and English prints. In October 1800 he says: 'I know a deal of Latin,' and in December he is reading Burns's poems, 'which I am very fond of.' Influence or accident, the coincidence is singular, and at least shows us something in Blake's brain working like the brain of a precocious child.

In 1806 Blake wrote a generous and vigorous letter to the editor of the *Monthly Review* (July 1, 1806) in reply to a criticism which had appeared in *Bell's Weekly Messenger* on Fuseli's picture of Count Ugolino in the Royal Academy. In 1808 he had himself, and for the fifth and last time, two pictures in the Academy, and in that year he wrote the letter to Ozias Humphrey, describing one of his many 'Last Judgments,' which is given, with a few verbal errors, by J. T. Smith. In December he wrote to George Cumberland, who had written to order for a friend 'a complete set of all you have published in the way of books coloured as mine are,' that 'new varieties, or

rather new pleasures, occupy my thoughts;
new profits seem to arise before me so
tempting that I have already involved
myself in engagements that preclude all
possibility of promising anything.'   Does
this refer to the success of Blair's *Grave*,
which had just been published?   He goes
on : 'I have, however, the satisfaction to
inform you that I have myself begun to
print an account of my various inventions
in Art, for which I have procured a publisher, and am determined to pursue the
plan of publishing, that I may get printed
without disarranging my time, which in
future must alone be designing and painting.'   To this project, which was never
carried out, he refers again in the prospectus
printed in anticipation of his exhibition, a
copy of which, given to Ozias Humphreys,
exists with the date May 15, 1809.   A
second prospectus is given by Gilchrist as
follows :—

'Blake's Chaucer, the Canterbury Pil-
grims. This Fresco Picture, representing
Chaucer's Characters, painted by William
Blake, as it is now submitted to the public.

'The designer proposes to engrave in a

correct and finished line manner of engraving, similar to those original copper-plates
of Albert Durer, Lucas Van Leyden, Alde-
grave, and the old original engravers, who
were great masters in painting and designing; whose methods alone can delineate
Character as it is in this Picture, where
all the lineaments are distinct.

'It is hoped that the Painter will be
allowed by the public (notwithstanding
artfully disseminated insinuations to the
contrary) to be better able than any other
to keep his own characters and expressions;
having had sufficient evidence in the works
of our own Hogarth, that no other artist
can reach the original spirit so well as the
Painter himself, especially as Mr. B. is an
old, well-known, and acknowledged graver.

'The size of the engraving will be three feet
one inch long by one foot high. The artist
engages to deliver it, finished, in one year
from September next. No work of art can
take longer than a year: it may be worked
backwards and forwards without end, and
last a man's whole life; but he will, at
length, only be forced to bring it back to
what it was, and it will be worse than it

was at the end of the first twelve months.
The value of this artist's year is the criterion
of Society; and as it is valued, so does
Society flourish or decay.

'The price to Subscribers, Four Guineas;
two to be paid at the time of subscribing,
the other two, on delivery of the print.

'Subscriptions received at No. 28, corner
of Broad Street, Golden Square, where the
Picture is now exhibiting, among other
works, by the same artist.

'The price will be considerably raised to
non-subscribers.'

The exhibition thus announced was held
at the house of James Blake, and contained
sixteen pictures, of which the first nine are
described as 'Frescoes' or 'experiment
pictures,' and the remaining seven as 'drawings,' that is, drawings in water-colour. The
Catalogue (which was included in the entrance fee of half a crown) is Blake's most
coherent work in prose, and can be read in
Gilchrist, ii. 139-163. It is called 'A
Descriptive Catalogue of Pictures, Poetical
and Historical Inventions, painted by
William Blake, in Water-Colours, being the
ancient Method of Fresco Painting Re-

stored; and Drawings, for Public Inspection, and for Sale by Private Contract.'
Crabb Robinson, from whom we have the
only detailed account of the exhibition, says
that the pictures filled 'several rooms of an
ordinary dwelling-house' (see p. 283 below).
He mentions Lamb's delight in the Catalogue,[1] and his declaring 'that Blake's
description was the finest criticism he had
ever read of Chaucer's poem.' In that
letter to Bernard Barton (May 15, 1824),
which is full of vivid admiration for Blake
('I must look on him as one of the most
extraordinary persons of the age'), Lamb
speaks of the criticism as 'most spirited, but
mystical and full of vision,' and says: 'His
pictures—one in particular, the "Canterbury Pilgrims" (far above Stothard's)—
have great merit, but hard, dry, yet
with grace.' Southey, we know from a
sneer in *The Doctor* at 'that painter of
great but insane genius, William Blake,'
also went to the exhibition, and found, he

---

[1] We know from Mr. Lucas's catalogue of Lamb's library
that Lamb bound it up in a thick 12mo volume with his own
Confessions of a Drunkard, Southey's *Wat Tyler*, and Lady
Winchilsea's and Lord Rochester's poems.

tells us, the picture of ' The Ancient Britons,'
' one of the worst pictures, which is saying
much.' A note to Mr. Swinburne's *William
Blake* tells us that in the competent opinion
of Mr. Seymour Kirkup this picture was
' the very noblest of all Blake's works.' It
is now lost; it was probably Blake's largest
work, the figures, Blake asserts, being ' full
as large as life.' Of the other pictures the
seventh, eighth, ninth, tenth, and sixteenth
are lost; the ninth exists in a replica in
' fresco,' and the sixteenth in what is probably a first sketch.

Blake's reason for giving this exhibition
was undoubtedly indignation at what he
took to be Stothard's treachery in the
matter of the ' Canterbury Pilgrims.' This
picture (now in the National Gallery, No.
1163) had been exhibited by Cromek
throughout the kingdom, and he had announced effusively, in a seven page advertisement at the end of Blair's *Grave*, the
issue of ' a print executed in the line manner
of engraving, and in the same excellent
style as the portrait of Mr. William Blake,
prefixed to this work, by Louis Schiavonetti,
Esq., V.A., the gentleman who has etched

the prints that at once illustrate and em-
bellish the present volume.' The *Descriptive Catalogue* is full of angry scorn of 'my
rival,' as Blake calls Stothard, and of the
'dumb dollies' whom he has 'jumbled
together' in his design, and of Hoppner for
praising them in the letter quoted in the
advertisement. 'If Mr. B.'s "Canterbury
Pilgrims" had been done by any other power
than that of the poetic visionary, it would
have been as dull as his adversary's,' Blake
assures us, and, no doubt, justly. The
general feeling of Blake's friends, I doubt
not, is summed up in an ill-spelled letter
from young George Cumberland to his
father, written from the Pay Office, White-
hall, October 14, 1809, which I copy in all its
literal slovenliness from the letter preserved
in the Cumberland Papers: 'Blakes has published a Catalogue of Pictures being the
ancient method of Frescoe Painting Restored. you should tell Mr. Barry to get it,
it may be the means of serving your friend.
It sells for 2/6 and may be had of J. Blake,
28 Broad St., Golden Square, at his Brothers
—the Book is a great curiosity. He as
given Stothard a compleet set down.'

The Catalogue is badly printed on poor
paper in the form of a small octavo book
of 66 pages. It is full of fierce, exuberant
wisdom, which plunges from time to time
into a bright, demonstrative folly; it is a
confession, a criticism, and a kind of gospel
of sanctity and honesty and imagination in
art. The whole thing is a thinking aloud.
One hears an impetuous voice as if saying :
'I have been scorned long enough by these
fellows, who owe to me all that they possess ;
it shall be so no longer.' As he thinks, his
pen follows; he argues with foes actually
visible to him ; never does he realise the
indifferent public that may glance at what
he has written, and how best to interest or
convince it if it does. He throws down a
challenge, and awaits an answer.

What answer came is rememberable among
the infamies of journalism. Only one news-
paper noticed the exhibition, and this was
again *The Examiner*. The notice appeared
under the title ' Mr. Blake's Exhibition ' in
No. 90, September 17, 1809, pp. 605-6,
where it fills two columns. It is unsigned,
but there can be no doubt that it was
written by the R. H. of the former article.

The main part of it is taken up by extracts from the *Descriptive Catalogue,* italicised and put into small capitals ' to amuse the reader, and satisfy him of the truth of the foregoing remarks.' This is all that need be quoted of the foregoing remarks :

' But when the ebullitions of a distempered brain are mistaken for the sallies of genius by those whose works have exhibited the soundest thinking in art, the malady has indeed attained a pernicious height, and it becomes a duty to endeavour to arrest its progress. Such is the case with the productions and admirers of William Blake, an unfortunate lunatic, whose personal inoffensiveness secures him from confinement, and, consequently, of whom no public notice would have been taken, if he was not forced on the notice and animadversion of *The Examiner,* in having been held up to public admiration by many esteemed amateurs and professors as a genius in some respect original and legitimate. The praises which these gentlemen bestowed last year on this unfortunate man's illustrations to Blair's *Grave* have, in feeding his vanity, stimulated him to publish his madness more largely, and thus again exposed him, if not to the derision, at least to the pity of the public. . . . Thus encouraged, the poor man fancies himself a great master, and has painted a few wretched pictures, some of which are unintelligible allegory, others an attempt at sober character by caricature representation, and the whole " blotted and blurred," and very badly drawn. These he calls an Exhibition, of which he has published a Catalogue, or rather a farrago of nonsense, unintelligibleness, and egregious vanity, the wild effusions of a distempered brain. One of the pictures represents Chaucer's Pilgrims, and is in every respect a striking contrast to the admirable picture of the same subject by Mr. Stothard, from which an exquisite print is forthcoming from the hand of Schiavonetti.'

The last great words of the Catalogue, ' If a man is master of his profession, he cannot be ignorant that he is so ; and, if he is not employed by those who pretend to encourage art, he will employ himself, and laugh in secret at the pretences of the ignorant, while he has every night dropped into his shoe, as soon as he puts it off, and puts out

the candle, and gets into bed, a reward
for the labours of the day such as the world
cannot give, and patience and time await
to give him all that the world can give ':
those noble, lovely, pathetic and prophetic
words, are quoted at the end of the article
without comment, as if to quote them was
enough.   It was.

In 1803 William Blake sold to Thomas
Butts eleven drawings for fourteen guineas.
In 1903 twelve water-colour drawings in
illustration of *L'Allegro* and *Il Penseroso*
were sold for £1960, and the twenty-one
water-colour drawings for *Job* for £5600.
These figures have their significance, but the
significance must not be taken to mean any
improvement in individual taste.   When a
selection from the pictures in the Butts collection was on view at Sotheby's I heard a
vulgar person with a loud voice, a dealer or
a dealer's assistant, say with a guffaw : 'It
would make me sick to have these things
round my room.'   That vulgar person represents the eternal taste of the multitude;
only, in the course of a hundred years, a
few men of genius have repeated after one
another that Blake was a man of genius, and

their united voices have carried further than
the guffaws of vulgar persons, repeated
generation after generation.   And so in due
course, when Blake has been properly dead
long enough, there is a little public which,
bidding against itself, gambles cheerfully for
the possession of the scraps of paper on
which he sent in his account, against the
taste of his age and the taste of all the ages.

Blake himself had never any doubt of his
own greatness as an artist, and some of the
proud or petulant things which he occasionally wrote (the only outbreaks of impatience
in a life wholly given up to unceasing and
apparently unrewarded labour) have been
quoted against him as petty or unworthy,
partly because they are so uncalculated and
so childlike.   Blake 'bore witness,' as he
might have said, that he had done his duty :
'for that I cannot live without doing my
duty, to lay up treasures in heaven, is certain and determined,' he writes from Felpham.
And he asserted the truth of his own genius,
its truth in the spiritual sense, its divine
origin, as directly and as emphatically as he
asserted everything which he had apprehended as truth.   He is merely stating

what seems to him an obvious but over-
looked fact when he says : 'In Mr. B.'s
Britons the blood is seen to circulate in
their limbs : he defies competition in colouring'; and again : 'I am, like other men,
just equal in invention and execution of my
work.' All art, he had realised, which is
true art, is equal, as every diamond is a
diamond. There is only true and false art.
Thus when he says in his prospectus of 1793
that he has been 'enabled to bring before
the Public works (he is not afraid to say) of
equal magnitude and consequence with the
productions of any age or country,' he means
neither more nor less than when he says
in the *Descriptive Catalogue* of 1809 : 'He
knows that what he does is not inferior to
the grandest antiques. Superior it cannot
be, for human power cannot go beyond either
what he does or what they have done ; it is
the gift of God, it is inspiration and vision.
. . . The human mind cannot go beyond the
gift of God, the Holy Ghost.' It is in
humility rather than in pride that he equals
himself with those who seemed to him the
genuine artists, the humility of a belief that
all art is only a portion of that 'Poetic Genius,

which is the Lord,' offered up in homage
by man, and returning, in mere gratitude,
to its origin.   When he says, 'I do not pretend to paint better than Rafael or Michael
Angelo, or Julio Romano, or Albert Durer,
but I do pretend to paint finer than Rubens,
or Rembrandt, or Titian, or Correggio,' he
merely means, in that odd coupling and
contrasting of names, to assert his belief
in the supremacy of strong, clear, masculine
execution over what seemed to him (to his
limited knowledge, not false instinct) the
heresy and deceit of 'soft and effeminate'
execution, the 'broken lines, broken masses,
and broken colours' of the art which 'loses
form.'   In standing up for his ideal of art, he
stands up himself, like a champion.   'I am
hid,' he writes on the flyleaf of Reynolds's
Discourses, and, in the last sentence of that
'Public Address' which was never printed,
he declares : 'Resentment for personal in-
juries has had some share in this public
address, but love to my art, and zeal for my
country, a much greater.'   And in the last sentence of the *Descriptive Catalogue*, he sums
up the whole matter, so far as it concerned
him, finally, and with a 'sure and certain

hope' which, now that it has been realised, so long afterwards, comes to us like a reproach.

'Shall Painting,' asks Blake in his *Descriptive Catalogue*, 'be confined to the sordid drudgery of facsimile representations of merely mortal and perishing substances, and not be, as poetry and music are, elevated into its own proper sphere of invention and visionary conception? No, it shall not be so! Painting, as well as poetry and music, exists and exults in immortal thoughts.' It was to restore this conception of art to England that Blake devoted his life. 'The Enquiry in England,' he said, in his marginalia to Reynolds, 'is not whether a Man has Talents and Genius, but whether he is Passive and Polite and a Virtuous Ass.' He says there: 'Ages are all Equal, but Genius is always above the Age.' He looks on Bacon and Locke and Burke and Reynolds as men who 'mock Inspiration and Vision.' 'Inspiration and Vision,' he says, 'was then, and now is, and I hope will always Remain, my Element, my Eternal Dwelling-place.' 'The Ancients did not mean to Impose when they affirmed their belief in Vision and Revelation. Plato was

in Earnest. Milton was in Earnest. They
believed that God did visit Man Really
and Truly.' Further, 'Knowledge of Ideal
Beauty is not to be Acquired. It is born
with us. . . . Man is Born Like a Garden
ready Planted and Sown. This World is
too poor to produce one Seed.'

What Blake meant by vision, how signifi-
cantly yet cautiously he interchanged the
words 'seen' and 'imagined,' has been
already noted in that passage of the *Descriptive Catalogue*, where he answers his ob-
jectors : ' The connoisseurs and artists who
have made objections to Mr. B.'s mode of
representing spirits with real bodies would
do well to consider that the Venus, the
Minerva, the Jupiter, the Apollo, which they
admire in Greek statues are, all of them,
representations of spiritual existences, of
Gods immortal, to the ordinary perishing
organ of sight ; and yet they are embodied
and organised in solid marble. Mr. B.
requires the same latitude, and all is well.'
Then comes the great definition, which I
will not repeat : ' He who does not imagine
in stronger and better lineaments.'

'The world of imagination,' he says else-

where, ' is infinite and eternal, whereas the
world of generation or vegetation is finite
and temporal. There exist in that eternal
world the eternal realities of everything
which we see reflected in this vegetable
glass of nature.' What is said here, trans-
muted by an instinct wholly an artist's into
a great defence of the reality of imagination
in art, is a form of the central doctrine of
the mystics, formulated by Swedenborg in
something very like Blake's language, though
with errors or hesitations which is what
Blake sets himself to point out in his marginalia to Swedenborg. As, in those marginalia, we see Blake altering every allusion to
God into an allusion to ' the Poetic Genius,'
so, always, we shall find him understanding every promise of Christ, or Old Testament prophecy, as equally translatable into
terms of the imaginative life, into terms of
painting, poetry, or music. In the rendering of vision he required above all things
that fidelity which can only be obtained
through ' minutely particular' execution.
' Invention depends Altogether upon Execution or Organisation; as that is right or
wrong, so is the Invention perfect or imper-

fect. Whoever is set to Undermine the
Execution of Art is set to destroy Art.
Michael Angelo's Art depends on Michael
Angelo's Execution Altogether. . . . He
who admires Rafael Must admire Rafael's
Execution. He who does not admire
Rafael's Execution can not admire Rafael.'
Finally, 'the great and golden rule of
art as well as of life,' he says in the
Descriptive Catalogue, 'is this : that the
more distinct, sharp, and wiry the bounding
line, the more perfect the work of art ; and
the less keen and sharp, the greater is the
evidence of weak imagination, plagiarism,
and bungling. . . . What is it that dis-
tinguishes honesty from knavery, but the
hard and wiry line of rectitude and certainty
in the actions and intentions ? Leave out
this line, and you leave out life itself. All
is chance again, and the line of the Almighty
must be drawn out upon it again, before
man or beast can exist.'

In Blake's work a great fundamental conception is rarely lacking, and the conception is not, as it has often been asserted, a
literary, but always a pictorial, one. At
times imagination and execution are wholly

untired, as in the splendid water-colour of 'Death on the Pale Horse,' in which not only every line and colour is alive with passionate idea, the implacable and eternal joy of destruction, but also with a realised beauty, a fully grasped invention. No detail has been slurred in vision, or in the setting down of the vision : the crowned old man with the sword, the galloping horse, the pestilential figure of putrid scales and flames below, and the wide-armed angel with the scroll above. In the vision of ' Fire ' there is grandeur and, along with it, something inadequately seen, inadequately rendered. Flame and smoke embrace, coil, spire, swell in bellying clouds, divide into lacerating tongues, tangle and whirl ecstatically upward and onward, like a venomous joy in action, painting the air with all the colour of all the flowers of evil. But the figures in the foreground are partly academic studies, partly archaic dolls, in which only the intention is admirable. In ' Job Confessing his Presumption to God ' one sees all that is great and all that is childish in Blake's genius. I have never seen so sufficing a suggestion of disembodied

divine forces as in this whirling cloud of
angels, cast out and swept round by the
wind of God's speed, like a cascade of veined
and tapering wings, out of which ecstatic
and astonished heads leap forward. But in
the midst of the wheel a fierce old man, with
outstretched arms (who is an image of God
certainly not corrected out of any authentic
vision), and, below, the extinguished figure
of Job's friends, and Job, himself one of
Blake's gnome-like old men with a face of
rigid awe and pointing fingers of inarticulate
terror, remain no more than statements,
literal statements, of the facts of the
imagination. They are summarised remembrances of vision, not anything 'imagined
in stronger and better lineaments, and in
stronger and better light, than the perishing mortal eye can see.'

Or, might it not be said that it is precisely through this minute accuracy to the
detail of imagination that this visionary
reality comes to seem to us unreal ? In
Blake every detail is seen with intensity,
and with equal intensity. No one detail is
subordinated to another, every inch of his
surface is equally important to him; and
from this unslackening emphasis come alike

his arresting power and the defect which
leaves us, though arrested, often uncon-
vinced. In his most splendid things, as in
'Satan exulting over Job' and 'Cain
fleeing from the Grave of Abel,' which are
painted on wood, as if carved or graved,
with a tumult of decorative colour, detail
literally overpowers the sense of sight, like
strong sunlight, and every outline seizes
and enters into you simultaneously. At
times, as in 'The Bard of Gray,' and 'The
Spiritual Form of Pitt' in the National
Gallery, he is mysteriously lyrical in his
paint, and creates a vague emotion out of a
kind of musical colour, which is content to
suggest. Still more rarely, as in the ripe
and admirable 'Canterbury Pilgrims,' which
is a picture in narrative, as like Chaucer
as Chaucer himself, but unlike any other
picture, he gives us a vision of worldly
reality; but it was of this picture that he
said: 'If Mr. B.'s "Canterbury Pilgrims" had
been done by any other power than that of
the poetic visionary, it would have been as
dull as his adversary's.' Pure beauty and
pure terror creep and flicker in and out of all
his pictures, with a child's innocence; and he
is unconscious of how far he is helped or

hindered, as an artist, by that burden of a divine message which is continually upon him. He is unconscious that with one artist the imagination may overpower the technique, as awe overpowers the senses, while to another artist the imagination gives new life to the technique. Blake did not understand Rembrandt, and imagined that he hated him; but there are a few of his pictures in which Rembrandt is strangely suggested. In 'The Adoration of the Three Kings' and in 'The Angel appearing to Zacharias' there is a lovely depth of colour, bright in dimness, which has something of the warmth and mystery of Rembrandt, and there are details in the design of 'The Three Kings' (the door open on the pointing star in the sky and on the shadowy multitude below) which are as fine in conception as anything in the Munich 'Adoration of the Shepherds.' But in these, or in the almost finer 'Christ in the Garden, sustained by an Angel' (fire flames about the descending angel, and the garden is a forest of the night), how fatal to our enjoyment is the thought of Rembrandt! To Rembrandt, too, all things were visions, but they were visions that he saw with unflinching eyes; he saw them with his hands; he saw them with the faces and forms of men, and with the lines of earthly habitations.

And, above all, Rembrandt, all the greatest painters, saw a picture as a whole, composed every picture consciously, giving it unity by his way of arranging what he saw. Blake was too humble towards vision to allow himself to compose or arrange what he saw, and he saw in detail, with an unparalleled fixity and clearness. Every picture of Blake, quite apart from its meaning to the intelligence, is built up in detail like a piece of decoration; and, widely remote as are both intention and result, I am inclined to think he composed as Japanese artists compose, bit by bit, as he saw his picture come piece by piece before him. In every picture there is a mental idea, and there is also a pictorial conception, working visually and apart from the mental idea. In the greatest pictures (in the tremendous invention, for instance, of the soldiers on Calvary casting lots for the garments of Christ), the two are fused, with overwhelming effect; but it happens frequently that the two fail to unite, and we see the picture, and also the idea, but not the idea embodied in the picture.

Blake's passion for detail, and his refusal
to subordinate any detail for any purpose,
is to be seen in all his figures, of which the
bodies seem to be copied from living statues,
and in which the faces are wrung into masks
of moods which they are too urgent to
interpret. A world of conventional patterns,
in which all natural things are artificial and
yet expressive, is peopled by giants and
dolls, muscular and foolish, in whom strength
becomes an insane gesture and beauty a
formal prettiness. Not a flower or beast
has reality, as our eyes see it, yet every
flower and beast is informed by an almost
human soul, not the mere vitality of animal
or vegetable, but a consciousness of its own
lovely or evil shape. His snakes are not
only wonderful in their coils and colours,
but each has his individual soul, visible in
his eyes, and interpreting those coils and
colours. And every leaf, unnatural yet alive,
and always a piece of decoration, peers with
some meaning of its own out of every corner,
not content to be forgotten, and so uneasily
alive that it draws the eye to follow it.
'As poetry,' he said, 'admits not a letter
that is insignificant, so painting admits not

a grain of sand or a blade of grass insignificant—much less an insignificant blur or
mark.' The stones with which Achan has
been martyred live each with a separate and
evil life of its own, not less vivid and violent
than the clenched hands raised to hurl other
stones; there is menacing gesture in the
cloud of dust that rises behind them. And
these human beings and these angels, and
God (sometimes an old bowed Jew, fitted
into a square or lozenge of winged heads)
are full of the energy of a life which is betrayed by their bodies. Sometimes they
are mere child's toys, like a Lucifer of bright
baubles, painted chromatically, with pink
hair and blushing wings, hung with bursting stars that spill out animalculæ. Sometimes the whole man is a gesture and con-
vulses the sky; or he runs, and the earth
vanishes under him. But the gesture de-
vours the man also; his force as a cipher
annihilates his very being.

In greatness of conception Blake must be
compared with the greatest among artists,
but the difference between Blake and
Michelangelo is the difference between the
artist in whom imagination overpowers

technique, as awe overpowers the senses, and the artist in whom imagination gives new life to technique. No one, as we have seen, was more conscious of the identity which exists in the work of the greatest artists between conception and execution. But in speaking of invention and execution as equal, he is assuming, as he came to do, the identity of art and inspiration, the sufficiency of first thoughts in art. 'Be assured,' he writes to Mr. Butts from Felpham, 'that there is not one touch in those drawings and pictures but what came from my head and heart in unison. . . . If I were to do them over again, they would lose as much as they gained, because they were done in the heat of my spirit.' He was an inexhaustible fountain of first thoughts, and to him first thoughts only were of importance. The one draughtsman of the soul, he drew, no doubt, what he saw as he saw it; but he lacked the patience which is a part of all supreme genius. Having seen his vision, he is in haste to record what he has seen hastily; and he leaves the first rough draft as it stands, not correcting it by a deliberate seeing over again from the

beginning, and a scrupulous translation of
the terms of eternity into the terms of time.
I was once showing Rodin some facsimiles of
Blake's drawings, and telling him about
Blake, I said : ' He used to literally see
these figures ; they are not mere inventions.'
' Yes,' said Rodin, ' he saw them once ; he
should have seen them three or four times.'
There, it seems to me, is the fundamental
truth about the art of Blake : it is a record
of vision which has not been thoroughly
mastered even as vision. ' No man,' said
Blake, ' can improve an original invention ;
nor can an original invention exist without
execution organised, delineated, and articulated, either by God or man.' And he said
also : ' He who does not imagine in stronger
and better lineaments, and in stronger and
better light, than his perishing mortal eye
can see, does not imagine at all.' But Blake's
imagination is in rebellion, not only against
the limits of reality, but against the only
means by which he can make vision visible
to others. And thus he allows himself to be
mastered by that against which he rebels :
that power of the hand by which art begins
where vision leaves off.

IX

NOTHING is known of Blake's life between 1809, the date of his exhibition, and 1818, when he met the chief friend and helper of his later years, John Linnell. Everything leads us to believe that those nine years were years of poverty and neglect. Between 1815 and 1817 we find him doing engraver's task-work for Flaxman's *Hesiod*, and for articles, probably written by Flaxman, on Armour and Sculpture in Rees's *Encyclopædia*. Gilchrist tells a story, on the authority of Tatham, of Blake copying the cast of the Laocoon among the students at the Royal Academy, and of Fuseli, then the keeper, coming up with the just and pleasant remark that it was they who should learn of him, not he of them. The *Milton* and the *Jerusalem*, both dated 1804, were printed at some time during this period. Gilchrist suggests that the reason why Blake issued no more engraved books from his press was probably his inability to pay for the copper required in engraving; and his suggestion is confirmed in a letter to Dawson Turner, a Norfolk antiquary, dated June 9, 1818, a few days before the meeting with Linnell. Blake writes: 'I send you a list of the different works you have done me the honour to inquire after. They are unprofitable enough to me, though expensive to the buyer. Those I printed for Mr. Humphry are a selection from the different books of such as could be printed without the writing, though to the loss of some of the best things; for they, when printed perfect, accompany poetical personifications and acts, without which poems they never could have been executed :—

	£	s.	d.
America, 18 prints folio, .	5	5	0
Europe, 17 do. do., .	5	5	0
Visions, 8 do. do., .	3	3	0
Thel, 6 do. quarto, .	2	2	0
Songs of Innocence, 28 prints octavo, ...	3	3	0
Songs of Experience, 26 do. octavo, ...	3	3	0

	£	s.	d.
Urizen, 28 prints quarto, .	5	5	0
Milton, 50 do. do., .	10	10	0
12 large prints, size of each about 2 ft. by 1½ ft., historical and poetical, printed in colours, each . .	5	5	0

The last twelve prints are unaccompanied by any writing. The few I have printed and sold are sufficient to have gained me great reputation as an artist, which was the chief thing intended. But I have never been able to produce a sufficient number for general sale by means of a regular publisher. It is therefore necessary to me that any person wishing to have any or all of them should send me their order to print them on the above terms, and I will take care that they shall be done at least as well as any I have yet produced.'

If we compare this list with the printed list of twenty-five years back (see p. 60) we shall see that the prices are now half as many guineas as they were once shillings; in a letter to Cumberland, nine years later, they have gone up by one, two, or three guineas apiece, and Blake tells Cumberland that 'having none remaining of all that I had printed, I cannot print more except at a great loss. For at the time I printed these things I had a little house to range in. Now I am shut up in a corner, therefore I am forced to ask a price for them that I can scarce expect to get from a stranger. I am now printing a set of the *Songs of Innocence and Experience* for a friend at ten guineas, which I cannot do under six months consistent with my other work, so that I have little hope of doing any more of such things. The last work is a poem entitled *Jerusalem, the Emanation of the Giant Albion,* but find that to print it will cost my time to the value of twenty guineas. One I have finished. It contains 100 plates, but it is not likely that I shall get a customer for it.' [1]

Gilchrist tells us, by an error which was pointed out in the life of Palmer by his son, in 1892, that Blake met Linnell in 1813. It was in 1818, and the first entry relating to Blake in Linnell's journal is dated June 24. In a letter communicated to me by Mr.

---

[1] I take the text of this letter, not from Mr. Russell's edition, but from the fuller text printed by Mr. Ellis in *The Real Blake.*

Sampson, Mr. John Linnell, junior, states
that his father took in October or November
1817 the greater part of a house at 38 Rathbone Place, where he lived till the end of
1818; he then took a house at Cirencester
Place, Fitzroy Square. Mr. Linnell gives
the following extract from his father's auto-
biographical notes: 'At Rathbone Place,
1818 . . . here I first became acquainted with
William Blake, to whom I paid a visit in
company with the younger Mr. Cumberland.
Blake lived then in South Molton Street, Oxford Street, second floor. We soon became
intimate, and I employed him to help me
with an engraving of my portrait of Mr. Up-
ton, a Baptist preacher, which he was glad to
do, having scarcely enough employment to
live by at the prices he could obtain; everything in Art was at a low ebb then. . . . I
soon encountered Blake's peculiarities, and
somewhat taken aback by the boldness of
some of his assertions, I never saw anything
the least like madness, for I never opposed
him spitefully, as many did, but being really
anxious to fathom, if possible, the amount of
truth which might be in his most startling
assertions, generally met with a sufficiently

rational explanation in the most really friendly and conciliatory tone.'

From 1818 Linnell became, in his own independent way, the chief friend and disciple of Blake. Himself a man of narrow but strong individuality, he realised and accepted Blake for what he was, worked with him and for him, introduced him to rich and appreciative buyers like Sir Thomas Lawrence, and gave him, out of his own carefully controlled purse, a steady price for his work, which was at least enough for Blake to live on. There are notes in his journal of visits to picture-galleries together; to the Academy, the British Gallery, the Water-Colour Exhibition, the Spring Gardens Exhibition ; 'went with Mr. Blake to see Harlow's copy of the Transfiguration' (August 20, 1819), 'went with Mr. Blake to British Museum to see prints' (April 4 and 24, 1823). In 1820 there are notes of two visits to Drury Lane Theatre. It was probably early in 1819 that Linnell introduced Blake to his friend John Varley, the water-colour painter and astrologer, for whom Blake did the famous 'visionary heads.' A vivid sketch of the two arguing,

drawn by Linnell, is given in Mr. Story's
Life of Linnell. Varley, though an astrologer on the mathematical side, was no
visionary. He persuaded Blake to do a
series of drawings, naming historical or
legendary people to him, and carefully
writing down name and date of the imaginary portraits which Blake willingly drew,
and believing, it has been said, in the reality
of Blake's visions more than Blake himself.
Cunningham, in his farcical way, tells the
story as he may have got it from Varley
(see p. 420 below), for he claims in a letter
to Linnell to have 'received much valuable
information from him.' But the process has
been described, more simply, by Varley himself in his *Treatise of Zodiacal Physiognomy*
(1828), where the 'Ghost of a Flea' and the
'Constellation Cancer' are reproduced in
engraving. Some of the heads are finely
symbolical, and I should have thought the
ghost of a flea, in the sketch, an invention
more wholly outside nature if I had not
seen, in Rome and in London, a man in
whom it is impossible not to recognise the
type, modified to humanity, but scarcely
by a longer distance than the men from the

animals in Giovanni della Porta's ' Fisonomia dell' Huomo.'

It was in 1820, the year in which Blake began his vast picture of the 'Last Judgment,' only finished in the year of his death, that he did the seventeen woodcuts to Thornton's *Virgil*, certainly one of his greatest, his most wholly successful achievements. The book was for boys' schools, and we find Blake returning without an effort to the childlike mood of the *Songs of Innocence and Experience*. The woodcuts have all the natural joy of those early designs, an equal simplicity, but with what added depth, what richness, what passionate strength ! Blake was now engraving on wood for the first time, and he had to invent his own way of working. Just what he did has never been better defined than in an article which appeared in the *Athenæum* of January 21, 1843, one of the very few intelligent references to Blake which can be found in print between the time of his death and the date of Gilchrist's *Life*. ' We hold it impossible,' says the writer, ' to get a genuine work of art, unless it come pure and unadulterated from the mind that conceived it. . . . Still more

strongly is the author's meaning marked in
the few wood-engravings which that wonderful man Blake cut himself for an edition of
Thornton's *Pastorals of Virgil*. In token
of our faith in the principle here announced,
we have obtained the loan of one of Blake's
original blocks, from Mr. Linnell, who possesses the whole series, to print, as an illustration of our argument, that, amid all
drawbacks, there exists a power in the work
of the man of genius, which no one but
himself can utter fully. Side by side we
have printed a copy of an engraver's improved version of the same subject. When
Blake had produced his cuts, which were,
however, printed with an apology, a shout
of derision was raised by the wood-engravers.
"This will never do!" said they; "we will
show what it ought to be"—that is, what
the public taste would like—and they produced the above amendment! The engravers
were quite right in their estimate of public
taste; and we dare say many will agree
with them even now : yet, to our minds,
Blake's rude work, utterly without preten-
sion, too, as an engraving — the merest
attempt of a fresh apprentice—is a work

of genius; whilst the latter is but a piece
of smooth, tame mechanism.'

Blake lived at South Molton Street for
seventeen years. In 1821, 'on his landlord's
leaving off business, and retiring to France,'
says Linnell, he removed to Fountain Court,
in the Strand, where he took the first floor
of 'a private house kept by Mr. Banes, whose
wife was a sister of Mrs. Blake.' Linnell
tells us that he was at this time 'in want
of employment,' and, he says, 'before I knew
his distress he had sold all his collection
of old prints to Messrs. Colnaghi and Co.'
Through Linnell's efforts, a donation of £25
was about the same time sent to him from
the Royal Academy.

Fountain Court (the name is still per-
petuated on a metal slab) was called so until
1883, when the name was changed to Southampton Buildings. It has all been pulled
down and rebuilt, but I remember it fifteen
years ago, when there were lodging-houses
in it, by the side of the stage-door of Terry's
Theatre. It was a narrow slit between the
Strand and the river, and, when I knew it,
was dark and comfortless, a blind alley.
Gilchrist describes the two rooms on the

first floor, front and back, the front room used as a reception-room; a smaller room opened out of it at the back, which was workroom, bedroom, and kitchen in one. The side window looked down through an opening between the houses, showing the river and the hills beyond; and Blake worked at a table facing the window. There seems to be no doubt, from the testimony of many friends, that Crabb Robinson's description, which will be seen below, on p. 261, with fuller detail than has yet been printed, conveys the prejudiced view of a fastidious person, and Palmer, roused by the word 'squalor,' wrote to Gilchrist, asserting 'himself, his wife, and his rooms, were clean and orderly; everything was in its place.' Tatham says that 'he fixed upon these lodgings as being more congenial to his habits, as he was very much accustomed to get out of his bed in the night to write for hours, and return to bed for the rest of the night.' He rarely left the house, except to fetch his pint of porter from the public-house at the corner of the Strand. It was on one of these occasions that he is said to have been cut by a Royal Academician whom he had recently

met in society. Had not the Royal Academy
been founded (J. T. Smith tells us in his
Book for a Rainy Day, under date 1768)
by 'members who had agreed to withdraw
themselves from various clubs, not only in
order to be more select as to talent, but
perfectly correct as to gentlemanly conduct'?

It was about this time that Blake was
discovered, admired, and helped by one who
has been described as 'not merely a poet
and a painter, an art-critic, an antiquarian,
and a writer of prose, an amateur of beautiful
things, and a dilettante of things delightful,
but also a forger of no mean or ordinary
capabilities, and as a subtle and secret
poisoner almost without rival in this or
any age.' This was Lamb's 'kind, light-
hearted Wainewright,' who in the intervals
of his strange crimes found time to buy a
fine copy of the *Songs of Innocence* and to
give a jaunty word of encouragement or
advertisement to *Jerusalem*. Palmer remembers Blake stopping before one of
Wainewright's pictures in the Academy
and saying, 'Very fine.'

In 1820 Blake had carried out his last
commission from Butts in a series of twenty-

one drawings in illustration of the Book of
Job. In the following year Linnell commissioned from him a duplicate set, and in
September 1821 traced them himself from
Butts's copies; they were finished, and in parts
altered, by Blake. By an agreement dated
March 25, 1823, Blake undertook to engrave
the designs, which were to be published by
Linnell, who gave £100 for the designs and
copyright, with the promise of another £100
out of the profits on the sale. There were
no profits, but Linnell gave another £50,
paying the whole sum of £150 in weekly
sums of £2 or £3. The plates are dated
March 8, 1825, but they were not published
until the date given on the cover, March
1826. Gilchrist intimates that 'much must
be lost by the way' in the engraving of the
water-colour drawings; but Mr. Russell, a
better authority, says that 'marvellous as
the original water-colour drawings unquestionably were, they are in every case inferior
to the final version in the engraving.' It is
on these engravings that the fame of Blake
as an artist rests most solidly; invention
and execution are here, as he declared that
they must always be in great art, equal;

imagination at its highest here finds adequate
expression, without even the lovely strange-
ness of a defect. They have been finally
praised and defined by Rossetti, in the
pages contributed to Gilchrist's life (i. 330-
335), of which Mr. Swinburne has said, with
little exaggeration, that 'Blake himself,
had he undertaken to write notes on his
designs, must have done them less justice
than this.'

Before Blake had finished engraving the
designs to 'Job' he had already begun a
new series of illustrations to Dante, also a
commission from Linnell; and, with that
passionate conscientiousness which was part
of the foundation of his genius, he set to
work to learn enough Italian to be able to
follow the original with the help of Cary's
translation. Linnell not only let Blake do
the work he wanted to do, paying him for
it as he did it, but he took him to see
people whom it might be useful for him to
know, such as the Aders, who had a house
full of books and pictures, and who entertained artists and men of letters. Mrs.
Aders had a small amateur talent of her
own for painting, and from a letter of Car-

lyle's, which is preserved among the Crabb
Robinson papers, seems to have had literary
knowledge as well. 'Has not Mrs. Aders
(the lady who lent me *Wilhelm Meister*)
great skill in such things?' he asks in a
letter full of minute inquiries into German
novels. Lamb and Coleridge went to the
house, and it was there that Crabb Robinson
met Blake in December 1825. Mr. Story,
in his Life of Linnell, tells us that one of
Linnell's 'most vivid recollections of those
days was of hearing Crabb Robinson recite
Blake's poem, "The Tiger," before a distinguished company gathered at Mrs. Aders's
table. It was a most impressive performance.' We find Blake afterwards at a
supper-party at Crabb Robinson's, with
Linnell, who notes in his journal going with
Blake to Lady Ford's, to see her pictures;
in 1820 we find him at Lady Caroline
Lamb's.

Along with this general society Blake
now gathered about him a certain number
of friends and disciples, Linnell being the
steadiest friend, and Samuel Palmer, Edward
Calvert, and George Richmond the chief
disciples. To these must be added, in 1826,

Frederick Tatham, a young sculptor, who was to be the betrayer among the disciples. They called Blake's house 'the House of the Interpreter,' and in speaking of it afterwards speak of it always as of holy ground. Thus we hear of Richmond, finding his invention flag, going to seek counsel, and how Blake, who was sitting at tea with his wife, turned to her and said : 'What do we do, Kate, when the visions forsake us?' 'We kneel down and pray, Mr. Blake.' It is Richmond who records a profoundly significant saying of Blake : 'I can look at a knot in a piece of wood till I am frightened at it.' Palmer tells us that Blake and his wife would look into the fire together and draw the figures they saw there, hers quite unlike his, his often terrible. On Palmer's first meeting that Blake, on October 9, 1824, he tells us how Blake fixed his eyes upon him and said : 'Do you work with fear and trembling?' 'Yes, indeed,' was the reply. 'Then,' said Blake, 'you 'll do.'

The friends often met at Hampstead, where Linnell had, in 1824, taken Collins's Farm, at North End, now again known by its old name of 'Wyldes.' Blake disliked

the air of Hampstead, which he said always
made him ill; but he often went there to
see Linnell, and loved the aspect from his
cottage, and to sit and hear Mrs. Linnell
sing Scotch songs, and would sometimes
himself sing his own songs to tunes of his
own making. The children loved him, and
would watch for him as he came, generally
on foot, and one of them says that she
remembers 'the cold winter nights when
Blake was wrapped up in an old shawl by
Mrs. Linnell, and sent on his homeward
way, with the servant, lantern in hand,
lighting him across the heath to the main
road.' It is Palmer's son who reports it,
and he adds : 'It is a matter of regret that
the record of these meetings and walks and
conversations is so imperfect, for in the
words of one of Blake's disciples, to walk
with him was like "walking with the
Prophet Isaiah."' Once when the Palmers
were staying at Shoreham, the whole party
went down into the country in a carrier's
van drawn by eight horses : Calvert tells
the story, with picturesque details of Blake's
second-sight, and of the hunt with lanterns
in Shoreham Castle after a ghost, who

turned out to be a snail tapping on the broken glass of the window.

From the end of 1825 Blake's health began to fail, and most of his letters to Linnell contain apologies for not coming to Hampstead, as he is in bed, or is suffering from a cold in the stomach. It was the beginning of that sickness which killed him, described as the mixing of the gall with the blood. He worked persistently, whether he was well or ill, at the Dante drawings, which he made in a folio book given him by Linnell. There were a hundred pages in the book, and he did a drawing on every page, some completely finished, some a mere outline; of these he had only engraved seven at the time of his death. He sat propped up in bed, at work on his drawings, saying, 'Dante goes on the better, which is all I care about.' In a letter to George Cumberland, on April 12, 1827, he writes: 'I have been very near the gates of death, and have returned very weak and an old man, feeble and tottering, but not in the spirit and life, not in the real man, the imagination, which liveth for ever.' And indeed there is no sign of age or weakness in these last great inventions of a dying man. 'Flaxman is gone,' he adds, 'and we must soon follow, every one to his own eternal house, leaving the delusive Goddess Nature to her laws, to get into freedom from all law of the numbers, into the mind, in which every one is king and priest in his own house. God send it so on earth, as it is in heaven.'

Blake died on August 12, 1827, and the ecstasy of his death has been recorded by many witnesses. Tatham tells us how, as he put the finishing touches to a design of 'The Ancient of Days' which he had been colouring for him, he 'threw it down suddenly and said: "Kate, you have been a good wife; I will draw your portrait." She sat near his bed, and he made a drawing which, though not a likeness, is finely touched and expressed. He then threw that down, after having drawn for an hour, and began to sing Hallelujahs and songs of joy and triumph which Mrs. Blake described as being truly sublime in music and in verse.' Smith tells us that he said to his wife, as she stood to hear him, 'My beloved, they are not mine, no, they are not mine.' And a friend quoted by Gilchrist says: 'He

died on Sunday night, at six o'clock, in a
most glorious manner. He said he was
going to that country he had all his life
wished to see, and expressed himself happy,
hoping for salvation through Jesus Christ.
Just before he died his countenance became
fair, his eyes brightened, and he burst out
into singing of the things he saw in heaven.'
'Perhaps,' he had written not long before,
'and I verily believe it, every death is an
improvement of the state of the departed.'

Blake was buried in Bunhill Fields, where
all his family had been buried before him,
but with the rites of the Church of England,
and on August 17 his body was followed to
the grave by Calvert, Richmond, Tatham,
and Tatham's brother, a clergyman. The
burial register reads: 'Aug. 17, 1827.
William Blake. Age, 69 years. Brought
from Fountain Court, Strand. Grave, 9 feet;
E. & W. 77 : N. & S. 32. 19/.' The grave,
being a 'common grave,' was used again,
and the bones scattered; and this was the
world's last indignity against William Blake.

Tatham tells us that, during a marriage
of forty-five years, Mrs. Blake had never
been separated from her husband 'save for

a period that would make altogether about
five weeks.' He does not remind us, as
Mr. Swinburne, on the authority of Seymour
Kirkup, reminds us, of Mrs. Blake's one
complaint, that her husband was incessantly
away ' in Paradise.' Tatham adds : ' After
the death of her husband she resided for
some time with the author of this, whose
domestic arrangements were entirely undertaken by her, until such changes took place
that rendered it impossible for her strength
to continue in this voluntary office of sincere affection and regard.' Before going to
Tatham's she had spent nine months at
Linnell's house in Cirencester Place, only
leaving it in the summer of 1828, when
Linnell let the house. After leaving Tatham
she took lodgings in 17 Upper Charlotte
Street, Fitzroy Square, where she died at
half-past seven on the morning of October
18, 1831, four years after the death of her
husband, and within three months of his
age. Tatham says : ' Her death not being
known but by calculation, sixty-five years
were placed upon her coffin,' and in the
burial register at Bunhill Fields we read :
' Oct. 23, 1831. Catherine Sophia Blake.

Age, 65 yrs.   Brought from Upper Charlotte
Street, Fitzroy Square.   Grave, 12 feet;
E. & W. 7 : N. & S. 31, 32.   £1, 5s.'   She
was born April 24, 1762, and was thus
aged sixty-nine years and six months.

Mr. Swinburne tells us, on the authority
of Seymour Kirkup, that, after Blake's
death, a gift of £100 was sent to his widow
by the Princess Sophia, which she grate-
fully returned, as not being in actual need
of it.   Many friends bought copies of Blake's
engraved books, some of which Mrs. Blake
coloured, with the help of Tatham.   After
her death all the plates and manuscripts
passed into Tatham's hands.   In his memoir
Tatham says that Blake on his death-bed
'spoke of the writer of this as a likely
person to become the manager' of Mrs.
Blake's affairs, and he says that Mrs. Blake
bequeathed to him 'all of his works that
remained unsold at his death, being writings,
paintings, and a very great number of copper-
plates, of whom impressions may be obtained.'
Linnell says that Tatham never showed anything in proof of his assertion that they
had been left to him.   Tatham had passed
through various religious phases, and from

being a Baptist, had become an 'angel' of
the Irvingite Church. He is supposed to
have destroyed the whole of the manuscripts
and drawings in his possession on account
of religious scruples; and in the life of
Calvert by his son we read: 'Edward
Calvert, fearing some fatal *dénouement*, went
to Tatham and implored him to reconsider
the matter and spare the good man's precious
work; notwithstanding which, blocks, plates,
drawings, and MSS., I understand, were
destroyed.'

Such is the received story, but is it
strictly true? Did Tatham really destroy
these manuscripts for religious reasons, or
did he keep them and surreptitiously sell
them for reasons of quite another kind? In
the *Rossetti Papers* there is a letter from
Tatham to Mr. W. M. Rossetti, dated
Nov. 6, 1862, in which he says: 'I have
sold Mr. Blake's works for thirty years';
and a footnote to Dr. Garnett's monograph
on Blake in the *The Portfolio* of 1895 relates
a visit from Tatham which took place about
1860. Dr. Garnett told me that Tatham
had said, without giving any explanation,
that he had destroyed some of Blake's manu-

scripts and kept others by him, which he
had sold from time to time. Is there not
therefore a possibility that some of these
lost manuscripts may still exist? whether
or not they may turn out to be, as Crabb
Robinson tells us that Blake told him, 'six
or seven epic poems as long as Homer, and
twenty tragedies as long as *Macbeth.*'

X

THERE are people who still ask seriously if
Blake was mad. If the mind of Lord
Macaulay is the one and only type of sanity,
then Blake was mad. If imagination, and
ecstasy, and disregard of worldly things,
and absorption in the inner world of the
mind, and a literal belief in those things
which the whole 'Christian community'
professes from the tip of its tongue; if
these are signs and suspicions of madness,
then Blake was certainly mad. His place
is where he saw Teresa, among 'the gentle
souls who guide the great wine-press
of Love'; and, like her, he was 'drunk
with intellectual vision.' That drunkenness
illuminated him during his whole life, yet
without incapacitating him from any needful
attention to things by the way. He lived
in poverty because he did not need riches;
but he died without leaving a debt. He
was a steady, not a fitful worker, and his

wife said of him that she never saw his
hands still unless he was reading or asleep.
He was gentle and sudden; his whole nature
was in a steady heat which could blaze at
any moment into a flame. 'A saint amongst
the infidels and a heretic with the orthodox,'
he has been described by one who knew him
best in his later years, John Linnell; and
Palmer has said of him : 'His love of art
was so great that he would see nothing but
art in anything he loved; and so, as he loved
the Apostles and their divine Head (for so
I believe he did), he must needs say that
they were all artists.' 'When opposed by
the superstitious, the crafty, or the proud,'
says Linnell again, 'he outraged all common-
sense and rationality by the opinions he
advanced'; and Palmer gives an instance
of it : 'Being irritated by the exclusively
scientific talk at a friend's house, which talk
had turned on the vastness of space, he cried
out, " It is false. I walked the other evening
to the end of the heath, and touched the
sky with my finger." '

It was of the essence of Blake's sanity
that he could always touch the sky with his
finger. 'To justify the soul's frequent joy

in what cannot be defined to the intellectual part, or to calculation' : that, which is Walt Whitman's definition of his own aim, defines Blake's. Where others doubted he knew; and he saw where others looked vaguely into the darkness. He saw so much further than others into what we call reality, that others doubted his report, not being able to check it for themselves; and when he saw truth naked he did not turn aside his eyes. Nor had he the common notion of what truth is, or why it is to be regarded. He said : ' When I tell a truth it is not for the sake of convincing those who do not know it, but for the sake of defending those who do.' And his criterion of truth was the inward certainty of instinct or intuition, not the outward certainty of fact. ' God forbid,' he said, 'that Truth should be confined to mathematical demonstration. He who does not know Truth at sight is unworthy of her notice.' And he said : ' Error is created, truth is eternal. Error or creation will be burned up, and then, not till then, truth or eternity will appear. It is burned up the moment men cease to behold it.'

It was this private certainty in regard to truth and all things that Blake shared with the greatest minds of the world, and men doubted him partly because he was content to possess that certainty and had no desire to use it for any practical purpose, least of all to convince others. He asked to be believed when he spoke, told the truth, and was not concerned with argument or experiment, which seemed to him ways of evasion. He said:

'It is easy to acknowledge a man to be great and good, while we
  Derogate from him in the trifles and small articles of that goodness,
  Those alone are his friends who admire his minutest powers.'

He spoke naturally in terms of wisdom, and made no explanations, bridged none of the gulfs which it seemed to him so easy to fly over. Thus when he said that Ossian and Rowley were authentic, and that what Macpherson and Chatterton said was ancient was so, he did not mean it in a strictly literal sense, but in the sense in which ancient meant authentic: true to ancient truth. Is a thing true as poetry? then it is true in the minutest because the most essential sense. On the other hand, in saying that part of Wordsworth's Preface was written by another hand, he was merely expressing in a bold figure a sane critical opinion. Is a thing false among many true things? then it is not the true man who is writing it, but some false section of his brain. It may be dangerous practically to judge all things at an inner tribunal; but it is only by such judgments that truth moves.

And truth has moved, or we have. After *Zarathustra, Jerusalem* no longer seems a wild heresy. People were frightened because they were told that Blake was mad, or a blasphemer. Nietzsche, who has cleared away so many obstructions from thought, has shamed us from hiding behind these treacherous and unavailing defences. We have come to realise, what Rossetti pointed out long ago, that, as a poet, Blake's characteristic is above all things that of 'pure perfection in *writing verse*.' We no longer praise his painting for its qualities as literature, or forget that his design has greatness as design. And of that unique creation of an art out of the mingling of many arts which we see in the 'illuminated printing' of the engraved books, we have come to realise what Palmer meant when he said long ago : 'As a picture has been said to be something between a thing and a thought, so, in some of these type books over which Blake had long brooded with his brooding of fire, the very paper seems to come to life as you gaze upon it—not with a mortal life, but an indestructible life.' And we have come to realise what Blake meant by the humble and arrogant things which he said about himself. 'I doubt not yet,' he writes in one of those gaieties of speech which illuminate his letters, 'to make a figure in the great dance of life that shall amuse the spectators in the sky.' If there are indeed spectators there, amused by our motions, what dancer among us are they more likely to have approved than this joyous, untired, and undistracted dancer to the eternal rhythm ?

II

RECORDS FROM CONTEMPORARY SOURCES

(I.) EXTRACTS FROM THE DIARY, LETTERS, AND REMINISCENCES OF HENRY CRABB ROBINSON, transcribed from the Original MSS. in Dr. Williams's Library. 1810-1852.

'OF all the records of these his latter years,' says Mr. Swinburne in his book on Blake, 'the most valuable, perhaps, are those furnished by Mr. Crabb Robinson, whose cautious and vivid transcription of Blake's actual speech is worth more than much vague remark, or than any commentary now possible to give.' Through the kind permission of the Librarian of Dr. Williams's Library, where the Crabb Robinson MSS. are preserved, I am able to give, for the first time, an accurate and complete text of every reference to Blake in the *Diary*, *Letters*, and *Reminiscences*, which have hitherto been printed only in part, and with changes as well as omissions. In an entry in his Diary for May 13, 1848, Crabb Robinson says : 'It is strange that I, who have no imagination, nor any power beyond that of a logical understanding, should yet have great respect for the mystics.' This respect for the mystics, to which we owe the notes on Blake, was part of an inexhaustible curiosity in human things, and in things of the mind, which made of Crabb Robinson the most searching and significant reporter of the nineteenth century. Others may have understood Blake better than he did, but no one else was so attentive to his speech, and thus so faithful an interpreter of his meaning.

In copying from the MS. I have followed the spelling, not however preserving abbreviations such as 'Bl:' for 'Blake,' due merely to haste, and I have modified the punctuation and added commas of quotation only when the writer's carelessness in these matters was likely to be confusing. Otherwise the transcript is literal and verbatim, and I have added in footnotes any readings of possible interest which have been crossed out in the manuscript.

(1) FROM CRABB ROBINSON'S DIARY

1825

December

10 . . . Dined with Aders. A very remarkable
and interesting evening. The party *Blake* the
painter and Linnell—also a painter and engraver—
to dinner. In the evening came Miss Denman
and Miss Flaxman.

10*th December* 1825

BLAKE

I will put down as they occur to me without
method all I can recollect of the conversation of
this remarkable man. Shall I call him Artist or
Genius—or Mystic—or Madman? Probably he
is all. He has a most interesting appearance.
He is now old—pale with a Socratic countenance,
and an expression of great sweetness, but bordering
on weakness—except when his features are ani-
mated by [1] expression, and then he has an air of
inspiration about him. The conversation was on

---

[1] 'Any' crossed out.

art, and on poetry, and on religion; but it was my
object, and I was successful, in drawing him out,
and in so getting from him an avowal of his
peculiar sentiments.   I was aware before of the
nature of his impressions, or I should at times
have been at a loss to understand him.   He was
shewn soon after he entered the room some compositions of Mrs. Aders which he cordially praised.
And he brought with him an engraving of his
Canterbury Pilgrims for Aders.   One of the figures
ressembled one in one of Aders's pictures.   'They
say I stole it from this picture, but I did it 20
years before I knew of the picture—however, in
my youth I was always studying this kind of
paintings.   No wonder there is a resemblence.'
In this he seemed to explain *humanly* what he had
done, but he at another time spoke of his paintings
as being what he had seen in his visions.   And
when he said *my visions* it was in the ordinary
unemphatic tone in which we speak of trivial
matters that every one understands and cares
nothing about.   In the same tone he said repeatedly, the 'Spirit told me.'   I took occasion to
say—You use the same word as Socrates used.
What resemblance do you suppose is there between
your spirit and the spirit of Socrates?   'The same
as between our countenance.'   He paused and
added—'I was Socrates.'   And then, as if correcting himself, 'A sort of brother.   I must have
had conversations with him.   So I had with Jesus

Christ.   I have an obscure recollection of having been with both of them.'

It was before this, that I had suggested on very obvious philosophical grounds the *impossibility* of supposing an immortal being created—an eternity *a parte post* without an eternity *a parte ante*.   This is an obvious truth I have been many (perhaps 30) years fully aware of.   His eye brightened on my saying this, and he eagerly concurred—'To be sure it is impossible.   We are all co-existent with God—members of the Divine body.   We are all partakers of the Divine nature.'   In this, by the bye, Blake has but adopted an ancient Greek idea—query of Plato?   As connected with this idea I will mention here (though it formed part of our talk, walking homeward) that on my asking in what light he viewed the great question concerning the Divinity of Jesus Christ, he said—'*He is the only God.*'   But then he added—'And so am I and so are you.'   Now he had just before (and this occasioned my question) been speaking of the errors of Jesus Christ—He was wrong in suffering Himself to be crucified.   He should not have attacked the Government.   He had no business with such matters.   On my inquiring how he reconciled this with the sanctity and divine qualities of Jesus, he said He was not then become the Father.   Connecting as well as one can these fragmentary sentiments, it would be hard to give Blake's station between Christianity, Platonism, and Spinosism. Yet he professes to be very hostile to Plato, and reproaches Wordsworth with being not a Christian but a Platonist.

It is one of the subtle remarks of Hume on certain religious speculations that the tendency of them is to make men indifferent to whatever takes place by destroying all ideas of good and evil. I took occasion to apply this remark to something Blake said. If so, I said, there is no use in discipline or education, no difference between good and evil. He hastily broke in on me—'There is no use in education. I hold it wrong. It is the great sin.[1] It is eating of the tree of the knowledge of good and evil. That was the fault of Plato— he knew of nothing but of the virtues and vices and good and evil. There is nothing in all that. Every thing is good in God's eyes.' On my putting the obvious question—Is there nothing absolutely evil in what men do? 'I am no judge of that. Perhaps not in God's Eyes.' Though on this and other occasions he spoke as if he denied altogether the existence of evil, and as if we had nothing to do with right and wrong. It being sufficient to consider all things as alike the work of God. [I interposed with the German word objectively, which he approved of.] Yet at other times he spoke of error as being in heaven. I asked about the *moral* character of Dante in writing his Vision: was he pure? '*Pure*,' said Blake. 'Do you think there

---

[1] 'By which evil' crossed out.

is any purity in God's eyes? The angels in heaven are no more so than we—"he chargeth his angels with folly."' He afterwards extended this to the Supreme Being—he is liable to error too. Did he not repent him that he had made Nineveh?

It is easier to repeat the personal remarks of Blake than these metaphysical speculations so nearly allied to the most opposite systems. He spoke with seeming complacency of himself—said he acted by command. The spirit said to him, 'Blake, be an artist and nothing else.' In this there is felicity. His eye glistened while he spoke of the joy of devoting himself solely to divine art. 'Art is inspiration. When Michael Angelo or Raphael or Mr. Flaxman does any of his fine things, he does them in the spirit.' Blake said, 'I should be sorry if I had any earthly fame, for whatever natural glory a man has is so much detracted from his spiritual glory. I wish to do nothing for profit. I wish to live for art. I want nothing whatever. I am quite happy.'

Among the [1] unintelligible sentiments which he was continually expressing is his distinction between the natural and the spiritual world. The natural world must be consumed. Incidentally *Swedenborg* was spoken of. He was a divine teacher—he has done much good, and will do much good—he has corrected many errors of Popery, and also of Luther and Calvin. Yet he

---

[1] 'More remarkable' crossed out.

also said that *Swedenborg* was wrong in endeavouring to explain to the *rational* faculty what the
reason cannot comprehend : he should have left
that.   As Blake mentioned *Swedenborg* and *Dante*
together I wished to know whether he considered
their visions of the same kind.   As far as I could
collect, he does.   *Dante* he said was the greater
poet.   He had *political* objects.   Yet this, though
wrong, does not appear in Blake's mind to affect
the truth of the vision.   Strangely inconsistent with
this was the language of Blake about Wordsworth.
Wordsworth he thinks is no Christian but a
Platonist.   He asked me, ' Does he believe in the
Scriptures ? '   On my answering in the affirmative
he said he had been much pained by reading the
introduction to the Excursion.   It brought on a
fit of illness.   The passage was produced and
read :

> ' Jehovah—with his thunder, and the choir
>   Of shouting Angels, and the empyreal thrones,
>   I *pass* them unalarmed.'

This *pass them unalarmed* greatly offended
Blake.   ' Does Mr. Wordsworth think his mind
can *surpass* Jehovah ? '   I tried to twist this passage
into a sense corresponding with Blake's own
theories, but filled [*sic* = failed], and Wordsworth
was finally set down as a pagan.   But still with
great praise as the greatest poet of the age.
   Jacob Boehmen was spoken of as a divinely

inspired man.   Blake praised, too, the figures in
Law's translation as being very beautiful.
Michael Angelo could not have done better.
Though he spoke of his happiness, he spoke of past
sufferings, and of sufferings as necessary.   'There
is suffering in heaven, for where there is the capacity
of enjoyment, there is the capacity of pain.'

I have been interrupted by a call from Talfourd
in writing this account—and I can not now recollect any distinct remarks—but as Blake has invited
me to go and see him I shall possibly have an
opportunity again of noting what he says, and I
may be able hereafter to throw connection, if not
system, into what I have written above.

I feel great admiration and respect for him—he
is certainly a most amiable man—a good creature
—and of his poetical and pictorial genius there is
no doubt, I believe, in the minds of judges.
Wordsworth and Lamb like his poems, and the
Aders his paintings.

A few other detached thoughts occur to me.

Bacon, *Locke*, and *Newton* are the three great
teachers of Atheism or of Satan's doctrine.

Every thing is *Atheism* which assumes the
reality of the natural and unspiritual world.

Irving.   He is a highly gifted man—he is a
sent man—but they who are sent sometimes[1] go
further than they ought.

[1] ' Exceed their commission ' crossed out.

Dante saw Devils where I see none. I see only good. I saw nothing but good in *Calvin's* house— better than in Luther's; he had harlots.

Swedenborg. Parts of his scheme are dangerous. His sexual religion is dangerous.

I do not believe that the world is round. I believe it is quite flat. I objected the circumnavigation. We were called to dinner at the moment, and I lost the reply.

The *Sun*. ' I have conversed with the Spiritual Sun—I saw him on Primrose-hill. He said, " Do you take me for the Greek Apollo ? " " No," I said, " that " [and Blake pointed to the sky] " that is the Greek Apollo. He is Satan." '

' I know what is true by internal conviction. A doctrine is told me—my heart says it must be true.' I corroborated this by remarking on the impossibility of the unlearned man judging of what are called the *external* evidences of religion, in which he heartily concurred.

I regret that I have been unable to do more than set down these seeming idle and rambling sentences. The tone and manner are incommunicable. There is a natural sweetness and gentility about Blake which are delightful. And when he is not referring to his Visions he talks sensibly and acutely.

His friend Linnel seems a great admirer.

Perhaps the best thing he said was his comparison of moral with natural evil. ' Who shall

say what God thinks evil ?   That is a wise tale of
the Mahometans—of the Angel of the Lord that
murdered the infant' [alluding to the Hermit of
Parnel, I suppose]. ' Is not every infant that dies of
disease in effect murdered by an angel ? '

17th December.   For the sake of connection I
will here insert a minute of a short call I this
morning made on Blake.   He dwells in Fountain
Court in the Strand.   I found him in a small
room, which seems to be both a working-room and
a bedroom.   Nothing could exceed the squalid air
both of the apartment and his dress, but in spite
of dirt—I might say filth—an air of natural
gentility is diffused over him.   And his wife, notwithstanding the same offensive character of her
dress and appearance, has a good expression of
countenance, so that I shall have a pleasure in
calling on and conversing with these worthy
people.

But I fear I shall not make any progress in
ascertaining his opinions and feelings—that there
being really no system or connection in his mind,
all his future conversation will be but varieties of
wildness and incongruity.

I found [*sic*] at work on Dante.   The book
(Cary) and his sketches both before him.   He
shewed me his designs, of which I have nothing to
say but that they evince a power of grouping and
of throwing grace and interest over conceptions

most monstrous and disgusting, which I should not have anticipated.

Our conversation began about Dante. 'He was an "Atheist," a mere politician busied about this world as Milton was, till in his old age he returned back to God whom he had had in his childhood.'

I tried to get out from Blake that he meant this charge only in a higher sense, and not using the word Atheism in its popular meaning. But he would not allow this. Though when he in like manner charged Locke with Atheism and I remarked that Locke wrote on the evidences of piety and lived a virtuous life, he had nothing to reply to me nor reiterated the charge of wilful deception. I admitted that Locke's doctrine leads to Atheism, and this seemed to satisfy him. From this subject we passed over to that of good and evil, in which he repeated his former assertions more decidedly. He allowed, indeed, that there is error, mistake, etc., and if these be evil—then there is evil, but these are only negations. Nor would he admit that any education should be attempted except that of cultivation of the imagination and fine arts. 'What are called the vices in the natural world are the highest sublimities in the spiritual world.' When I asked whether if he had been a father he would not have grieved if his child had become vicious or a great criminal, he answered, 'I must not regard when I am endeavouring to think rightly my own any more than other people's weaknesses.' And when I again remarked that this doctrine puts an end to all exertion or even wish to change anything, he had no reply. We spoke of the Devil, and I observed that when a child I thought the Manichæan doctrine or that of the two principles a rational one. He assented to this, and in confirmation asserted that he did not believe in the *omnipotence* of God. 'The language of the Bible on that subject is only poetical or allegorical.' Yet soon after he denied that the natural world is anything. 'It is all nothing, and Satan's empire is the empire of nothing.'

He reverted soon to his favourite expression, my Visions. 'I saw Milton in imagination, and he told me to beware of being misled by his Paradise Lost. In particular he wished me to show the falsehood of his doctrine that the pleasures of *sex* arose from the fall. The fall could not produce any pleasure.' I answered, the fall produced a state of *evil* in which there was a mixture of good or pleasure. And in that sense the fall may be said to produce the pleasure. But he replied that the fall produced only generation and death. And then he went off upon a rambling state of a union of sexes in man as in Ovid, an androgynous state, in which I could not follow him.

As he spoke of Milton's appearing to him, I asked whether he resembled the prints of him. He answered, 'All.' Of what age did he appear to be? 'Various ages—sometimes a very old man.' He spoke of Milton as being at one time a sort of classical Atheist, and of Dante as being now with God.

Of the faculty of Vision, he spoke as one he has had from early infancy. He thinks all men partake of it, but it is lost by not being cultivated. And he eagerly assented to a remark I made, that all men have all faculties to a greater or less degree. I am to renew my visits, and to read Wordsworth to him, of whom he seems to entertain a high idea.

[Here R. has added *vide* p. 174, *i.e.* Dec. 24, below.]

Sunday 11*th.* The greater part of the forenoon was spent in writing the preceding account of my interview with Blake in which I was interrupted by a call from Talfourd. . . .

17*th.* Made a visit to Blake of which I have written fully in a preceding page.

20*th.* . . . Hundleby took coffee with me *tête à tête.* We talked of his personal concerns, of Wordsworth, whom I can't make him properly enjoy ; of Blake, whose peculiarities he can as little relish. . . .

Saturday 24*th.* A call on *Blake.* My third interview. I read him Wordsworth's incomparable ode, which he heartily enjoyed. The same half crazy crotchets about the two worlds—the eternal rèpetition of what must in time become tiresome. Again he repeated to day, ' I fear

Wordsworth loves Nature—and Nature is the work of the Devil. The Devil is in us, as far as we are Nature.' On my enquiring whether the Devil would not be destroyed by God as being of less power, he denied that God has any power—asserted that the Devil is eternally created not by God, but by God's permission. And when I objected that permission implies power to prevent, he did not seem to understand me. It was remarked that the parts of Wordworth's ode which he most enjoyed were the most obscure and those I the least like and comprehend. . . .

January 1826

6*th.* A call on Blake. I hardly feel it worth while to write down his conversation, it is so much a repetition of his former talk. He was very cordial to-day. I had procured him two subscriptions for his Job from Geo. Procter and Bas. Montague. I paid £1 on each. This, probably, put him in spirits, more than he was aware of—he spoke of his being richer than ever on having learned to know me, and he told Mrs. A. he and I were nearly of an opinion. Yet I have practised no deception intentionally, unless silence be so. He renewed his complaints, blended with his admiration of Wordsworth. The oddest thing he said was that he had been commanded to do certain things, that is, to write about Milton, and that he was applauded for refusing—he struggled with the Angels and was victor. His wife joined in the conversation. . . .

8*th*. . . . Then took tea with Basil Montague, Mrs. M. there. A short chat about Coleridge, Irving, etc. She admires Blake—*Encore une excellence là de plus.* . . .

February

18*th*. Jos. Wedd breakfasted with me. Then called on *Blake*. An amusing chat with him, but still no novelty. The same round of extravagant and mad doctrines, which I shall not now repeat, but merely notice their application.

He gave me, copied out by himself, Wordsworth's preface to his Excursion. At the end he has added this note :—

' Solomon, when he married Pharaoh's daughter, became a convert to the Heathen Mythology, talked exactly in this way of Jehovah as a very inferior object of man's contemplations ; he also passed him by unalarmed, and was permitted. Jehovah dropped a tear and followed him by his Spirit into the abstract void. It is called the divine Mercy. Satan dwells in it, but mercy does not dwell in him.'

Of Wordsworth he talked as before. Some of his writings proceed from the Holy Ghost, but then others are the work of the Devil. However, I

found on this subject Blake's language more in
conformity with Orthodox Christianity than before.
He talked of the being under the direction of *Self*;
and of *Reason* as the creature of man and opposed
to God's grace.   And warmly declared that all he
knew was in the Bible, but then he understands by
the Bible the spiritual sense.   For as to the
natural sense, that Voltaire was commissioned by
God to expose.   ' I have had much intercourse with
Voltaire, and he said to me I blasphemed the Son
of Man, and it shall be forgiven me.   But they (the
enemies of Voltaire) blasphemed the Holy Ghost
in me, and it shall not be forgiven them.'   I asked
in what language Voltaire spoke—he gave an
ingenious answer.   'To my sensation it was
English.   It was like the touch of a musical key.
He touched it probably French, but to my ear it
became English.'   I spoke again of the *form* of the
persons who appear to him.   Asked why he did
not *draw* them, ' It is not worth while.   There are
so many, the labour would be too great.   Besides
there would be no use.   As to Shakespeare, he is
exactly like the *old* engraving—which is called a
bad one.   I think it very good.'

I enquired about his writings.   ' I have written
more than Voltaire or Rousseau—six or seven
epic poems as long as Homer, and 20 tragedies
as long as Macbeth.'   He showed me his Vision
(for so it may be called) of Genesis—'as understood by a Christian Visionary,' in which in a

style resembling the Bible the spirit is given. He read a passage at random. It was striking. He will not print any more.[1] 'I write,' he says, ' when commanded by the spirits, and the moment I have written I see the words fly about the room in all directions. It is then published, and the spirits can read. My MSS. of no further use. I have been tempted to burn my MSS., but my wife won't let me.' She is right, said I—and you have written these, not from yourself, but by a higher order. The MSS. are theirs and your property. You cannot tell what purpose they may answer—unforeseen to you. He liked this, and said he would not destroy them. His philosophy he repeated—denying causation, asserting everything to be the work of God or the Devil—that there is a constant falling off from God—angels becoming devils. Every man has a devil in him, and the conflict is eternal between a man's self and God, etc. etc. etc. He told me my copy of his songs would be 5 guineas, and was pleased by my manner of receiving this information. He spoke of his horror of money—of his turning pale when money had been offered him, etc. etc. etc.

May

Thursday 11*th.* Calls this morning on Blake, on Thornton [etc.] . . .

12*th* . . . Tea and supper at home. The Flaxmans,

---

[1] 'For the writer' crossed out.

Masqueriers (a Miss Forbes), Blake, and Sutton
Sharpe.

On the whole the evening went off tolerably.
Masquerier not precisely the man to enjoy Blake,
who was, however, not in an *exalted* state.   Allusions only to his particular notions while Masquerier commented on his opinions as if they were
those of a man of ordinary notions.   Blake asserted
that the oldest painter poets were the best.   Do
you deny all progression? says Masquerier.   'Oh
yes!'   I doubt whether Flaxman sufficiently
tolerates Blake.   But Blake appreciates Flaxman
as he ought.   Blake relished my Stone drawings.
They staid till eleven.

Blake is more and more convinced that Wordsworth worships *nature* and is not a Bible Christian.
I have sent him the Sketches.   We shall see
whether they convert him.

June

13*th*.   Another idle day.   Called early on
Blake.   He was as wild as ever, with no great
novelty, except that he confessed a *practical* notion
which would do him more injury than any other I
have heard from him.   He says that from the
Bible he has learned that *eine Gemeinschaft der
Frauen statt finden sollte*.   When I objected that
Ehestand seems to be a divine institution, he
referred to the Bible—'that from the beginning it

was not so.' He talked as usual of the spirits,
asserted that he had committed many murders,
that reason is the only evil or sin, and that careless,
gay people are better than those who think, etc.
etc. etc.

December

Thursday 7th. I sent Britt. to enquire after Mr.
Flaxman's health, etc., and was engaged looking
over the Term Reports while he was gone. On
his return, he brought the melancholy intelligence
of his death early in the morning ! ! ! The country
has lost one of its greatest and best of men. As
an artist he has spread the fame of the country
beyond any others of his age. As a man he exhibited a rare specimen of Christian and moral
excellence.

I walked out and called at Mr. Soane's. He
was from home. I then called on Blake, desirous
to see how, with his peculiar feelings and opinions,
he would receive the intelligence. It was much
as I expected—he had himself been very ill during
the summer, and his first observation was with a
smile—'I thought I should have gone first.' He then
said, 'I cannot consider death as anything but [1] a
removing from one room to another.' One thing
led to another, and he fell into his wild rambling
way of talk. 'Men are born with a devil and an

[1] 'A passage from' crossed out.

angel,' but this he himself interpreted body and soul. Of the Old Testament he seemed to think not favourably. 'Christ,' said he, 'took much after his mother (the law), and in that respect was one of the worst of men.' On my requiring an explanation, he said, 'There was his turning the money changers out of the Temple. He had no right to do that.' Blake then declared against those who sat in judgement on others. 'I have never known a very bad man who had not something very good about him.' He spoke of the Atonement. Said, 'It is a horrible doctrine. If another man pay your debt, I do not forgive it,' etc. etc. etc. He produced *Sintram* by Fouqué—'This is better than my things.'

1827

February

Friday, 2nd. Götzenberger, the young painter from Germany, called on me, and I accompanied him to Blake. We looked over Blake's Dante. Götzenberger seemed highly gratified by the designs, and Mrs. Aders says Götzenberger considers Blake as the first and Flaxman as the second man he had seen in England. The conversation was slight —I was interpreter between them. And nothing remarkable was said by Blake—he was interested apparently by Götzenberger. . . .

1828

January

    8th. Breakfasted with Shott—Talfourd and B. Field there. Walked with Field to Mrs. Blake. The poor old lady was more affected than I expected, yet she spoke of her husband as dying like an angel. She is the housekeeper of Linnell the painter and engraver, and at present her services might well pay for her board. A few of her husband's works are all her property. We found that the Job is Linnell's property, and the print of Chaucer's pilgrimage hers. Therefore Field bought a proof and I two prints at $2\frac{1}{2}$ guineas each. I mean one for Lamb. Mrs. Blake is to look out some engravings for me hereafter. . . .

(2) FROM A LETTER OF CRABB ROBINSON TO DOROTHY WORDSWORTH

In a letter to Dorothy Wordsworth, not dated, but bearing the postmark of February 20, 1826, there is the following reference to Blake. No earlier reference to him occurs in the letter, in spite of the sentence which follows :—

    'I have above mentioned *Blake.* I forget

whether I ever mentioned to you this very interesting man, with whom I am now become acquainted. Were the "Memorials" at my hand, I should quote a fine passage in the Sonnet on the Cologne Cathedral as applicable to the contemplation of this singular being.

' I gave your brother some poems in MS. by him, and they interested him—as well they might, for there is an affinity between them, as there is between the regulated imagination of a wise poet and the incoherent dreams of a poet. Blake is an engraver by trade, a painter and a poet also, whose works have been subject of derision to men in general; but he has a few admirers, and some of eminence have eulogised his designs. He has lived in obscurity and poverty, to which the constant hallucinations in which he lives have doomed him. I do not mean to give you a detailed account of him. A few words will suffice to inform you of what class he is. He is not so much a disciple of Jacob Böhmen and Swedenborg as a fellow Visionary. He lives, as they did, in a world of his own, enjoying constant intercourse with the world of spirits. He receives visits from Shakespeare, Milton, Dante, Voltaire, etc. etc. etc., and has given me repeatedly their very words in their conversations. His paintings are copies of what he saw in his Visions. His books (and his MSS. are immense in quantity) are dictations from the spirits. He told me yesterday that when he writes it is for the spirits only; he sees the words fly about the room the moment he has put them on paper, and his book is then published. A man so favoured, of course, has sources of wisdom and truth peculiar to himself. I will not pretend to give you an account of his religious and philosophical opinions. They are a strange compound of Christianity, Spinozism, and Platonism. I must confine myself to what he has said about your brother's works, and [1] I fear this may lead me far enough to fatigue you in following me. After what I have said, Mr. W. will not be flattered by knowing that Blake deems him the *only poet* of the age, nor much alarmed by hearing that, like Muley Moloch, Blake thinks that he is often in his works an *Atheist*. Now, according to Blake, Atheism consists in worshipping the natural world, which same natural world, properly speaking, is nothing real, but a mere illusion produced by Satan. Milton was for a great part of his life an Atheist, and therefore has fatal errors in his Paradise Lost, which he has often begged Blake to confute. Dante (though now with God) lived and died an Atheist. He was the slave of the world and time. But Dante and Wordsworth, in spite of their Atheism, were inspired by the Holy Ghost. Indeed, all real poetry is the work of the Holy Ghost, and Wordsworth's poems (a large pro-

---

[1] 'And as I am requested to copy what he has written for the purpose' crossed out.

portion, at least) are the work of divine inspiration. Unhappily he is left by God to his own illusions, and then the Atheism is apparent. I had the pleasure of reading to Blake in my best style (and you know I am vain on that point, and think I read W.'s poems particularly well) the Ode on Immortality. I never witnessed greater delight in any listener; and in general Blake loves the poems. What appears to have disturbed his mind, on the other hand, is the Preface to the Excursion. He told me six months ago that it caused him a bowel complaint which nearly killed him. I have in his hand a copy of the extract [with the][1] following note at the end : "Solomon, when he married Pharaoh's daughter and became a convert to the Heathen Mythology, talked exactly in this way of Jehovah as a very inferior object of man's contemplation; he also passed him by unalarmed, and was permitted. Jehovah dropped a tear, and followed him by his Spirit into the abstract void. It is called the divine mercy. Satan dwells in it, but Mercy does not dwell in him, he knows not to forgive." When I first saw Blake at Mrs. Aders's he very earnestly asked me, "Is Mr. W. a sincere real Christian ? " In reply to my answer he said, " If so, what does he mean by 'the worlds to which the heaven of heavens is but a veil,' and who is he that shall 'pass Jehovah unalarmed ' ? " It is since then that I have lent Blake all the

[1] The MS. is here torn.

works which he but imperfectly knew. I doubt
whether what I have written will excite your and
Mr. W.'s curiosity ; but there is something so delightful about the man—though in great poverty,
he is so perfect a gentleman, with such genuine
dignity and independence, scorning presents, and
of such native delicacy in words, etc. etc. etc., that
I have not scrupled promising introducing him
and Mr. W. together. He expressed his thanks
strongly, saying, "You do me honour, Mr. W. is
a great man. Besides, he may convince me I am
wrong about him. I have been wrong before now,"
etc. Coleridge has visited Blake, and, I am told,
talks finely about him. That I might not encroach
on a third sheet I have compressed what I had to
say about Blake. You must *see* him one of these
days and he will interest you at all events, whatever character you give to his mind.'

The main part of the letter is concerned with
Wordsworth's arrangement of his poems, which
Crabb Robinson says that he agrees with Lamb in
disliking. He then says : ' It is a sort of intellectual suicide in your brother not to have continued his admirable series of poems " dedicated to
liberty," he might add, "and public virtue." I
assure you it gives me real pain when I think that
some future commentator may possibly hereafter
write, "This great poet survived to the fifth
decennary of the nineteenth century, but he appears
to have dyed in the year 1814 as far as life con-

sisted in an active sympathy with the temporary welfare of his fellow-creatures. . . ."

[More follows, and then] 'I had no intention, I assure you, to make so long a parenthesis or indeed to advert to such a subject. And I wish you not to read any part of this letter which might be thought impertinent. . . . In favour of my affectionate attachment to your brother's fame, do forgive me this digression, and, as I said above, keep it to yourself.'

[At the end he says] 'My best remembrances to Mr. W. And recollect again that you are not to read *all* this letter to any one if it will offend, and you are yourself to forgive it as coming from one who is affly. your friend,   H. C. R.'

On April 6, Wordsworth answers the letter from Rydal Mount, saying : 'My sister had taken flight for Herefordshire when your letter, for such we guessed it to be, arrived—it was broken open—(pray forgive the offense) and your charges of concealment and reserve frustrated. We are all, at all times, so glad to hear from you that we could not resist the temptation to purchase the pleasure at the expense of the peccadillo, for which we beg pardon with united voices. You are kind enough to mention my poems.'

[All the rest of the letter is taken up with them, and it ends, with no mention of Blake] 'I can write no more. T. Clarkson is going. Your sup-

posed Biography entertained me much.   I could
give you the other side.   Farewell.'

[There is no signature.]

(3)—FROM CRABB ROBINSON'S

REMINISCENCES

1810

I was amusing myself this spring by writing an
account of the insane poet, painter, and engraver,
Blake.   Perthes of Hamburg had written to me
asking me to send him an article for a new German
magazine, entitled Vaterländische Annalen, which
he was about to set up, and Dr. *Malkin* having in
his Memoirs of his son given an account of this
extraordinary genius with specimens of his poems,
I resolved out of these to compile a paper.   And
this I did,[1] and the paper was translated by Dr.

---

[1] The article appeared under the title : 'William Blake,
Künstler, Dichter und religiöser Schwärmer' (aus dem
Englischen) on pp. 107-131 of the *Vaterländisches Museum*,
Zweiter Band, Erstes Heft.   Hamburg, bey Friedrich Perthes.
1811.'   It has the motto :

'The lunatic, the lover, and the poet
Are of imagination all compact.'
                                    SHAKESPEARE.

Five of Blake's poems, 'To the Muses,' 'Piping down the

Julius, who, many years afterwards, introduced himself to me as my translator. It appears in the single number of the second volume of the Vaterländische Annalen. For it was at this time that Buonaparte united Hamburg to the French Empire, on which Perthes manfully gave up the magazine, saying, as he had no longer a Vaterland, there could be no Vaterländische Annalen. But before I drew up the paper, I went to see a gallery of Blake's paintings, which were exhibited by his brother, a hosier in Carnaby Market. The entrance was 2s. 6d., catalogue included. I was deeply interested by the catalogue as well as the pictures. I took 4—telling the brother I hoped he would let me come in again. He said, ' Oh ! as often as you please.' I dare say such a thing had never happened before or did afterwards. I afterwards became acquainted with Blake, and will postpone till hereafter what I have to say of this extraordinary character, whose life has since been written very inadequately by Allan Cunningham in his *Lives of the English Artists*.

[At the side is written]—*N.B.* What I have written about Blake will appear at the end of the year 1825.

valleys wild,' ' Holy Thursday,' ' The Tyger,' ' The Garden of Love,' together with ten lines from the Prophetic Books, are quoted, with German versions in the metres of the original by Dr. Julius, the translator of the article. On p. 101 there is an article, ' Von der neuesten englischen Poesie,' containing notices of ' Poems by W. Cowper' (1803), ' Works of R. Burns,' and ' Southey's Poems ' (1801) and ' Metrical Tales ' (1803).

1825

WILLIAM BLAKE   19/2/52.

IT was at the latter end of the year 1825 that
I put in writing my recollections of this most
remarkable man. The larger portions are under
the date of the 18th of December. He died in the
year 1827. I have therefore now revised what I
wrote on the 10th of December and afterwards, and
without any attempt to reduce to order, or make
consistent the wild and strange rhapsodies uttered
by this insane man of genius, thinking it better
to put down what I find as it occurs, though I am
aware of the objection that may justly be made to
the recording the ravings of insanity in which it
may be said there can be found no principle, as
there is no ascertainable law of mental association
which is obeyed; and from which therefore
nothing can be learned.

This would be perfectly true of *mere* madness—
but does not apply to that form of insanity ordin-
arily called monomania, and may be disregarded in
a case like the present in which the subject of the
remark was unquestionably what a German would
call a *Verunglückter Genie,* whose theosophic dreams
bear a close resemblance to those of *Swedenborg*—
whose genius as an artist was praised by no less
men than *Flaxman* and *Fuseli*—and whose poems
were thought worthy republication by the bio-
grapher of *Swedenborg* (*Wilkinson*), and of which

Wordsworth said after reading a number—they were the 'Songs of Innocence and Experience showing the two opposite sides of the human soul '— 'There is no doubt this poor man was mad, but there is something in the madness of this man which interests me more than the sanity of Lord Byron and Walter Scott!' The German painter *Götzenberger* (a man indeed who ought not to be named *after the others* as an authority for my writing about Blake) said, on his returning to Germany about the time at which I am now arrived, ' I saw in England many men of talents, but only three men of genius, Coleridge, Flaxman, and Blake, and of these Blake was the greatest.' I do not mean to intimate my assent to this opinion, nor to do more than supply such materials as my intercourse with him furnish to an uncritical narative to which I shall confine myself. I have written a few sentences in these reminiscences already, those of the year 1810. I had not then begun the regular journal which I afterwards kept. I will therefore go over the ground again and introduce these recollections of 1825 by a reference to the slight knowledge I had of him before, and what occasioned my taking an interest in him, not caring to repeat what Cunningham has recorded of him in the volume of his *Lives of the British Painters*, etc. etc., except thus much. It appears that he was born

[The page ends here.]

Dr. Malkin, our Bury Grammar School Head-master, published in the year 1806 a Memoir of a very precocious child who died . . . years old, and he prefixed to the Memoir an account of Blake, and in the volume he gave an account of Blake as a painter and poet, and printed some specimens of his poems, viz. ' The Tyger,' and ballads and mystical lyrical poems, all of a wild character, and M. gave an account of Visions which Blake related to his acquaintance.   I knew that Flaxman thought highly of him, and though he did not venture to extol him as a genuine seer, yet he did not join in the ordinary derision of him as a madman.   Without having seen him, yet I had already conceived a high opinion of him, and thought he would furnish matter for a paper interesting to Germans, and therefore when *Fred. Perthes,* the patriotic publisher at Hamburg, wrote to me in 1810 requesting me to give him an article for his Patriotische Annalen, I thought I could do no better than send him a paper on Blake, which was translated into German by *Dr. Julius,* filling, with a few small poems copied and translated, 24 pages.   These appeared in the first and last No. of volume 2 of the Annals.   The high-minded editor boldly declared that as the Emperor of France had annexed Hamburg to France he had no longer a country, and there could no longer be any patriotical Annals ! ! !   Perthes' Life has been written since, which I have not seen.   I am told there is in it a civil mention of me. This *Dr. Julius* introduced himself to me as such translator a few years ago. He travelled as an Inspector of Prisons for the Prussian Government into the United States of America. In order to enable me to write this paper, which, by the bye, has nothing in it of the least value, I went to see an exhibition of Blake's original paintings in Carnaby Market, at a hosier's, Blake's brother. These paintings filled several rooms of an ordinary dwelling-house, and for the sight a half-crown was demanded of the visitor, for which he had a catalogue. This catalogue I possess, and it is a very curious exposure of the state of the artist's mind. I wished to send it to Germany and to give a copy to Lamb and others, so I took four, and giving 10s., bargained that I should be at liberty to go again. 'Free! as long as you live,'[1] said the brother, astonished at such a liberality, which he had never experienced before, nor I dare say did afterwards. *Lamb* was delighted with the catalogue, especially with the description of a painting afterwards engraved, and connected with which is an anecdote that, unexplained, would reflect discredit on a most amiable and excellent man, but which Flaxman considered to have been not the wilful act of *Stodart*. It was after the friends of Blake had circulated a subscription paper for an engraving of his *Canterbury Pilgrims*, that *Stodart* was made a party to an

---

[1] 'Like' is first written, and replaced by 'live.'

engraving of a painting of the same subject by
himself. Stodart's work is well known, Blake's is
known by very few. Lamb preferred it greatly to
Stodart's, and declared that Blake's description
was the finest criticism he had ever read of
Chaucer's poem.

In this catalogue Blake writes of himself in the
most outrageous language—says, ' This artist defies
all competition in colouring '—that none can beat
him, for none can beat the Holy Ghost—that he
and Raphael and Michael Angelo were under
divine influence — while Corregio and Titian
worshipped a lascivious and therefore cruel deity
—Reubens a proud devil, etc. etc. He declared,
speaking of colour, Titian's men to be of leather
and his women of chalk, and ascribed his own perfection in colouring to the advantage he enjoyed in
seeing daily the primitive men walking in their native
nakedness in the mountains of Wales. There were
about thirty oil-paintings, the colouring excessively
dark and high, the veins black, and the colour of
the primitive men very like that of the Red
Indians. In his estimation they would probably
be the primitive men. Many of his designs were
unconscious imitations. This appears also in his
published works—the designs of *Blair's Grave*,
which Fuseli and Schiavonetti highly extolled—
and in his designs to illustrate *Job*, published after
his death for the benefit of his widow.

To this catalogue and in the printed poems, the small pamphlet which appeared in 1783, the edition put forth by Wilkinson of 'The Songs of Innocence,' and other works already mentioned, to which I have to add the first four books of Young's Night Thoughts, and Allan Cunningham's Life of him, I now refer, and will confine myself to the memorandums I took of his conversation. I had heard of him from Flaxman, and for the first time dined in his company at the Aders'. *Linnell* the painter also was there—an artist of considerable talent, and who professed to take [1] a deep interest in Blake and his work, whether of a perfectly disinterested character may be doubtful, as will appear hereafter. This was on the 10th of December.

I was aware of his idiosyncracies and therefore to a great degree prepared for the sort of conversation which took place at and after dinner, an altogether unmethodical rhapsody on art, poetry, and religion—he saying the most strange things in the most unemphatic manner, speaking of his *Visions* as any man would of the most ordinary occurrence. He was then 68 years of age. He had a broad, pale face, a large full eye with a benignant expression—at the same time a look of languor,[2] except when excited, and then he had an air of

---

[1] 'Took' crossed out.
[2] 'With an air of feebleness' crossed out.

inspiration. But not such as without a previous acquaintance with him, or attending to *what* he said, would suggest the notion that he was insane. There was nothing *wild* about his look, and though very ready to be drawn out to the assertion of his favourite ideas, yet with no warmth as if he wanted to make proselytes. Indeed one of the peculiar features of his scheme, as far as it was consistent, was indifference and a very extraordinary degree of tolerance and satisfaction with what had taken place.[1]   A sort of pious and humble optimism, not the scornful optimism of Candide. But at the same time that he was very ready to praise he seemed incapable of envy, as he was of discontent.   He warmly praised some composition of Mrs. Aders, and having brought for Aders an engraving of his Canterbury Pilgrims, he remarked that one of the figures resembled a figure in one of the works then in Aders's room, so that he had been accused of having stolen from it.   But he added that he had drawn the figure in question 20 years before he had seen the *original* picture.   However, there is 'no wonder in the resemblance, as in my youth I was always studying that class of painting.'   I have forgotten what it was, but his taste was in close conformity with the old German school.

    [1] After 'indifference and' 'the entire absence of anything like blame ['reproach' crossed out], and I do not think that I ever heard him blame anything, then or afterwards' crossed out.

This was somewhat at variance with what he
said both this day and afterwards—implying that
he copies his Visions. And it was on this first day
that, in answer to a question from me, he said, ' *The
Spirits told me.*' This lead me to say: Socrates
used pretty much the same language. He spoke
of his Genius. Now, what affinity or resemblance
do you suppose was there between the *Genius*
which inspired Socrates and your *Spirits?* He
smiled, and for once it seemed to me as if he had
a feeling of vanity gratified.[1] ' The same as in
our countenances.' He paused and said, ' I was
Socrates '—and then as if he had gone too far in
that—' or a sort of brother. I must have had
conversations with him. So I had with Jesus
Christ. I have an obscure recollection of having
been with both of them.' As I had for many years
been familiar with the idea that an eternity *a
parte post* was inconceivable without an eternity *a
parte ante*, I was naturally led to express that
thought on this occasion. His eye brightened on
my saying this. He eagerly assented: ' To be
sure. We are all coexistent with God; members
of the Divine body, and partakers of the Divine
nature.' Blake's having adopted this Platonic
idea led me on our *tête-à-tête* walk home at night
to put the popular question to him, concerning the
imputed Divinity of Jesus Christ. He answered:
' He is the only God ' — but then he added —

[1] ' Pretty much ' crossed out.

'And so am I and so are you.' He had before said—and that led me to put the question—that Christ ought not to have suffered himself to be crucified.' 'He should not have attacked the Government. He had no business with such matters.' On my representing this to be inconsistent with the sanctity of divine qualities, he said Christ was not yet become the Father. It is hard on bringing together these fragmentary recollections[1] to fix Blake's position in relation to Christianity, Platonism, and Spinozism.

It is one of the subtle remarks of *Hume* on the tendency of certain religious notions to reconcile us to whatever occurs, as God's will. And applying this to something Blake said, and drawing the inference that there is no use in education, he hastily rejoined : 'There *is* no use in education. I hold it wrong. It is the great Sin. It is eating of the tree of knowledge of Good and Evil. That was the fault of Plato : he knew of nothing but the Virtues and Vices. There is nothing in all that. Everything is good in God's eyes.' On my asking whether there is nothing absolutely evil in what man does, he answered : 'I am no judge of that —perhaps not in God's eyes.' Notwithstanding this, he, however, at the same time spoke of error as being in heaven; for on my asking whether Dante was pure in writing his *Vision*, 'Pure,' said Blake. 'Is there any purity in God's eyes? No.

---

[1] 'Comparing these fragmentary memoranda' crossed out.

"He chargeth his angels with folly."' He even extended this liability to error to the Supreme Being. 'Did he not repent him that he had made Nineveh?' My journal here has the remark that it is easier to retail his personal remarks than to reconcile those which seemed to be in conformity with the most opposed abstract systems. He spoke with seeming complacency of his own life in connection with Art. In becoming an artist he 'acted by command.' The Spirits said to him, 'Blake, be an artist.' His eye glistened while he spoke of the joy of devoting himself to *divine art* alone. 'Art is inspiration. When Mich. Angelo or Raphael, in their day, or Mr. Flaxman, does any of his fine things, he does them in the Spirit.' Of fame he said: 'I should be sorry if I had any earthly fame, for whatever natural glory a man has is so much detracted from his spiritual glory. I wish to do nothing for profit. I want nothing— I am quite happy.' This was confirmed to me on my subsequent interviews with him. His distinction between the Natural and Spiritual worlds was very confused. Incidentally, Swedenborg was mentioned—he declared him to be a Divine Teacher. He had done, and would do, much good. Yet he did wrong in endeavouring to explain to the *reason* what it could not comprehend. He seemed to consider, but that was not clear, the visions of Swedenborg and Dante as of the same kind. Dante was the greater poet. He too was wrong in occupying his mind about political objects. Yet this did not appear to affect his estimation of Dante's genius, or his opinion of the truth of Dante's visions. Indeed, when he even declared Dante to be an Atheist, it was accompanied by expression of the highest admiration; though, said he, Dante saw Devils where I saw none.[1]

I put down in my journal the following insulated remarks. *Jacob Böhmen* was placed among the divinely inspired men. He praised also the designs to Law's translation of Böhmen. Michael Angelo could not have surpassed them.

' *Bacon, Locke,* and *Newton* are the three great teachers of Atheism, or Satan's Doctrine,' he asserted.

' *Irving* is a highly gifted man—he is a *sent* man;

---

[1] Crossed out :
' Yet this did not appear to] affect the truth of his Visions. I could not reconcile this with his blaming Wordsworth for being a Platonist—not a Christian. He asked whether Wordsworth acknowledged the Scriptures as Divine, and declared on my answering in the affirmative that the Introduction to the Excursion had troubled him so as to bring on a fit of illness. The passage that offended Blake was

> ' Jehovah with his thunder and the choir
> Of shouting Angels and the empyreal throne,
> I pass them unalarmed.

' " Does Mr. Wordsworth," said Blake, "think his mind can *surpass* Jehovah's." I tried in vain to rescue Wordsworth from the imputation of being a Pagan or perhaps an Atheist, but this did not rob him of the character of being the great poet. Indeed Atheism meant but little in Blake's mind as will hereafter appear. Therefore when he declared [Dante to be an Atheist, etc.'

In the margin : See of Wordsworth as Blake judged of him, p. 46 *et seq.* (*i. e.* p. 296 below).

but they who are sent sometimes go further than they ought.'[1]

Calvin. I saw nothing but good in *Calvin's* house. In *Luther's* there were *Harlots*. He declared his opinion that the earth is flat, not round, and just as I had objected the circumnavigation dinner was announced. But objections were seldom of any use. The wildest of his assertions was made with the veriest indifference of tone,[2] as if altogether insignificant. It respected the natural and spiritual worlds. By way of example of the difference between them, he said, ' *You* never saw the spiritual Sun. I have. I saw him on Primrose Hill.' He said, ' Do you take me for the Greek Apollo?' ' No!' I said. ' *That* (pointing to the sky) that is the Greek Apollo. He is Satan.'

Not everything was thus absurd. There were glimpses and flashes of truth and beauty: as when he compared moral with physical evil. 'Who shall say what God thinks evil? That is a wise tale of the Mahometans—of the Angel of the Lord who murdered the Infant.'—The Hermit of Parnell, I suppose.—' Is not every infant that dies of a natural death in reality slain by an Angel?'

And when he joined to the assurance of his happiness, that of his having suffered, and that it was necessary, he added, 'There is suffering in

---

[1] ' Dante saw Devils where I saw none' crossed out.
[2] ' Most unconscious simplicity ' crossed out.

Heaven ; for where there is the capacity of enjoyment, there is the capacity of pain.[1]

I include among the glimpses of truth this assertion, ' I know what is true by internal conviction. A doctrine is stated. My heart tells me It *must* be true.' I remarked, in confirmation of it, that, to an unlearned man, what are called the *external* evidences of religion can carry no conviction with them ; and this he assented to.

After my first evening with him at Aders's, I made the remark in my journal, that his observations, apart from his Visions and references to the spiritual world, were sensible and acute. In the sweetness of his countenance and gentility of his manner he added an indescribable grace to his conversation. I added my regret, which I must now repeat, at my inability to give more than incoherent thoughts. Not altogether my fault perhaps.

25/2/52.

On the 17th I called on him in his house in Fountain's Court in the Strand. The interview was a short one, and what I saw was more remarkable than what I heard. He was at work engraving in a small bedroom, light, and looking out on a mean yard. Everything in the room squalid and indicating poverty, except himself. And there was

---

[1] ' It was after my first interview with him that I expressed what I must repeat now—my regret ' crossed out.

a natural gentility about him, and an insensibility
to the seeming poverty, which quite removed the
impression. Besides, his linen was clean, his hand
white, and his air quite unembarrassed when he
begged me to sit down as if he were in a palace.
There was but one chair in the room besides that
on which he sat. On my putting my hand to it,
I found that it would have fallen to pieces if I had
lifted it, so, as if I had been a Sybarite, I said with
a smile, 'Will you let me indulge myself?' and I
sat on the bed, and near him,[1] and during my short
stay there was nothing in him that betrayed that
he was aware of what to other persons might have
been even offensive, not in his person, but in all
about him.

His wife I saw at this time, and she seemed to
be the very woman to make him happy. She had
been formed by him. Indeed, otherwise, she could
not have lived with him. Notwithstanding her
dress, which was poor and dirty, she had a good
expression in her countenance, and, with a dark
eye, had remains [2] of beauty in her youth. She
had that virtue of virtues in a wife, an implicit
reverence of her husband. It is quite certain that
she believed in all his visions. And on one
occasion, not this day, speaking of his Visions, she
said, 'You know, dear, the first time you saw God
was when you were four years old, and he put his
head to the window and set you a-screaming.' In

---

[1] 'He smiled' omitted.   [2] 'Marks' crossed out.

a word, she was formed on the Miltonic model, and like the first Wife Eve worshipped God in her husband. He being to her what God was to him. Vide Milton's Paradise Lost—*passim.*

26/2/52.

He was making designs or engravings, I forget which. Carey's Dante was before [*sic*]. He showed me some of his designs from Dante, of which I do not presume to speak. They were too much above me. But Götzenberger, whom I afterwards took to see them, expressed the highest admiration of them. They are in the hands of *Linnell* the painter, and, it has been suggested, are reserved by him for publication when Blake may have become[1] an object of interest to a greater number than he could be at this age. *Dante* was again the subject of our conversation. And Blake declared him a mere politician and atheist, busied about this world's affairs; as Milton was till, in his (M.'s) old age, he returned back to the God he had abandoned in childhood.[2] I in vain endeavoured to obtain from him a qualification of the term atheist, so as not to include him in the ordinary reproach. And yet he afterwards spoke of Dante's being *then* with God. I was more successful when he also called Locke an atheist, and imputed to him wilful deception, and seemed

[1] 'More' crossed out.
[2] 'And yet he afterwards said that he was *then* with God' crossed out.

satisfied with my admission, that Locke's philosophy
led to the Atheism of the French school. He
reiterated his former strange notions on morals—
would allow of no other education than what lies
in the cultivation of the fine arts and the imagination. 'What are called the Vices in the natural
world, are the highest sublimities in the spiritual
world.' And when I supposed the case of his
being the father of a vicious son and asked him
how he would feel, he evaded the question by
saying that in trying to think correctly he must
not regard his own weaknesses any more than
other people's. And he was silent to the observation that his doctrine denied evil. He seemed not
unwilling to admit the Manichæan doctrine of two
principles, as far as it is found in the idea of the
Devil. And said expressly said [sic] he did not
believe in the omnipotence of God. The language
of the Bible is only poetical or allegorical on the
subject, yet he at the same time denied the *reality*
of the natural world. Satan's empire is the empire
of nothing.

As he spoke of frequently seeing Milton, I
ventured to ask, half ashamed at the time, which
of the three or four portraits in *Hollis's* Memoirs
(vols. in 4to) is the most like. He answered, 'They
are all like, at different ages. I have seen him as
a youth and as an old man with a long flowing
beard. He came lately as an old man—he said
he came to ask a favour of me. He said he had

committed an error in his Paradise Lost, which he
wanted me to correct, in a poem or picture; but I
declined. I said I had my own duties to perform.'
It is a presumptuous question, I replied—might
I venture to ask—what that could be. 'He wished
me to expose the falsehood of his doctrine, taught
in the Paradise Lost, that[1] sexual intercourse arose
out of the Fall. Now that cannot be, for no good
can spring out of evil.' But, I replied, if the consequence were evil, mixed with good, then the
good might be ascribed to the common cause. To
this he answered by a reference to the *androgynous*
state, in which I could not possibly follow him.
At the time that he asserted his own possession of
this gift of Vision, he did not boast of it as
peculiar to himself; all men might have it if they
would.

1826

27/2/52.

On the 24th I called a second time on him.
And on this occasion it was that I read to him
Wordsworth's Ode on the supposed pre-existent
State, and the subject of Wordsworth's religious
character was discussed when we met on the
18th of Feb., and the 12th of May. I will here
bring together Blake's declarations concerning
Wordsworth, and set down his marginalia in the
8vo. edit. A.D. 1815, vol. i. I had been in the

---

[1] 'The plea' crossed out.

habit, when reading this marvellous Ode to friends, to omit one or two passages, especially that beginning:

'But there's a Tree, of many one,'

lest I should be rendered ridiculous, being unable to explain precisely *what* I admired. Not that I acknowledged this to be a fair test. But with Blake I could fear nothing of the kind. And it was this very stanza which threw him almost into a hysterical rapture. His delight in Wordsworth's poetry was intense.[1] Nor did it seem less, notwithstanding the reproaches he continually cast on Wordsworth for his imputed worship of nature;[2] which in the mind of Blake constituted Atheism [p. 46].

28/2/52.

The combination of the warmest praise with imputations which from another would assume the most serious character, and the liberty he took to interpret as he pleased, rendered it as difficult to be offended as to reason with him. The eloquent descriptions of Nature in Wordsworth's poems were conclusive proofs of atheism, for whoever believes in Nature, said Blake, disbelieves in God. For Nature is the work of the

---

[1] 'And seemingly undisturbed by the' crossed out.
[2] 'Which I have anticipated, and which he characterised as Atheism, that is, in worshipping Nature. See page' crossed out.

Devil. On my obtaining from him the declaration
that the Bible was the Word of God, I referred to
the commencement of Genesis—In the beginning
God created the Heavens and the Earth. But I
gained nothing by this, for I was triumphantly
told that this God was not Jehovah, but the
Elohim; and the doctrine of the Gnostics repeated
with sufficient consistency to silence one so
unlearned as myself.

The Preface to the Excursion, especially the
verses quoted from book i. of the Recluse, so
troubled him as to bring on a fit of illness. These
lines he singled out :

> Jehovah with his thunder, and the Choir
> Of shouting Angels, and the Empyreal throne,
> I pass them unalarmed.'

Does Mr. Wordsworth think he can surpass
Jehovah ? There was a copy of the whole
passage in his own hand,[1] in the volume of
Wordsworth's poems sent to my chambers after his
death. There was this note at the end : 'Solomon,
when he married Pharaoh's daughter, and became a
convert to the Heathen Mythology, talked exactly
in this way of Jehovah, as a very inferior object of
Man's contemplations; he also passed him unalarmed, and was permitted. Jehovah dropped a
tear and followed him by his Spirit into the abstract

---

[1] ' He gave me a copy of these lines in his hand, with this
note at the end ' crossed out.

void. It is called the Divine Mercy. Sarah
dwells in it, but Mercy does not dwell in Him.'

Some of Wordsworth's poems he maintained
were from the Holy Ghost, others from the Devil.
I lent him the 8vo edition, two vols., of Wordsworth's poems, which he had in his possession at
the time of his death. They were sent me then.
I did not recognise the pencil notes he made in
them to be his for some time, and was on the point
of rubbing them out under that impression, when I
made the discovery.

The following are found in the 3rd vol., in the
fly-leaf under the words : Poems referring to the
Period of Childhood.

29/2/52.

' I see in Wordsworth the Natural man rising up
against the Spiritual man continually, and then he
is no poet, but a Heathen Philosopher at Enmity
against all true poetry or inspiration.'

Under the first poem :

> ' And I could wish my days to be
> Bound each to each by natural piety,'

he had written, ' There is no such thing as natural
piety, because the natural man is at enmity with
God.' P. 43, under the Verses ' To H. C., six
years old '—' This is all in the highest degree
imaginative and equal to any poet, but not superior.
I cannot think that real poets have any competi-

tion. None are greatest in the kingdom of heaven. It is so in poetry.' P. 44, ' On the Influence of Natural Objects,' at the bottom of the page. ' Natural objects always did and now do weaken, deaden, and obliterate imagination in me. Wordsworth must know that what he writes valuable is not to be found in Nature. Read Michael Angelo's sonnet, vol. iv. p. 179.' That is, the one beginning

> ' No mortal object did these eyes behold
> When first they met the placid light of thine.' [1]

It is remarkable that Blake, whose judgements were on most points so very singular, on one subject closely connected with Wordsworth's poetical reputation should have taken a very commonplace view. Over the heading of the ' Essay Supplementary to the Preface ' at the end of the vol. he wrote, ' I do not know who wrote these Prefaces ; they are very mischievous, and direct contrary to Wordsworth's own practice ' (p. 341). This is not the defence of his own style in opposition to what is called Poetic Diction, but a sort of historic vindication of the *unpopular* poets. On Macpherson, p. 364, Wordsworth wrote with the severity with which all great writers have written of him. Blake's comment below was, ' I believe both Macpherson and Chatterton, that what they say is ancient is so.' And in the following page, ' I own myself an admirer of Ossian equally

---

[1] ' An admirable assertion of the ideal' crossed out.

with any other poet whatever.   Rowley and Chatterton also.'   And at the end of this Essay he wrote,
' It appears to me as if the last paragraph beginning
"Is it the spirit of the whole," etc., was written
by another hand and mind from the rest of these
Prefaces; they are the opinions of [   ] land-
scape-painter.   Imagination is the divine vision
not of the world, nor of man, nor from man as he
is a natural man, but only as he is a spiritual man.
Imagination has nothing to do with memory.'

1826

1/3/52.

19*th Feb.*   It was this day in connection with
the assertion that[1] the Bible is the Word of God and
all truth is to be found in it, he using language
concerning man's reason being opposed to grace
very like that used by the Orthodox Christian,
that he qualified, and as the same Orthodox would
say utterly nullified all he said by declaring that
he understood the Bible in a Spiritual sense.   As
to the natural sense, he said *Voltaire* was commissioned by God to expose that.   'I have had,' he
said, ' much intercourse with Voltaire, and he said
to me, "I blasphemed the Son of Man, and it shall
be forgiven me, but they (the enemies of Voltaire)
blasphemed the Holy Ghost in me, and it shall not
be forgiven to them."   'I ask him in what language

[1] 'Some of Wordsworth's' crossed out.

Voltaire spoke. His answer was ingenious and gave no encouragement to cross-questioning : ' To my sensations it was English. It was like the touch of a musical key ; he touched it probably French, but to my ear it became English.' I also enquired as I had before about the form of the persons [1] who appeared to him, and asked why he did not *draw* them. ' It is not worth while,' he said. ' Besides there are so many that the labour would be too great. And there would be no use in it.' In answer to an enquiry about Shakespeare, ' he is exactly like the old engraving—which is said to be a bad one. I think it very good.' I enquired about his own writings. ' I have written,' he answered, ' more than Rousseau or Voltaire— six or seven Epic poems as long as Homer and 20 Tragedies as long as Macbeth.' He shewed me his ' Version of Genesis,' [2] for so it may be called, as understood by a Christian Visionary. He read a wild passage in a sort of Bible style. ' I shall print [2] no more,' he said. ' When I am commanded by the Spirits, then I write, and the moment I have written, I see the words fly about the room in all directions. It is then published. The Spirits can read, and my MS. is of no further use. I have been tempted to burn my MS., but my wife won't let me.' She is right, I answered ; you write not

---

[1] ' Spirits ' crossed out.
[2] ' Vision of Genesis ' crossed out.
[3] ' Write ' crossed out.

from yourself but from higher order. The MSS.
are their property, not yours. You cannot tell
what purpose they may answer. This was
addressed *ad hominem*. And it indeed amounted
only to a deduction from his own principles. He
incidentally denied *causation*, every thing being the
work of God or Devil. Every man has a Devil in
himself, and the conflict between his *Self* and God
is perpetually going on. I ordered of him to-day
a copy of his songs for 5 guineas. My [1] manner of
receiving his mention of price pleased him. He
spoke of his horror of money and of turning pale
when it was offered him, and this was certainly
unfeigned.

In the No. of the *Gents. Magazine* for last Jan.
there is a letter by *Cromek* to Blake printed in
order to convict Blake of selfishness. It cannot
possibly be substantially true. I may elsewhere
notice it.

13th June. I saw him again in June. He was
as wild as ever, says my journal, but he was led to-
day to make assertions more palpably mischievous,
if capable of influencing other minds, and immoral,
supposing them to express the will [2] of a responsible agent, than anything he had said before. As,
for instance, that he had learned from the Bible
that Wives should be in common. And when I
objected that marriage was a Divine institution, he

---

[1] 'Immediate' crossed out.
[2] 'Character' crossed out.

referred to the Bible—'that from the beginning it was not so.' He affirmed that he had committed many murders, and repeated his doctrine, that reason is the only sin, and that careless, gay people are better than those who think, etc. etc.

It was, I believe, on the 7th of December that I saw him last. I had just heard of the death of Flaxman, a man whom he professed to admire, and was curious to know how he would receive the intelligence. It was as I expected.[1] He had been ill during the summer, and he said with a smile, 'I thought I should have gone first.' He then said, 'I cannot think of death as more than the going out of one room into another.' And Flaxman was no longer thought of. He relapsed into his ordinary train of thinking. Indeed I had by this time learned that there was nothing to be gained by frequent intercourse. And therefore it was that after this interview I was not anxious to be frequent in my visits. This day he said, 'Men are born with an Angel and a Devil.' This he himself interpreted as Soul and Body, and as I have long since said of the strange sayings of a man who enjoys a high reputation, 'it is more in the language than the thought that this singularity is to be looked for.' And this day he spoke of the Old Testament as if [sic] were the evil element. Christ, he said, took much after his mother, and in so far was one of the worst of men. On my asking him for

---

[1] 'As might have been expected' crossed out.

an instance, he referred to his turning the money-changers out of the Temple—he had no right to do that. He digressed into a condemnation of those who sit in judgement on others. ' I have never known a very bad man who had not something very good about him.'

Speaking of the Atonement in the ordinary Calvinistic sense, he said, ' It is a horrible doctrine; if another pay your debt, I do not forgive it.'

I have no account of any other call—but there is probably an omission. I took Götzenberger to see him, and he met the Masqueriers in my chambers. Masquerier was not the man to meet him. He could not humour Blake nor understand the peculiar sense in which he was to be received.[1]

1827

My journal of this year contains nothing about Blake. But in January 1828 Barron Field and myself called on Mrs. Blake. The poor old lady was more affected than I expected she would be at the sight of me. She spoke of her husband as dying like an angel. She informed me that she was going to live with Linnell as his housekeeper. And we understood that she would live with him, and he, as it were, to farm her services and take all she had. The engravings of Job were his already. Chaucer's Canterbury Pilgrims were hers.

[1] ' Understood' crossed out.

I took two copies—one I gave to C. Lamb. Barron
Field took a proof.

Mrs. Blake died within a few years, and since
Blake's death Linnell has not found the market
I took for granted he would seek for Blake's
works.   Wilkinson   printed   a   small   edition
of his poems, including the 'Songs of Innocence
and Experience,'[1] a few years ago, and Monkton
Mylne talks of printing an edition.   I have a few
coloured engravings—but Blake is still an object
of interest exclusively to men of imaginative taste
and psychological curiosity.   I doubt much whether
these mems. will be of any use to this small
class.   I have been reading since the Life of Blake
by Allan Cuningham, vol. ii. p. 143 of his Lives of
the Painters.   It recognises more perhaps of
Blake's merit than might be expected of a *Scotch*
realist.

                                    22/3/52.

[1] 'And some other poems' crossed out.

(II.) FROM 'A FATHER'S MEMOIRS OF HIS CHILD,' BY BENJAMIN HEATH MALKIN

1806

[THIS, the first printed account of Blake, is taken from the dedicatory epistle of 'A Father's Memoirs of his Child,' by Benj. Heath Malkin, Esq., M.A., F.A.S. (London: Printed for Longmans, Hurst, Rees, and Orme, Paternoster Row, by T. Bensley, Bolt Court, Fleet Street, 1806), to Thomas Johnes, the translator of Froissart. I have given everything that relates to Blake, with enough of the remainder to explain the purpose of the dedication. Malkin was himself, perhaps, already engaged on the translation of *Gil Blas*, which he brought out in 1809. The frontispiece to the Memoirs, designed by Blake, and engraved by Cromek, consists of a portrait of little Malkin, from a miniature, surrounded by a design of the child saying good-bye to his mother, and floating up to heaven, hand in hand with an ample and benign angel.]

To Thomas Johnes, of Hafod, Esq., M.P., Lord
Lieutenant of the County of Cardigan,
etc. etc. etc.

My dear Friend,

I have been influenced by several motives, in
prefixing your name to the following pages. My
pen seems destined to owe its employment, in
some shape or other, to Hafod. . . .

You may perhaps recollect, that while I was
staying with you last summer, our conversations
were nearly as rambling and as various, as our
rides over your new mountain-farms, or as the
subject matter of these preliminary remarks seems
likely to be. . . . It would have been unnatural,
to have concealed the mark of an afflicting dispensation, in society so capable of consoling the
survivor, and appreciating the merit of the departed. In the interchange of our thoughts on
this subject, the task of furnishing the public with
the following facts was urged upon me, at once as
a tribute to the latter, and a relief to the feelings

of the former. . . . On mentioning my design to some of my friends, they expressed their regret, that I had not determined on it sooner. . . . In every other respect, but that of catching attention while the object is still before the eye, the interval must be considered as an advantage. . . . I have been asked, 'How could you get over such a loss?' I need not say, that this was not your question, for you could never have found it on the list of possible interrogatories: and to you, for that very reason, will I answer it.

I got over this great loss, by considering at once what I had left; how unavailing the lengthened and excessive indulgence of grief would have been to myself, and how useless it would have rendered me to others. . . .

Besides this comparison of my own, with the probable or actual circumstances of others, I bore my disappointment the better for the recollection, that personal regards are selfish. If my thoughts were disposed to dwell on the mortifying idea, that society might have lost an ornament derived to it through me, they were soon checked, and ashamed of their presumption. Topics of private bewailing or condolence, of whatever magnitude they may appear to the individual, can never be modestly transferred to general interest. But it was my principal consolation, that the change to him must have been for the better. Supposing the opinion to have been rational and probable, that the pro-

mise of this child would have ripened into something more than fair capacity and marketable
talent, the prolongation of life was to himself
perhaps the less desirable on that very account.
It rarely happens, that the world affords even the
ordinary allowance of happiness to men of tran-
scendent faculties. Their merits are too frequently
denied the protection and encouragement, to which
they feel themselvs entitled, from the private
intimations of their own scrutinising spirit.
When they are most successful, the composure of
their minds does not always keep pace with the
prosperity of their fortunes. They necessarily
have but few companions; few, who are capable
of appreciating their high endowments, and entering into the grandeur of their conceptions. Of
these few, those who come the nearest to their
own rank and standard, those who might be the
associates of their inmost thoughts, and the
partners of their dearest interests, are too often
envious of their fame. It is a common remark,
that great men are not gregarious. This is but
too just; and so much of man's happiness depends
upon society, that the comparative solitude, to
which a commanding genius condemns its possessor, detracts considerably from the sum of his
personal enjoyment.

While I am on this subject, I cannot forbear
enlarging somewhat on an instance the more
apposite, as being casually connected with the

subsequent pages. Hitherto, it has confirmed the observation just hazarded, on the probable fate of stubborn originality in human life. There seems now indeed some prospect, that the current will turn : and I shall be eager, on the evidence of the very first deponent, to disencumber myself of an opinion, which pays so ill a compliment to our nature. In the meantime, I am confident that you, and my other readers of taste and feeling, will readily forgive my travelling a little out of the record, for the purpose of descanting on merit, which ought to be more conspicuous, and which must have become so long since, but for opinions and habits of an eccentric kind.

It is, I hope, unnecessary to call your attention to the ornamental device, round the portrait in this book ; but I cannot so easily refrain from introducing to you the designer.

Mr. William Blake, very early in life, had the ordinary opportunities of seeing pictures in the houses of noblemen and gentlemen, and in the king's palaces. He soon improved such casual occasions of study, by attending sales at Langford's, Christie's, and other auction-rooms. At ten years of age he was put to Mr. Pars's drawing-school in the Strand, where he soon attained the art of drawing from casts in plaster of the various antiques. His father bought for him the Gladiator, the Hercules, the Venus of Medicis, and various heads, hands and feet. The same indulgent parent soon supplied him with money to buy prints ; when he immediately began his collection, frequenting the shops of the print-dealers, and the sales of the auctioneers. Langford called him his little connoisseur ; and often knocked down to him a cheap lot, with friendly precipitation. He copied Raphael and Michael Angelo, Martin Hemskerck and Albert Durer, Julio Romano, and the rest of the historic class, neglecting to buy any other prints, however celebrated. His choice was for the most part contemned by his youthful companions, who were accustomed to laugh at what they called his mechanical taste. At the age of fourteen, he fixed on the engraver of Stuart's Athens and West's Pylades and Orestes for his master, to whom he served seven years' apprenticeship. Basire, whose taste was like his own, approved of what he did. Two years passed over smoothly enough, till two other apprentices were added to the establishment, who completely destroyed its harmony. Blake, not choosing to take part with his master against his fellow apprentices, was sent out to make drawings. This circumstance he always mentions with gratitude to Basire, who said that he was too simple and they too cunning.

He was employed in making drawings from old buildings and monuments, and occasionally, especially in winter, in engraving from those drawings. This occupation led him to an acquaintance with those neglected works of art, called Gothic monuments. There he found a treasure, which he knew how to value. He saw the simple and plain road to the style of art at which he aimed, unentangled in the intricate windings of modern practice. The monuments of Kings and Queens in Westminster Abbey, which surround the chapel of Edward the Confessor, particularly that of King Henry the Third, the beautiful monument and figure of Queen Elinor, Queen Philippa, King Edward the Third, King Richard the Second and his Queen, were among his first studies. All these he drew in every point he could catch, frequently standing on the monument, and viewing the figures from the top. The heads he considered as portraits; and all the ornaments appeared as miracles of art, to his Gothicised imagination. He then drew Aymer de Valence's monument, with his fine figure on the top. Those exquisite little figures which surround it, though dreadfully mutilated, are still models for the study of drapery. But I do not mean to enumerate all his drawings, since they would lead me over all the old monuments in Westminster Abbey, as well as over other churches in and about London.

Such was his employment at Basire's. As soon as he was out of his time, he began to engrave two designs from the History of England, after drawings which he had made in the holiday hours of his

apprenticeship. They were selected from a great
number of historical compositions, the fruits of his
fancy. He continued making designs for his own
amusement, whenever he could steal a moment
from the routine of business; and began a course
of study at the Royal Academy, under the eye of
Mr. Moser. Here he drew with great care, perhaps
all, or certainly nearly all the noble antique figures
in various views. But now his peculiar notions
began to intercept him in his career. He professes
drawing from life always to have been hateful to
him; and speaks of it as looking more like death,
or smelling of mortality. Yet still he drew a good
deal from life, both at the academy and at home.
In this manner has he managed his talents, till
he is himself almost become a Gothic monument.
On a view of his whole life, he still thinks himself
authorised to pronounce, that practice and opportunity very soon teach the language of art: but
its spirit and poetry, which are seated in the
imagination alone, never can be taught; and these
make an artist.

Mr. Blake has long been known to the order
of men among whom he ranks; and is highly
esteemed by those, who can distinguish excellence
under the disguise of singularity. Enthusiastic
and high-flown notions on the subject of religion
have hitherto, as they usually do, prevented his
general reception, as a son of taste and of the muses.
The sceptic and the rational believer, uniting their

forces against the visionary, pursue and scare a warm and brilliant imagination, with the hue and cry of madness. Not contented with bringing down the reasonings of the mystical philosopher, as they well may, to this degraded level, they apply the test of cold calculation and mathematical proof to departments of the mind, which are privileged to appeal from so narrow and rigorous a tribunal. They criticise the representations of corporeal beauty, and the allegoric emblems of mental perfections; the image of the visible world, which appeals to the senses for a testimony to its truth, or the type of futurity and the immortal soul, which identifies itself with our hopes and with our hearts, as if they were syllogisms or theorems, demonstrable propositions or consecutive corollaries. By them have the higher powers of this artist been kept from public notice, and his genius tied down, as far as possible, to the mechanical department of his profession. By them, in short, has he been stigmatised as an engraver, who might do tolerably well, if he was not mad. But men, whose names will bear them out, in what they affirm, have now taken up his cause. On occasion of Mr. Blake engaging to illustrate the poem of The Grave, some of the first artists in this country have stept forward, and liberally given the sanction of ardent and enco-miastic applause. Mr. Fuseli, with a mind far superior to that jealousy above described, has written some introductory remarks in the Prospectus of the work. To these he has lent all the penetration of his understanding, with all the energy and descriptive power characteristic of his style. Mr. Hope and Mr. Locke have pledged their character as connoisseurs, by approving and patronising these designs. Had I been furnished with an opportunity of showing them to you, I should, on Mr. Blake's behalf, have requested your concurring testimony, which you would not have refused me, had you viewed them in the same light.

Neither is the capacity of this untutored proficient limited to his professional occupation. He has made several irregular and unfinished attempts at poetry. He has dared to venture on the ancient simplicity ; and feeling it in his own character and manners, has succeeded better than those, who have only seen it through a glass. His genius in this line assimilates more with the bold and careless freedom, peculiar to our writers at the latter end of the sixteenth, and former part of the seventeenth century, than with the polished phraseology, and just, but subdued thought of the eighteenth. As the public have hitherto had no opportunity of passing sentence on his poetical powers, I shall trespass on your patience, while I introduce a few specimens from a collection, circulated only among the author's friends, and richly embellished by his pencil.

LAUGHING SONG

When the green woods laugh with the voice of joy,
And the dimpling stream runs laughing by,
When the air does laugh with our merry wit,
And the green hill laughs with the noise of it,

When the meadows laugh with lively green,
And the grasshopper laughs in this merry scene,
When Mary and Susan and Emily,
With their sweet round mouths, sing Ha, ha, he!

When the painted birds laugh in the shade,
Where our table with cherries and nuts is spread,
Come live and be merry and join with me,
To sing the sweet chorus of Ha, ha, he!

The Fairy Glee of Oberon, which Stevens's
exquisite music has familiarised to modern ears,
will immediately occur to the reader of these
laughing stanzas. We may also trace another less
obvious resemblance to Jonson, in an ode gratu-
latory to the Right Honourable Hierome, Lord
Weston, for his return from his embassy, in the
year 1632. The accord is to be found, not in the
words nor in the subject; for either would betray
imitation: but in the style of thought, and, if I
may so term it, the date of the expression.

Such pleasure as the teeming earth
Doth take in easy nature's birth,
When she puts forth the life of every thing:
And in a dew of sweetest rain,
She lies delivered without pain,
Of the prime beauty of the year, the spring.

The rivers in their shores do run,
The clouds rack clear before the sun,
The rudest winds obey the calmest air :
 Rare plants from every bank do rise,
 And every plant the sense surprise,
Because the order of the whole is fair !

The very verdure of her nest,
Wherein she sits so richly drest,
As all the wealth of season there was spread ;
 Doth show the graces and the hours
 Have multiplied their arts and powers,
In making soft her aromatic bed.

Such joys, such sweets, doth your return
Bring all your friends, fair lord, that burn
With love, to hear your modesty relate
 The bus'ness of your blooming wit,
 With all the fruit shall follow it,
Both to the honour of the king and state.

The following poem of Blake is in a different
character. It expresses with majesty and pathos
the feelings of a benevolent mind, on being present
at a sublime display of national munificence and
charity.

HOLY THURSDAY

'Twas on a Holy Thursday, their innocent faces clean,
The children walking two and two, in red and blue and
  green ;
Grey-headed beadles walked before, with wands as white
  as snow ;
Till into the high dome of Paul's, they, like Thames'
  waters, flow.

Oh! What a multitude they seemed, these flowers of
    London town!
Seated in companies they sit, with radiance all their own!
The hum of multitudes was there, but multitudes of lambs;
Thousands of little boys and girls, raising their innocent
    hands.

Now like a mighty wind they raise to heaven the voice
    of song,
Or like harmonious thunderings, the seats of heaven
    among!
Beneath them sit the aged men, wise guardians of the
    poor:
Then cherish pity, lest you drive an angel from your door.

The book of Revelation, which may well be
supposed to engross much of Mr. Blake's study,
seems to have directed him, in common with
Milton, to some of the foregoing images. 'And I
heard as it were the voice of a great multitude, and
as the voice of many waters, and as the voice of
mighty thunderings, saying, Alleluia: for the Lord
God omnipotent reigneth.' Milton comprises the
mighty thunderings in the epithet 'loud,' and
adopts the comparison of many waters, which
image our poet, having in the first stanza appropriated differently, to their flow rather than to
their sound, exchanges in the last for that of a
mighty wind.

He ended; and the heav'nly audience loud
Sung hallelujah, as the sound of sees,
Through multitude that sung.
           Paradise Lost, Book x. 641.

It may be worth a moment's consideration,
whether Dr. Johnson's remarks on devotional
poetry, though strictly just where he applies them,
to the artificial compositions of Waller and Watts,
are universally and necessarily true. Watts seldom
rose above the level of a mere versifier. Waller,
though entitled to the higher appellation of poet,
had formed himself rather to elegance and delicacy,
than to passionate emotions or a lofty and dignified
deportment. The devotional pieces of the Hebrew
bards are clothed in that simple language, to which
Johnson with justice ascribes the character of
sublimity. There is no reason therefore why the
poets of other nations should not be equally successful, if they think with the same purity, and
express themselves in the same unaffected terms.
He says indeed with truth, that 'Repentance
trembling in the presence of the judge, is not at
leisure for cadences and epithets.' But though
we should exclude the severer topics from our
catalogue, mercy and benevolence may be treated
poetically, because they are in unison with the
mild spirit of poetry. They are seldom treated
successfully ; but the fault is not in the subject.
The mind of the poet is too often at leisure for
the mechanical prettinesses of cadence and epithet,
when it ought to be engrossed by higher thoughts.
Words and numbers present themselves unbidden,
when the soul is inspired by sentiment, elevated
by enthusiasm, or ravished by devotion. I leave it

to the reader to determine, whether the following stanzas have any tendency to vindicate this species of poetry; and whether their simplicity and sentiment at all make amends for their inartificial and unassuming construction.

THE DIVINE IMAGE

To Mercy, Pity, Peace, and Love,
All pray in their distress,
And to these virtues of delight
Return their thankfulness.

For Mercy, Pity, Peace, and Love
Is God our Father dear:
And Mercy, Pity, Peace, and Love,
Is man, his child and care.

For Mercy has a human heart;
Pity, a human face;
And Love, the human form divine,
And Peace, the human dress.

Then every man, of every clime,
That prays in his distress,
Prays to the human form divine,
Love, Mercy, Pity, Peace.

And all must love the human form,
In Heathen, Turk, or Jew!
Where Mercy, Love, and Pity dwell,
There God is dwelling too.

Shakespeare's Venus and Adonis, Tarquin and Lucrece, and his Sonnets, occasioned it to be said by a contemporary, that, 'As the soul of Euphorbus was thought to live in Pythagoras, so the sweet witty soul of Ovid lives in mellifluous honey-tongued Shakespeare.' These poems, now little read, were favourite studies of Mr. Blake's early days. So were Jonson's Underwoods and Miscellanies, and he seems to me to have caught his manner, more than that of Shakespeare in his trifles. The following song is a good deal in the spirit of the Hue and Cry after Cupid, in the Masque on Lord Haddington's marriage. It was written before the age of fourteen, in the heat of youthful fancy, unchastised by judgment. The poet, as such, takes the very strong liberty of equipping himself with wings, and thus appropriates his metaphorical costume to his corporeal fashion and seeming. The conceit is not unclassical; but Pindar and the ancient lyrics arrogated to themselves the bodies of swans for their august residence. Our Gothic songster is content to be encaged by Cupid; and submits, like a young lady's favourite, to all the vagaries of giddy curiosity and tormenting fondness.

How sweet I roamed from field to field,
    And tasted all the summer's pride,
Till I the prince of love beheld,
    Who in the sunny beams did glide !

He showed me lilies for my hair,
    And blushing roses for my brow;
He led me through his gardens fair,
    Where all his golden pleasures grow.

With sweet May dews my wings were wet,
 And Phœbus fired my vocal rage ;
He caught me in his silken net,
 And shut me in his golden cage.

He loves to sit and hear me sing,
 Then, laughing, sports and plays with me ;
Then stretches out my golden wing,
 And mocks my loss of liberty.

The playful character ascribed to the prince of
love, especially his wanton and fantastic action
while sporting with his captive, in the two last
stanzas, render it probable that the author had
read the Hue and Cry after Cupid. If so, it had
made its impression ; but the lines could scarcely
have been remembered at the time of writing, or
the resemblance would have been closer. The
stanzas to which I especially allude, are these.

Wings he hath, which though ye clip,
 He will leap from lip to lip,
 Over liver, lights, and heart,
 But not stay in any part ;
 And, if chance his arrow misses,
 He will shoot himself, in kisses.

Idle minutes are his reign ;
 Then the straggler makes his gain,
 By presenting maids with toys,
 And would have ye think 'em joys :
 'Tis th' ambition of the elf,
 To have all childish as himself.

The two following little pieces are added, as

well by way of contrast, as for the sake of their
respective merits.   In the first, there is a simple
and pastoral gaiety, which the poets of a refined
age have generally found much more difficult of
attainment, than the glitter of wit, or the affectation of antithesis.   The second rises with the subject.   It wears that garb of grandeur, which the
idea of creation communicates to a mind of the
higher order.   Our bard, having brought the topic
he descants on from warmer latitudes than his
own, is justified in adopting an imagery, of almost
oriental feature and complexion.

SONG

I love the jocund dance,
The softly breathing song,
Where innocent eyes do glance,
    And where lisps the maiden's tongue.

I love the laughing gale,
I love the echoing hill,
Where mirth does never fail,
    And the jolly swain laughs his fill.

I love the pleasant cot,
I love the innocent bower,
Where white and brown is our lot,
    Or fruit in the midday hour.

I love the oaken seat,
Beneath the oaken tree,
Where all the old villagers meet,
    And laugh our sports to see.

I love our neighbours all,
But, Kitty, I better love thee ;
And love them I ever shall ;
But thou art all to me.

THE TIGER

Tiger, Tiger, burning bright,
In the forest of the night !
What immortal hand or eye
Could frame thy fearful symmetry ?

In what distant deeps or skies,
Burnt the fire of thine eyes ?
On what wings dare he aspire ?
What the hand dare seize the fire ?

And what shoulder, and what art,
Could twist the sinews of thy heart ?
When thy heart began to beat,
What dread hand forged thy dread feet ?

What the hammer ? What the chain ?
In what furnace was thy brain ?
What the anvil ? What dread grasp
Dared its deadly terrors clasp ?

When the stars threw down their spears,
And watered heaven with their tears,
Did he smile his work to see ?
Did he, who made the lamb, make thee ?

Tiger, tiger, burning bright,
In the forest of the night ;
What immortal hand or eye
Dare frame thy fearful symmetry ?

Besides these lyric compositions, Mr. Blake has given several specimens of blank verse. Here, as might be expected, his personifications are bold, his thoughts original, and his style of writing altogether epic in its structure. The unrestrained measure, however, which should warn the poet to restrain himself, has not unfrequently betrayed him into so wild a pursuit of fancy, as to leave harmony unregarded, and to pass the line prescribed by criticism to the career of imagination.

But I have been leading you beside our subject, into a labyrinth of poetical comment, with as little method or ceremony, as if we were to have no witness of our correspondence. It is time we should return from the masquing regions of poetry, to the business with which we set out. Donne, in his Anatomy of the World, remarks the Egyptians to have acted wisely, in bestowing more cost upon their tombs than on their houses. This example he adduces, to justify his own Funeral Elegies: and I may perhaps be allowed to adopt it, as an additional plea, should my former be of no avail, for coming forward with this piece of almost infantine biography. . . .

I regret, my dear friend, that it was not in my power to furnish you and my readers with a portrait of a later date. We had often talked of allowing ourselves that indulgence; but we were not privy to the event, which was to have communicated to it an incalculable value. The engraving here given, though it might well be taken to represent a much older child, is from a very beautiful miniature, painted by Paye, when Thomas was not quite two years old. He then was only beginning to speak; but there was even at that early period an intelligence in his eye, and an expression about his mouth, which are, I hope, sufficiently characterised in the delineation to afford no inadequate idea of his physiognomy. . . .

At all events, this work, though it should escape censure, can rank no higher than a trifle. What apology must I make for addressing it to a fellow-labourer, who has accomplished the serious and difficult task of giving an English dress to Froissart? I think it was Gray who denominated your venerable original the Herodotus of a barbarous age. But surely that age is entitled to a more respectful epithet, when France could boast its Froissart, Italy its Petrarch, England its Wickliffe, the father of our reformation, and Chaucer, the father of our poetry. If I might slightly alter the designation of so complete a critic, I would prefer calling this simple and genuine historian, the Herodotus of chivalry. But by whatever title we are to greet him, the interesting minuteness of his recital, affording a strong pledge of its fidelity, the lively delineation of manners, and the charm of unadulterated language, all cor pire to place him in the first rank of early writers. The public began to revolt from that spirit of philosophising

on the most common occasions, in consequence of
which our modern historians seem to be more
ingenious in assigning causes and motives, than
assiduous to ascertain facts. We are returning
home to plain tales and first-hand authorities; and
you will share the honour of pointing out the way.
Froissart, hitherto inaccessible to English readers
in general, from the obsolete garb both of the
French and of Lord Berners's translation, may now
be read in such a form, as to unite a peculiar
thought and turn of the ancient with the intelligible phraseology of modern times. With my best
congratulations on your success, and my earnest
request to be forgiven for thus intruding on your
leisure, believe me to be, my dear friend, faithfully
yours, B. H. MALKIN.

HACKNEY, *January* 4, 1806.

(III.) FROM LADY CHARLOTTE BURY'S DIARY

1820

[THIS extract from the *Diary illustrative of the Times of George the Fourth*, by Lady Charlotte Bury, afterwards Lady Charlotte Campbell, published anonymously, and edited by John Galt, in four volumes, in 1839, was first noticed by Mr. W. M. Rossetti, who printed it in the *Athenæum*. It is from vol. iii. pp. 345-348.]

FROM LADY CHARLOTTE BURY'S DIARY

1820

Tuesday, the 20th of January [1820].—I dined at Lady C. L——'s. She had collected a strange party of artists and literati and one or two fine folks, who were very ill assorted with the rest of the company, and appeared neither to give nor receive pleasure from the society among whom they were mingled. Sir T. Lawrence, next whom I sat at dinner, is as courtly as ever. His conversation is agreeable, but I never feel as if he was saying what he really thought. . . .

Besides Sir T., there was also present of this profession Mrs. M., the miniature painter, a modest, pleasing person; like the pictures she executes, soft and sweet. Then there was another eccentric little artist, by name Blake; not a regular professional painter, but one of those persons who follow the art for its own sweet sake, and derive their happiness from its pursuit. He appeared to me to be full of beautiful imaginations and genius; but how far the execution of his

333

designs is equal to the conceptions of his mental
vision, I know not, never having seen them.
Main-d'œuvre is frequently wanting where the
mind is most powerful.　Mr. Blake appears unlearned in all that concerns this world, and, from
what he said, I should fear he is one of those
whose feelings are far superior to his situation in life.
He looks care-worn and subdued; but his countenance radiated as he spoke of his favourite pursuit,
and he appeared gratified by talking to a person
who comprehended his feelings.　I can easily
imagine that he seldom meets with any one who
enters into his views; for they are peculiar, and exalted above the common level of received opinions.
I could not help contrasting this humble artist
with the great and powerful Sir Thomas Lawrence,
and thinking that the one was fully if not more
worthy of the distinction and the fame to which
the other has attained, but from which *he* is far
removed.　Mr. Blake, however, though he may have
as much right, from talent and merit, to the
advantages of which Sir Thomas is possessed,
evidently lacks that worldly wisdom and that
grace of manner which make a man gain an
eminence in his profession, and succeed in society.
Every word he uttered spoke the perfect simplicity of his mind, and his total ignorance of all
worldly matters.　He told me that Lady C——
L—— had been very kind to him.　'Ah!' said
he, 'there is a deal of kindness in that lady.'　I

agreed with him, and though it was impossible not
to laugh at the strange manner in which she had
arranged this party, I could not help admiring the
goodness of heart and discrimination of talent
which had made her patronise this unknown artist.
Sir T. Lawrence looked at me several times whilst
I was talking with Mr. B., and I saw his lips curl
with a sneer, as if he despised me for conversing
with so insignificant a person.[1] It was very evident
Sir Thomas did not like the company he found
himself in, though he was too well-bred and too
prudent to hazard a remark upon the subject.

The literati were also of various degrees of
eminence, beginning with Lord B——, and ending
with ——. The grandees were Lord L——, who
appreciates talent, and therefore not so ill assorted
with the party as was Mrs. G—— and Lady
C——, who did nothing but yawn the whole
evening, and Mrs A——, who all looked with
evident contempt upon the surrounding company.

[1] There is surely some mistake in this supposition, for Sir
T. Lawrence was, afterwards at least, one of Mr. Blake's great
patrons and admirers.

(IV.) BLAKE'S HOROSCOPE

1825

[BLAKE's horoscope was cast during his lifetime in *Urania*, or, the Astrologer's Chronicle, and Mystical Magazine; edited by Merlinus Anglicanus, jun., the Astrologer of the Nineteenth Century, assisted by the Metropolitan Society of Occult Philosophers (No. 1, London, 1825), the first and only number of an astrological magazine, published under the pseudonym of Merlinus Anglicanus by R. C. Smith, an astrologer of the period, and it is highly probable, as Dr. Garnett suggests, that the date (confirmed by the birth register at St. James's, Westminster) was derived from Varley, who would have had it from Blake himself. I give the map, not as it is printed in the book, but in the clearer and simpler form in which it was copied and given to me by Dr. Garnett. I am told that the most striking thing in the map, from an astrological point of view, is the position and aspect of Uranus, the occult planet, which indicate in the highest degree 'an inborn and supreme instinct for things occult,' without showing the least tendency towards madness. The 'Nativity of Mr. Blake' is the last entry, p. 70.]

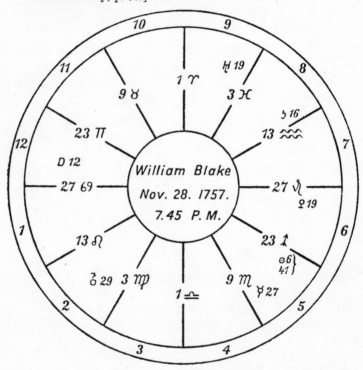

NATIVITY OF MR. BLAKE,

THE MYSTICAL ARTIST

Planets' Latitude

☽ 2.20 S. | ♄ 1.14 S. | ♃ 0.42 N. | ♂ 2.02 N.
| ♀ 2.10 S. | ☿ 0.40 N. |

THE above horoscope is calculated for the *estimate* time of birth, and Mr. Blake, the subject thereof, is well known amongst scientific characters, as having a most peculiar and extraordinary turn of genius and vivid imagination. His illustrations of the Book of Job have met with much and deserved praise; indeed, in the line which this artist has adopted, he is perhaps equalled by none of the present day. Mr. Blake is no less peculiar and *outré* in his ideas, as he seems to have some curious intercourse with the invisible world; and, according to his own account (in which he is certainly, to all appearance, perfectly sincere), he is continually surrounded by the spirits of the deceased of all ages, nations, and countries. He has, so he affirms, held actual conversations with Michael Angelo, Raphael, Milton, Dryden, and the worthies of antiquity. He has now by him a long poem nearly finished, which he affirms was recited to him by the spirit of Milton; and the mystical drawings of this gentleman are no less curious and worthy of notice, by all those whose minds soar above the cloggings of this terrestrial element, to which we are most of us too fastly chained to comprehend the nature and operations of the world of spirits.

Mr. Blake's pictures of the last judgment, his profiles of Wallace, Edward the Sixth, Harold, Cleopatra, and numerous others which we have seen, are really wonderful for the spirit in which they are delineated. We have been in company with this gentleman several times, and have frequently been not only delighted with his conversation, but also filled with feelings of wonder at his extraordinary faculties; which, whatever some may say to the contrary, are by no means tinctured with superstition, as he certainly believes what he promulgates. Our limits will not permit us to enlarge upon this geniture, which we merely give as an example worthy to be noticed by the astrological student in his list of remarkable nativities. But it is probable that the extraordinary faculties and eccentricities of idea which this gentleman possesses, are the effects of the Moon in Cancer in the twelfth house (both sign and house being mystical), in trine to Herschell from the mystical sign Pisces, from the house of science, and from the mundane trine to Saturn in the scientific sign Aquarius, which latter planet is in square to Mercury in Scorpio, and in quintile to the Sun and Jupiter, in the mystical sign Sagittarius. The square of Mars and Mercury, from fixed signs, also, has a remarkable tendency to sharpen the intellects, and lay the foundation of extraordinary ideas. There are also many other reasons for the strange peculiarities above noticed, but these the student will no doubt readily discover.

(V.) OBITUARY NOTICES IN THE 'LITER-
ARY GAZETTE' AND 'GENTLEMAN'S
MAGAZINE,' 1827.

[OBITUARY Notices of Blake appeared in the *Literary Gazette* of August 18, 1827 (pp. 540-41), the *Gentleman's Magazine* of October 1827 (pp. 377-8), and the *Annual Register* of 1827, in its Appendix of Deaths (pp. 253-4). The notice in the *Gentleman's Magazine* is largely condensed from that in the *Literary Gazette*, but with a different opening, which I have given after the notice in the *Literary Gazette*. The notice in the *Annual Register* is merely condensed from the *Gentleman's Magazine*.]

I

WILLIAM BLAKE

The Illustrator of the Grave, etc.

To those few who have sympathies for the ideal
and (comparatively speaking) the intellectual in
art, the following notice is addressed. Few persons
of taste are unacquainted with the designs by Blake,
appended as illustrations to a 4to edition of Blair's
Grave. It was borne forth into the world on the
warmest praises of all our prominent artists, Hoppner, Phillips, Stothard, Flaxman, Opie, Tresham,
Westmacott, Beechey, Lawrence, West, Nollekins,
Shee, Owen, Rossi, Thomson, Cosway, and Soane ;
and doubly assured with a preface by the learned
and severe Fuseli, the latter part of which we transcribe :—' The author of the moral series before us
has endeavoured to wake sensibility by touching
our sympathies with nearer, less ambiguous, and
less ludicrous imagery, than what mythology, Gothic
superstition, or symbols as far-fetched as inadequate
could supply. His invention has been chiefly employed to spread a familiar and domestic atmosphere round the most important of all subjects—

to connect the visible and the invisible world, without provoking probability—and to lead the eye from the milder light of time to the radiations of eternity. Such is the plan and the moral part of the author's invention ; the technic part, and the execution of the artist, though to be examined by other principles, and addressed to a narrower circle, equally claim approbation, sometimes excite our wonder, and not seldom our fears, when we see him play on the very verge of legitimate invention ; but wildness so picturesque in itself, so often redeemed by taste, simplicity, and elegance—what child of fancy, what artist, would wish to discharge ? The groups and single figures, on their own basis, abstracted from the general composition, and considered without attention to the plan, frequently exhibit those genuine and unaffected attitudes, those simple graces, which nature and the heart alone can dictate, and only an eye inspired by both discover. Every class of artists, in every stage of their progress and attainments, from the student to the finished master, and from the contriver of ornament to the painter of history, will here find materials of art, and hints of improvement ! '

When it is stated, that the pure-minded Flaxman pointed out to an eminent literary man the obscurity of Blake as a melancholy proof of English apathy towards the grand, the philosophic, or the enthusiastically devotional painter ; and that

he (Blake) has been several times employed for
that truly admirable judge of art, Sir T. Lawrence,
any further testimony to his extraordinary powers
is unnecessary. Yet has Blake been allowed to
exist in a penury which most artists [1]—beings
necessarily of a sensitive temperament—would
deem intolerable. Pent, with his affectionate wife,
in a close back-room in one of the Strand courts,
his bed in one corner, his meagre dinner in another,
a ricketty table holding his copper-plates in progress, his colours, books (among which his Bible,
a Sessi Velutello's Dante, and Mr. Carey's translation, were at the top), his large drawings, sketches,
and MSS.;—his ankles frightfully swelled, his chest
disordered, old age striding on, his wants increased,
but not his miserable means and appliances: even
yet was his eye undimmed, the fire of his imagination unquenched, and the preternatural, never-
resting activity of his mind unflagging. He had
not merely a calmly resigned, but a cheerful and
mirthful countenance; in short, he was a living
commentary on Jeremy Taylor's beautiful chapter
on Contentedness. He took no thought for his
life, what he should eat, or what he should drink;
nor yet for his body, what he should put on; but
had a fearless confidence in that Providence which
had given him the vast range of the world for his
recreation and delight.

----

[1] The term is employed in its generic and comprehensive
sense.

Blake died last Monday! Died as he lived! piously cheerful, talking calmly, and finally resigning himself to his eternal rest, like an infant to its sleep. He has left *nothing* except some pictures, copper-plates, and his principal work of a series of a hundred large designs from Dante.

William Blake was brought up under Basire, the eminent engraver. He was active in mind and body, passing from one occupation to another, without an intervening minute of repose. Of an ardent, affectionate, and grateful temper, he was simple in manner and address, and displayed an inbred courteousness, of the most agreeable character. Next November he would have been *sixty-nine*. At the age of sixty-six he commenced the study of Italian, for the sake of reading Dante in the original, which he accomplished!

His widow is left (we fear, from the accounts which have reached us) in a very forlorn condition, Mr. Blake having latterly been much indebted for succour and consolation to his friend Mr. Linnell, the painter. We have no doubt but her cause will be taken up by the distributors of those funds which are raised for the relief of distressed artists, and also by the benevolence of private individuals.

When further time has been allowed us for inquiry, we shall probably resume this matter; at present (owing the above information to the kindness of a correspondent) we can only record the death of a singular and very able man.

II

MR. WILLIAM BLAKE

Aug. 13, aged 68, Mr. William Blake, an excellent, but eccentric, artist.

He was a pupil of the engraver Basire; and among his earliest productions were eight beautiful plates in the Novelist's Magazine. In 1793 he published in 12mo, 'The Gates of Paradise,' a very small book for children, containing fifteen plates of emblems; and 'published by W. B., 13 Hercules Buildings, Lambeth'; also about the same time, 'Songs of Experience, with plates'; 'America; a Prophecy,' folio, and 'Europe, a Prophecy,' 1794, folio. These are now become very scarce. In 1797 he commenced, in large folio, an edition of Young's Night Thoughts, of which every page was a design, but only one number was published. In 1805 were produced in 8vo numbers, containing five engravings by Blake, some ballads by Mr. Hayley, but which also were abruptly discontinued. Few persons of taste are unacquainted with the designs by Blake, engraved by Schiavonetti, as illustrations to a 4to edition of Blair's Grave. They are twelve in number, and an excellent portrait of Blake, from a picture by T. Phillips, R.A., is prefixed. It was borne forth . . . [Here follows the third sentence, p. 345 above, to the end of the paragraph.]

In 1809 was published in 12mo, ' A Descriptive
Catalogue of [sixteen] pictures, poetical and historical inventions, painted by William Blake in water-
colours, being the ancient method of fresco painting
restored, and drawings, for public inspection, and
for sale by private contract.'   Among these was a
design of Chaucer's Pilgrimage to Canterbury,
from which an etching has been published.   Mr.
Blake's last publication is a set of engravings to
illustrate the Book of Job.   To Fuseli's testimony
of his merit above quoted, it is sufficient to add,
that he has been employed by that truly admirable
judge of art, Sir Thomas Lawrence ; and that the
pure-minded Flaxman. . . .

[The remainder is condensed from the *Literary
Gazette*, p. 346 above, with the occasional change
of a word, or the order of a sentence.]

(VI.) EXTRACT FROM VARLEY'S ZODIACAL PHYSIOGNOMY.   1828.

JOHN VARLEY, astrologer and water-colour painter, was introduced to Blake by Linnell, and it was for him that Blake did the 'visionary heads' described by Allan Cunningham, p. 420 below. 'The Ghost of a Flea' exists in both forms described by Varley, in a sketch of the head (which he reproduces, engraved by Linnell, in a plate at the end of his book, together with two other heads in outline), and in a full-length picture in tempera. The passage which follows is taken from pp. 54, 55 of 'A Treatise on Zodiacal Physiognomy; illustrated with engravings of heads and features; accompanied by tables of the times of rising of the twelve signs of the Zodiac; and containing also new and astrological explanation of some remarkable portions of Ancient Mythological History.' By John Varley. London : Printed for the Author, 1828.]

EXTRACT FROM VARLEY'S ZODIACAL PHYSIOGNOMY

WITH respect to the vision of the Ghost of the Flea, seen by Blake, it agrees in countenance with one class of people under Gemini, which sign is the significator of the Flea; whose brown colour is appropriate to the colour of the eyes in some full-toned Gemini persons. And the neatness, elasticity, and tenseness of the Flea are significant of the elegant dancing and fencing sign Gemini. This spirit visited his imagination in such a figure as he never anticipated in an insect. As I was anxious to make the most correct investigation in my power, of the truth of these visions, on hearing of this spiritual apparition of a Flea, I asked him if he could draw for me the resemblance of what he saw: he instantly said, 'I see him now before me.' I therefore gave him paper and a pencil, with which he drew the portrait, of which a facsimile is given in this number. I felt convinced by his mode of proceeding that he had a real image before him, for he left off, and began on another part of the paper to make a separate drawing of the mouth of the Flea, which the spirit having opened, he was prevented from proceeding with the first sketch, till he had closed it. During the time occupied in completing the drawing, the Flea told him that all fleas were inhabited by the souls of such men as were by nature blood-thirsty to excess, and were therefore providentially confined to the size and form of insects; otherwise, were he himself, for instance, the size of a horse, he would depopulate a great portion of the country. He added, that if in attempting to leap from one island to another, he should fall into the sea, he could swim, and should not be lost. This spirit afterwards appeared to Blake, and afforded him a view of his whole figure; an engraving of which I shall give in this work.

(VII.) BIOGRAPHICAL SKETCH OF BLAKE
BY J. T. SMITH. 1828

[THE Memoir of Blake by John Thomas Smith, Keeper of the Prints and Drawings in the British Museum, is the last of the 'Biographical Sketches and Anecdotes of several Artists and others contemporary with Nollekens,' contained in the second volume of 'Nollekens and his Times : comprehending a Life of that celebrated Sculptor ; and Memoirs of several contemporary Artists, from the time of Roubiliac, Hogarth, and Reynolds, to that of Fuseli, Flaxman, and Blake.' (London : Henry Colburn, New Burlington Street, 1828.) It contains more facts at first hand than any other account of Blake, and is really the foundation of all subsequent biographies. I have added a page, which is not without its significance, from a later book by Smith, 'A Book for a Rainy Day ; or, Recollections of the Events of the last Sixty-five Years' (1845), where it occurs under date 1784, on pp. 81, 82.]

BIOGRAPHICAL SKETCH OF BLAKE

I BELIEVE it has been invariably the custom of every age, whenever a man has been found to depart from the usual mode of thinking, to consider him of deranged intellect, and not unfrequently stark staring mad; which judgment his calumniators would pronounce with as little hesitation, as some of the uncharitable part of mankind would pass sentence of death upon a poor half-drowned cur who had lost his master, or one who had escaped hanging with a rope about his neck. Cowper, in a letter to Lady Hesketh, dated June 3, 1788, speaking of a dancing-master's advertisement, says, 'The author of it had the good hap to be crazed, or he had never produced anything half so clever; for you will ever observe, that they who are said to have lost their wits, have more than other people.'

Bearing this stigma of eccentricity, William Blake, with most extraordinary zeal, commenced his efforts in Art under the roof of No. 28 Broad Street, Carnaby Market; in which house he was born, and where his father carried on the business of a hosier. William, the subject of the following pages, who was his second son, showing an early stretch of mind, and a strong talent for drawing, being totally destitute of the dexterity of a London shopman, so well described by Dr. Johnson, was sent away from the counter as a booby, and placed under the late Mr. James Basire, an artist well known for many years as engraver to the Society of Antiquaries. From him he learned the mechanical part of his art, and as he drew carefully, and copied faithfully, his master frequently and confidently employed him to make drawings from monuments to be engraven.

After leaving his instructor, in whose house he had conducted himself with the strictest propriety, he became acquainted with Flaxman, the sculptor, through his friend Stothard, and was also honoured by an introduction to the accomplished Mrs. Mathew, whose house, No. 27, in Rathbone Place, was then frequented by most of the literary and talented people of the day. This lady—to whom I also had the honour of being known, and whose door and purse were constantly open and ready to cherish persons of genius who stood in need of assistance in their learned and arduous pursuits, worldly concerns, or inconveniences—was so extremely zealous in promoting the celebrity of Blake, that upon hearing him read some of his early efforts in poetry, she thought so well of them, as to request the Rev. Henry Mathew, her husband, to join Mr. Flaxman in his truly kind offer of defraying the expense of printing them ; in which he not only acquiesced, but, with his usual urbanity, wrote the following advertisement, which precedes the poems :

' The following sketches were the production of an untutored youth, commenced in his twelfth, and occasionally resumed by the author till his twentieth year ; since which time, his talents having been wholly directed to the attainment of excellence in his profession, he has been deprived of the leisure requisite to such a revisal of these sheets, as might have rendered them less unfit to meet the public eye.

' Conscious of the irregularities and defects to be found in almost every page, his friends have still believed that they possessed a poetical originality, which merited some respite from oblivion. These, their opinions, remain, however, to be now reproved or confirmed by a less partial public.'

The annexed Song is a specimen of the juvenile playfulness of Blake's muse, copied from page 10 of these Poems.[1]

SONG

' How sweet I roam'd from field to field,
    And tasted all the Summer's pride,
Till I the Prince of Love beheld,
    Who in the sunny beams did glide !

' He show'd me lilies for my hair,
    And blushing roses for my brow ;
He led me through his gardens fair,
    Where all his golden pleasures grow.

---

[1] The whole copy of this little work, entitled ' Poetical Sketches, by W. B.,' containing seventy pages, octavo, bearing the date of 1783, was given to Blake to sell to friends, or publish, as he might think proper.

' With sweet May-dews my wings were wet,
     And Phœbus fired my vocal rage ;
He caught me in his silken net,
     And shut me in his golden cage.

' He loves to sit and hear me sing,
     Then, laughing, sports and plays with me ;
Then stretches out my golden wing,
     And mocks my loss of liberty.'

But it happened, unfortunately, soon after this
period, that in consequence of his unbending deportment, or what his adherents are pleased to
call his manly firmness of opinion, which certainly
was not at all times considered pleasing by every
one, his visits were not so frequent. He, however,
continued to benefit by Mrs. Mathew's liberality,
and was enabled to continue in partnership, as a
printseller, with his fellow-pupil, Parker, in a shop,
No. 27, next door to his father's, in Broad Street ;
and being extremely partial to Robert, his youngest
brother, considered him as his pupil. Bob, as he
was familiarly called, was one of my playfellows,
and much beloved by all his companions.

Much about this time, Blake wrote many other
songs, to which he also composed tunes. These
he would occasionally sing to his friends ; and
though, according to his confession, he was entirely
unacquainted with the science of music, his ear
was so good, that his tunes were sometimes most
singularly beautiful, and were noted down by
musical professors. As for his later poetry, if it

may be so called, attached to his plates, though it was certainly in some parts enigmatically curious as to its application, yet it was not always wholly uninteresting; and I have unspeakable pleasure in being able to state, that though I admit he did not for the last forty years attend any place of Divine worship, yet he was not a Freethinker, as some invidious detractors have thought proper to assert, nor was he ever in any degree irreligious. Through life, his Bible was everything with him; and as a convincing proof how highly he reverenced the Almighty, I shall introduce the following lines with which he concludes his address to the Deists :

> ' For a tear is an intellectual thing ;
> And a sigh is the sword of an Angel-King ;
> And the bitter groan of a Martyr's woe
> Is an arrow from the Almighty's bow.'

Again, at page 77, in his address to the Christians :

> ' I give you the end of a golden string ;
> Only wind it into a ball,
> It will lead you in at Heaven's gate,
> Built in Jerusalem's wall.'

In his choice of subjects, and in his designs in Art, perhaps no man had higher claim to originality, nor ever drew with a closer adherence to his own conception ; and from what I knew of him, and have heard related by his friends, I most firmly believe few artists have been guilty of less plagiarisms than he. It is true, I have seen him admire

and heard him expatiate upon the beauties of Marc
Antonio and of Albert Dürer; but I verily believe
not with any view of borrowing an idea; neither
do I consider him at any time dependent in his
mode of working, which was generally with the
graver only; and as to printing, he mostly took off
his own impressions.

After his marriage, which took place at Battersea, and which proved a mutually happy one, he
instructed his *beloved*, for so he most frequently
called his Kate,[1] and allowed her, till the last
moment of his practice, to take off his proof impressions and print his works, which she did most
carefully, and ever delighted in the task: nay, she
became a draughtswoman; and as a convincing
proof that she and her husband were born for each
other's comfort, she not only entered cheerfully
into his views, but, what is curious, possessed a
similar power of imbibing ideas, and has produced
drawings equally original and, in some respects,
interesting.

Blake's peace of mind, as well as that of his

---

[1] A friend has favoured me with the following anecdotes,
which he received from Blake, respecting his courtship. He
states that ' Our Artist fell in love with a lively little girl, who
allowed him to say everything that was loving, but would not
listen to his overtures on the score of matrimony. He was
lamenting this in the house of a friend, when a generous-hearted
lass declared that she pitied him from her heart. "Do you
pity me?" asked Blake. "Yes; I do, most sincerely."—
"Then," said he, "I love you for that."—"Well," said the
honest girl, "and I love you." The consequence was, they
were married, and lived the happiest of lives.'

Catherine, was much broken by the death of their
brother Robert, who was a most amicable link in
their happiness; and, as a proof how much Blake
respected him, whenever he beheld him in his
visions, he implicitly attended to his opinion and
advice as to his future projected works. I should
have stated, that Blake was supereminently en-
dowed with the power of disuniting all other
thoughts from his mind, whenever he wished to
indulge in thinking of any particular subject; and
so firmly did he believe, by this abstracting power,
that the objects of his compositions were before him
in his mind's eye, that he frequently believed them
to be speaking to him. This I shall now illustrate
by the following narrative.

Blake, after deeply perplexing himself as to the
mode of accomplishing the publication of his illustrated songs, without their being subject to the
expense of letterpress, his brother Robert stood
before him in one of his visionary imaginations,
and so decidedly directed him in the way in which
he ought to proceed, that he immediately followed
his advice, by writing his poetry, and drawing his
marginal subjects of embellishments in outline upon
the copper-plate with an impervious liquid, and
then eating the plain parts or lights away with
aqua-fortis considerably below them, so that the
outlines were left as a stereotype. The plates in
this state were then printed in any tint that he
wished, to enable him or Mrs. Blake to colour the

marginal figures up by hand in imitation of drawings.

The following are some of his works produced in this manner, viz.; 'Songs of Innocence and Songs of Experience,' 'The Book of Jerusalem,' consisting of an hundred plates, 'The Marriage of Heaven and Hell,' 'Europe and America'; and another work, which is now very uncommon, a pretty little series of plates, entitled 'Gate of Paradise.'

Blake, like those artists absorbed in a beloved study, cared not for money beyond its use for the ensuing day; and indeed he and his 'beloved' were so reciprocally frugal in their expenses, that, never sighing for either gilded vessels, silver-laced attendants, or turtle's livers, they were contented with the simplest repast, and a little answered their purpose. Yet, notwithstanding all their economy, Dame Fortune being, as it is pretty well known to the world, sometimes a fickle jade, they, as well as thousands more, have had their intercepting clouds.

As it is not my intention to follow them through their lives, I shall confine myself to a relation of a few other anecdotes of this happy pair; and as they are connected with the Arts, in my opinion they ought not to be lost, as they may be considered worthy the attention of future biographers.

For his marginal illustrations of 'Young's Night Thoughts,' which possess a great power of imagination, he received so despicably low a price, that Flaxman, whose heart was ever warm, was determined to serve him whenever an opportunity offered itself; and with his usual voice of sympathy, introduced him to his friend Hayley, with whom it was no new thing to give pleasure, capricious as he was. This gentleman immediately engaged him to engrave the plates for his quarto edition of 'The Life of Cowper,' published in 1803-4; and for this purpose he went down to Felpham, in order to be near that highly respected *Hermit*.

Here he took a cottage, for which he paid twenty pounds a year, and was not, as has been reported, entertained in a house belonging to Mr. Hayley rent-free. During his stay he drew several portraits, and could have had full employment in that department of the Art; but he was born to follow his own inclinations, and was willing to rely upon a reward for the labours of the day.

Mr. Flaxman, knowing me to be a collector of autographs, among many others, gave me the following letter, which he received from Blake immediately after his arrival at Felpham, in which he styles him

' DEAR SCULPTOR OF ETERNITY,

' We are safe arrived at our cottage, which is more beautiful than I thought it, and more convenient. It is a perfect model for cottages, and, I think, for palaces of magnificence; only enlarging, not altering, its proportions, and adding ornaments and not principals. Nothing can be more grand than its simplicity and usefulness. Simple without intricacy, it seems to be the spontaneous effusion of humanity, congenial to the wants of man. No other-formed house can ever please me so well; nor shall I ever be persuaded, I believe, that it can be improved either in beauty or use.

'Mr. Hayley received us with his usual brotherly affection. I have begun to work. Felpham is a sweet place for study, because it is more spiritual than London. Heaven opens here on all sides her golden gates; her windows are not obstructed by vapours; voices of celestial inhabitants are more distinctly heard, and their forms more distinctly seen, and my cottage is also a shadow of their houses. My wife and sister are both well, courting Neptune for an embrace.

'Our journey was very pleasant; and though we had a great deal of luggage, no grumbling. All was cheerfulness and good-humour on the road, and yet we could not arrive at our cottage before half-past eleven at night, owing to the necessary shifting of our luggage from one chaise to another; for we had seven different chaises, and as many different drivers. We set out between six and seven in the morning of Thursday, with sixteen heavy boxes, and portfolios full of prints.

'And now begins a new life, because another covering of earth is shaken off. I am more famed in Heaven for my works than I could well conceive. In my brain are studies and chambers filled with books and pictures of old, which I wrote and painted in ages of eternity, before my mortal life; and those works are the delight and study of archangels. Why then should I be anxious about the riches or fame of mortality? The Lord, our father, will do for us and with us according to his Divine will for our good.

'You, O dear Flaxman! are a sublime Archangel, my friend and companion from eternity. In the Divine bosom is our dwelling-place. I look back into the regions of reminiscence, and behold our ancient days before this earth appeared in its vegetated mortality to my mortal-vegetated eyes. I see our houses of eternity which can never be separated, though our mortal vehicles should stand at the remotest corners of Heaven from each other.

'Farewell, my best friend! Remember me and my wife in love and friendship to our dear Mrs. Flaxman, whom we ardently desire to entertain beneath our thatched roof of rusted gold; and believe me for ever to remain,

'Your grateful and affectionate,

'WILLIAM BLAKE.

'FELPHAM, *Sept.* 21, 1800.

'Sunday morning.'

In a copy of Hayley's 'Triumphs of Temper,' illustrated by Stothard, which had been the one belonging to the Author's son, and which he gave after his death to Blake, are these verses in MS. by the hand of the donor:

'Accept, my gentle visionary, Blake,
    Whose thoughts are fanciful and kindly mild;
Accept, and fondly keep for friendship's sake,
    This favor'd vision, my poetic child.

'Rich in more grace than fancy ever won,
    To thy most tender mind this book will be,
For it belong'd to my departed son;
    So from an angel it descends to thee.

W. H.
'*July*, 1800.'[1]

Upon his return from Felpham, he addressed the public, in page 3 of his Book of Jerusalem, in these words, 'After my three years' slumber on the

[1] I copied the above from the book now in the possession of Mrs. Blake.

banks of the ocean, I again display my giant-forms to the public,' etc.

Some of the 'giant-forms,' as he calls them, are mighty and grand, and if I were to compare them to the style of any preceding artist, Michel Angelo, Sir Joshua's favourite, would be the one; and were I to select a specimen as a corroboration of this opinion, I should instance the figure personifying the 'Ancient of Days,' the frontispiece to his 'Europe, a Prophecy.' In my mind, his knowledge of drawing, as well as design, displayed in this figure, must at once convince the informed reader of his extraordinary abilities.

I am now under the painful necessity of relating an event promulgated in two different ways by two different parties; and as I entertain a high respect for the talents of both persons concerned, I shall, in order to steer clear of giving umbrage to the supporters of either, leave the reader to draw his own conclusions, unbiassed by any insinuation whatever of mine.

An engraver of the name of Cromek, a man who endeavoured to live by speculating upon the talents of others, purchased a series of drawings of Blake, illustrative of Blair's 'Grave,' which he had begun with a view of engraving and publishing. These were sold to Mr. Cromek for the insignificant sum of one guinea each, with the promise, and indeed under the express agreement, that Blake should be employed to engrave them; a task to which he looked forward with anxious delight. Instead of this negotiation being carried into effect, the drawings, to his great mortification, were put into the hands of Schiavonetti. During the time this artist was thus employed, Cromek had asked Blake what work he had in mind to execute next. The unsuspecting artist not only told him, but without the least reserve showed him the designs sketched out for a fresco picture ; the subject Chaucer's ' Pilgrimage to Canterbury ' ; with which Mr. Cromek appeared highly delighted. Shortly after this, Blake discovered that Stothard, a brother-artist to whom he had been extremely kind in early days, had been employed to paint a picture, not only of the same subject, but in some instances similar to the fresco sketch which he had shown to Mr. Cromek. The picture painted by Stothard became the property of Mr. Cromek, who published proposals for an engraving from it, naming Bromley as the engraver to be employed. However, in a short time, that artist's name was withdrawn, and Schiavonetti's substituted, who lived only to complete the etching ; the plate being finished afterwards by at least three different hands. Blake, highly indignant at this treatment, immediately set to work, and proposed an engraving from his fresco picture, which he publicly exhibited in his brother James's shop-window, at the corner of Broad Street, accompanied with an address to the public, stating what he considered to be improper conduct.

So much on the side of Blake.[1] On the part of Stothard, the story runs thus. Mr. Cromek had agreed with that artist to employ him upon a picture of the Procession of Chaucer's Pilgrimage to Canterbury, for which he first agreed to pay him sixty guineas, but in order to enable him to finish it in a more exquisite manner, promised him forty more, with an intention of engaging Bromley to engrave it; but in consequence of some occurrence, his name was withdrawn, and Schiavonetti was employed. During the time Stothard was painting the picture, Blake called to see it, and appeared so delighted with it, that Stothard, sincerely wishing to please an old friend with whom he had lived so cordially for many years, and from whose works he always most liberally declared he had received much pleasure and edification, expressed a wish to introduce his portrait as one of the party, as a mark of esteem.

Mr. Hoppner, in a letter to a friend, dated May 30, 1807, says of it,

'This intelligent group is rendered still more interesting

---

[1] In 1809, Blake exhibited sixteen poetical and historical inventions, in his brother's first-floor in Broad Street; eleven pictures in fresco, professed to be painted according to the ancient method, and seven drawings, of which an explanatory catalogue was published, and is perhaps the most curious of its kind ever written. At page 7, the description of his fresco painting of Geoffrey Chaucer's Pilgrimage commences. This picture, which is larger than the print, is now in the possession of Thomas Butts, Esq., a gentleman friendly to Blake, and who is in possession of a considerable number of his works.

by the charm of colouring, which though simple is strong, and most harmoniously distributed throughout the picture. The landscape has a deep-toned brightness that accords most admirably with the figures; and the painter has ingeniously contrived to give a value to a common scene and very ordinary forms, that would hardly be found, by unlearned eyes, in the natural objects.   He has expressed too, with great vivacity and truth, the freshness of morning, at that season when Nature herself is most fresh and blooming—the Spring; and it requires no great stretch of fancy to imagine we perceive the influence of it on the cheeks of the Fair Wife of Bath, and her rosy companions, the Monk and Friar.

' In respect of the execution of the various parts of this pleasing design, it is not too much praise to say, that it is wholly free from that vice which painters term *manner*; and it has this peculiarity beside, which I do not remember to have seen in any picture, ancient or modern, namely, that it bears no mark of the period in which it was painted, but might very well pass for the work of some able artist of the time of Chaucer.   This effect is not, I believe, the result of any association of ideas connected with the costume, but appears in primitive simplicity, and the total absence of all affectation, either of colouring or pencilling.

' Having attempted to describe a few of the beauties of this captivating performance, it remains only for me to mention one great defect.   The picture is, notwithstanding appearances, *a modern one*.   But if you can divest yourself of the general prejudice that exists against contemporary talents, you will see a work that would have done honour to any school, at any period.' [1]

In 1810, Stothard, to his great surprise, found that Blake had engraved and published a plate of the same size, in some respects bearing a similarity

[1] See the 'Artist,' by Prince Hoare, Esq., No. 13, vol. i. p. 13.

to his own.[1] Such are the outlines of this controversy.

Blake's ideas were often truly entertaining, and
after he had conveyed them to paper, his whimsical
and novel descriptions frequently surpassed his
delineations ; for instance, that of his picture of
the Transformation of the Flea to the form of a
Man, is extremely curious. This personification,
which he denominated a Cupper, or Blood-sucker,
is covered with coat of armour, similar to the
case of the flea, and is represented slowly pacing
in the night, with a thorn attached to his right
hand, and a cup in the other, as if ready to puncture
the first person whose blood he might fancy, like
Satan prowling about to seek whom he could devour.
Blake said of the flea, that were that lively little
fellow the size of an elephant, he was quite sure,
from the calculations he had made of his wonderful

---

[1] I must do Mr. Stothard the justice to declare, that the
very first time I saw him after he had read the announcement
of Blake's death, he spoke in the handsomest terms of his
talents, and informed me that Blake made a remarkably correct
and fine drawing of the head of Queen Philippa, from her monumental effigy in Westminster Abbey, for Gough's Sepulchral
Monuments, engraved by Basire. The collectors of Stothard's
numerous and elegant designs will recollect the name of Blake
as the engraver of several plates in the Novelist's Magazine,
the Poetical Magazine, and also others for a work entitled the
Wit's Magazine, from drawings produced by the same artist.
Trotter, the engraver, who received instructions from Blake,
and who was a pattern-draughtsman to the calico-printers,
introduced his friend Stothard to Blake, and their attachment
for each other continued most cordially to exist in the opinion
of the public, until they produced their rival pictures of
Chaucer's Canterbury Pilgrimage.

strength, that he could bound from Dover to Calais in one leap.[1] Whatever may be the public opinion hereafter of Blake's talents, when his enemies are dead, I will not presume to predict;[2] but this I am certain of, that on the score of industry at least, many artists must strike to him. Application was a faculty so engendered in him that he took little bodily exercise to keep up his health: he had few evening walks and little rest from labour, for his mind was ever fixed upon his art, nor did he at any time indulge in a game of chess, draughts, or backgammon; such amusements, considered as relaxations by artists in general, being to him distractions. His greatest pleasure was derived from the Bible—a work ever at his hand, and which he often assiduously consulted in several languages. Had he fortunately lived till the next year's exhibition at Somerset House, the public would then have been astonished at his exquisite

[1] This interesting little picture is painted in fresco. It is now the property of John Varley, the artist, whose landscapes will ever be esteemed as some of the finest productions in Art, and who may fairly be considered as one of the founders of the Society of Artists in Water-Colours; the annual exhibitions of which continue to surpass those of the preceding seasons.

[2] Blake's talent is not to be seen in his engravings from the designs of other artists, though he certainly honestly endeavoured to copy the beauties of Stothard, Flaxman, and those masters set before him by the few publishers who employed him; but his own engravings from his own mind are the productions which the man of true feeling must ever admire, and the predictions of Fuseli and Flaxman may hereafter be verified —'That a time will come when Blake's finest works will be as much sought after and treasured up in the portfolios of men of mind, as those of Michel Angelo are at present.'

finishing of a Fresco picture of the Last Judgment, containing upwards of one thousand figures, many of them wonderfully conceived and grandly drawn. The lights of this extraordinary performance have the appearance of silver and gold ; but upon Mrs. Blake's assuring me that there was no silver used, I found, upon a closer examination, that a blue wash had been passed over those parts of the gilding which receded, and the lights of the forward objects, which were also of gold, were heightened with a warm colour, to give the appearance of the two metals.

It is most certain, that the uninitiated eye was incapable of selecting the beauties of Blake; his effusions were not generally felt ; and in this opinion I am borne out in the frequent assertions of Fuseli and Flaxman. It would, therefore, be unreasonable to expect the booksellers to embark in publications not likely to meet remuneration. Circumstanced, then, as Blake was, approaching to threescore years and ten, in what way was he to persevere in his labours ? Alas, he knew not! until the liberality of Mr. Linnell, a brother-artist of eminence, whose discernment could well appreciate those parts of his designs which deserved perpetuity, enabled him to proceed and execute in comfort a series of twenty-one plates, illustrative of the Book of Job. This was the last work he completed, upon the merits of which he received the highest congratulations from the following Royal

Academicians: Sir Thomas Lawrence, Mr. Baily,
Mr. Philips, Mr. Chantrey, Mr. James Ward, Mr.
Arnald, Mr. Collins, Mr. Westmacott, and many
other artists of eminence.

As to Blake's system of colouring, which I have
not hitherto noticed, it was in many instances most
beautifully prismatic. In this branch of the art
he often acknowledged Apelles to have been his
tutor, who was, he said, so much pleased with his
style, that once when he appeared before him,
among many of his observations, he delivered the
following:—'You certainly possess my system of
colouring; and I now wish you to draw my person,
which has hitherto been untruly delineated.'

I must own that until I was favoured by Mr.
Upcott with a sight of some of Blake's works,
several of which I had never seen, I was not so
fully aware of his great depth of knowledge in
colouring. Of these most interesting specimens
of his art, which are now extremely rare, and
rendered invaluable by his death, as it is impossible
for any one to colour them with his mind, should
the plates remain, Mr. Richard Thomson, another
truly kind friend, has favoured me with the following descriptive lists.

Songs of Experience. The author and printer, W.
Blake. Small octavo; seventeen plates, including the
title-page. Frontispiece, a winged infant mounted on the
shoulders of a. youth. On the title-page, two figures
weeping over two crosses.

Introduction. Four Stanzas on a cloud, with a night-sky behind, and beneath, a figure of Earth stretched on a mantle.

Earth's Answer. Five Stanzas; a serpent on the ground beneath.

The Clod and the Pebble. Three Stanzas; above, a headpiece of four sheep and two oxen; beneath, a duck and reptiles.

A Poison Tree. Four Stanzas. The tree stretches up the right side of the page; and beneath, a dead body killed by its influence.

The Fly. Five Stanzas. Beneath, a female figure with two children.

Holy Thursday. Four Stanzas. Head-piece, a female figure discovering a dead child. On the right-hand margin a mother and two children lamenting the loss of an infant which lies beneath. Perhaps this is one of the most tasteful of the set.

The Chimney-Sweeper. Three Stanzas. Beneath, a figure of one walking in snow towards an open door.

London. Four Stanzas. Above, a child leading an old man through the street; on the right hand, a figure warming itself at a fire. If in any instance Mr. Blake has copied himself, it is in the figure of the old man upon this plate, whose position appears to have been a favourite one with him.

The Tiger. Six Stanzas. On the right-hand margin, the trunk of a tree; and beneath, a tiger walking.

A Little Boy Lost. Six Stanzas. Ivy-leaves on the right hand, and beneath, weeping figure before a fire, in which the verses state that the child had been burned by a Saint.

The Human Abstract. Six Stanzas. The trunk of a tree on the right-hand margin, and beneath, an old man in white drawing a veil over his head.

The Angel. Four Stanzas. Head-piece, a female figure lying beneath a tree, and pushing from her a winged boy.

My Pretty Rose-Tree. Two Stanzas: succeeded by a small vignette, of a figure weeping, and another lying reclined at the foot of a tree. Beneath, are two verses more, entitled, *Ah! Sun-Flower*; and a single stanza, headed *The Lily*.

Nurse's Song. Two Stanzas. Beneath, a girl with a youth and a female child at a door surrounded by vine-leaves.

A Little Girl Lost. Seven Stanzas; interspersed with birds and leaves, the trunk of a tree on the right-hand margin.

The whole of these plates are coloured in imitation of fresco. The poetry of these songs is wild, irregular, and highly mystical, but of no great degree of elegance or excellence, and their prevailing feature is a tone of complaint of the misery of mankind.

AMERICA: *a Prophecy.* Lambeth : Printed by William Blake, in the year 1793 ; folio ; eighteen plates or twenty pages, including the frontispiece and title-page. After a Preludium of thirty-seven lines commences the Prophecy of 226, which are interspersed with numerous head-pieces, vignettes, and tail-pieces, usually stretching along the left-hand margin and enclosing the text ; which sometimes appears written on a cloud, and at others environed by flames and water. Of the latter subject a very fine specimen is shown upon page 13, where the tail-piece represents the bottom of the sea, with various fishes coming together to prey upon a dead body. The head-piece is another dead body lying on the surface of the waters, with an eagle feeding upon it with out-stretched wings. Another instance of Mr. Blake's favourite figure of the old man entering at Death's door, is contained on page 12 of this poem. The subject of the text is a conversation between the Angel of Albion, the Angels of the Thirteen States, Washington, and some others of the American generals, and ' Red Orc,' the spirit of war and evil. The verses are without rhyme, and most resemble hexameters, though they are by no means exact ; and the expressions are mystical in a very high degree.

EUROPE: *a Prophecy.* Lambeth : Printed by William

Blake, 1794; folio; seventeen plates on the leaves, inclusive of the frontispiece and title-page. Coloured to imitate the ancient fresco painting. The Preludium consists of thirty-three lines, in stanzas without rhyme, and the Prophecy of two hundred and eight; the decorations to which are larger than most of those in the former book, and approach nearest to the character of paintings, since, in several instances, they occupy the whole page. The frontispiece is an uncommonly fine specimen of art, and approaches almost to the sublimity of Raffaelle or Michel Angelo. It represents 'The Ancient of Days,' in an orb of light surrounded by dark clouds, as referred to in Proverbs viii. 27, stooping down with an enormous pair of compasses to describe the destined orb of the world,[1] 'when he set a compass upon the face of the earth.'

> 'in His hand
> He took the golden compasses, prepar'd
> In God's eternal store, to circumscribe
> This universe, and all created things :
> One foot he centred, and the other turn'd
> Round through the vast profundity obscure ;
> And said, "Thus far extend, thus far thy bounds,
> This be thy just circumference, O World!"'
>
> Paradise Lost, book vii. line 236.

---

[1] He was inspired with the splendid grandeur of this figure, by the vision which he declared hovered over his head at the top of his staircase ; and he has been frequently heard to say, that it made a more powerful impression upon his mind than all he had ever been visited by. This subject was such a favourite with him, that he always bestowed more time and enjoyed greater pleasure when colouring the print, than anything he ever produced.

Mr. F. Tatham employed him to tint an impression of it, for which I have heard he paid him the truly liberal sum of three guineas and a half. I say liberal, though the specimen is worth any price, because the sum was so considerably beyond what Blake generally had been accustomed to receive as a remunera-

Another splendid composition in this work are the two angels pouring out the black-spotted plague upon England, on page 9 ; in which the fore-shortening of the legs, the grandeur of their positions, and the harmony with which they are adapted to each other and to their curved trumpets, are perfectly admirable. The subject-matter of the work is written in the same wild and singular measures as the preceding, and describes, in mystical language, the terrors of plague and anarchy which overspread England during the slumbers of Enitharmon for eighteen hundred years ; upon whose awaking, the ferocious spirit Orc burst into flames 'in the vineyards of red France.' At the end of this poem are seven separate engravings on folio pages, without letterpress, which are coloured like the former part of the work, with a degree of splendour and force, as almost to resemble sketches in oil-colours. The finest of these are a figure of an angel standing in the sun, a group of three furies surrounded by clouds and fire, and a figure of a man sitting beneath a tree in the deepest dejection ; all of which are peculiarly remarkable for their strength and splendour of colouring. Another publication by Mr. Blake consisted only of a small quarto volume of twenty-three engravings of various shapes and sizes, coloured as before, some of which are of extraordinary effect and beauty. The best

---

tion for his extraordinary talents. Upon this truly inestimable impression, which I have now before me, Blake worked when bolstered-up in his bed only a few days before he died ; and my friend F. Tatham has just informed me, that after Blake had frequently touched upon it, and had as frequently held it at a distance, he threw it from him, and with an air of exulting triumph exclaimed, 'There, that will do ! I cannot mend it.' However, this was not his last production ; for immediately after he had made the above declaration to his beloved Kate, upon whom his eyes were steadfastly fixed, he vociferated, 'Stay ! keep as you are ! *you* have ever been *an angel* to me, I will draw you' ; and he actually made a most spirited likeness of her, though within so short a period of his earthly termination.

plates in this series are—the first of an aged man, with a white beard sweeping the ground, and writing in a book with each hand, naked ; a human figure pressing out his brain through his ears ; and the great sea-serpent ; but perhaps the best is a figure sinking in a stormy sea at sunset, the splendid light of which, and the foam upon the black waves, are almost magical effects of colouring. Beneath the first design is engraven ' *Lambeth, printed by W. Blake,* 1794.'

Blake's modes of preparing his ground, and laying them over his panels for painting, mixing his colours, and manner of working, were those which he considered to have been practised by the earliest fresco painters, whose productions still remain, in numerous instances, vivid and permanently fresh. His ground was a mixture of whiting and carpenter's glue, which he passed over several times in thin coatings : his colours he ground himself, and also united them with the same sort of glue, but in a much weaker state. He would, in the course of painting a picture, pass a very thin transparent wash of glue-water over the whole of the parts he had worked upon, and then proceed with his finishing.[1]

[1] Loutherbourgh was also, in *his* way, very ingenious in his contrivances. To oblige his friend Garrick, he enriched a drama, entitled ' *The Christmas Tale,*' with scenery painted by himself, and introduced such novelty and brilliancy of effect, as formed a new era in that species of art. This he accomplished by means of differently coloured silks placed before the lamps at the front of the stage, and by the lights behind the side scenes. The same effects were used for distance and atmosphere. As for instance, Harlequin in a fog was produced by tiffany hung between the audience and himself. Mr. Seguire, the father of

This process I have tried, and find, by using my mixture warm, that I can produce the same texture as possessed in Blake's pictures of the Last Judgment, and others of his productions, particularly in Varley's curious picture of the personified Flea. Blake preferred mixing his colours with carpenter's glue, to gum, on account of the latter cracking in the sun, and becoming humid in moist weather. The glue-mixture stands the sun, and change of atmosphere has no effect upon it. Every carpenter knows that if a broken piece of stick be joined with good glue, the stick will seldom break again in the glued parts.

That Blake had many secret modes of working, both as a colourist and an engraver, I have no doubt. His method of eating away the plain copper, and leaving his drawn lines of his subjects and his words as stereotype, is, in my mind, perfectly original. Mrs. Blake is in possession of the secret, and she ought to receive something considerable for its communication, as I am quite certain it may be used to the greatest advantage both to artists and literary characters in general.

That Blake's coloured plates have more effect

the Keeper of the King's Pictures, and those of the National Gallery, purchased of Mr. Loutherbourgh ten small designs for the scenery of Omiah, for which scenes the manager paid him one thousand pounds. Mr. Loutherbourgh never would leave any paper or designs at the theatre, nor would he ever allow any one to see what he intended to produce ; as he secretly held small cards in his hand, which he now and then referred to in order to assist him in his recollections of his small drawings.

than others where gum has been used, is, in my opinion, the fact, and I shall rest my assertion upon those beautiful specimens in the possession of Mr. Upcott, coloured purposely for that gentleman's godfather, Ozias Humphrey, Esq., to whom Blake wrote the following interesting letter.

TO OZIAS HUMPHREY, Esq.

'THE design of The Last Judgment, which I have completed by your recommendation for the Countess of Egremont, it is necessary to give some account of; and its various parts ought to be described, for the accommodation of those who give it the honour of their attention.

'Christ seated on the Throne of Judgment: the Heavens in clouds rolling before him and around him, like a scroll ready to be consumed in the fires of the Angels; who descend before his feet, with their four trumpets sounding to the four winds.

'Beneath, the Earth is convulsed with the labours of the Resurrection. In the caverns of the earth is the Dragon with seven heads and ten horns, chained by two Angels; and above his cavern, on the earth's surface, is the Harlot, also seized and bound by two Angels with chains, while her palaces are falling into ruins, and her counsellors and warriors are descending into the abyss, in wailing and despair.

'Hell opens beneath the harlot's seat on the left hand, into which the wicked are descending.

'The right hand of the design is appropriated to the Resurrection of the Just: the left hand of the design is appropriated to the Resurrection and Fall of the Wicked.

'Immediately before the Throne of Christ are Adam and Eve, kneeling in humiliation, as representatives of

the whole human race; Abraham and Moses kneel on
each side beneath them; from the cloud on which Eve
kneels, and beneath Moses, and from the tables of stone
which utter lightning, is seen Satan wound round by the
Serpent, and falling headlong; the Pharisees appear on
the left hand pleading their own righteousness before the
Throne of Christ: The Book of Death is opened on clouds
by two Angels; many groups of figures are falling from
before the throne, and from the sea of fire, which flows
before the steps of the throne; on which are seen the
seven Lamps of the Almighty, burning before the throne.
Many figures chained and bound together fall through the
air, and some are scourged by Spirits with flames of fire
into the abyss, of Hell, which opens to receive them
beneath, on the left hand of the harlot's seat; where
others are howling and descending into the flames, and
in the act of dragging each other into Hell, and of con-
tending in fighting with each other on the brink of
perdition.

'Before the Throne of Christ on the right hand, the
Just, in humiliation and in exultation, rise through the air,
with their Children and Families; some of whom are
bowing before the Book of Life, which is opened by two
Angels on clouds: many groups arise with exultation;
among them is a figure crowned with stars, and the moon
beneath her feet, with six infants around her, she represents the Christian Church.   The green hills appear
beneath; with the graves of the blessed, which are seen
bursting with their births of immortality; parents and
children embrace and arise together, and in exulting
attitudes tell each other that the New Jerusalem is ready
to descend upon earth; they arise upon the air rejoicing;
others newly awaked from the graves, stand upon the
earth embracing and shouting to the Lamb, who cometh
in the clouds with power and great glory.

'The whole upper part of the design is a view of
Heaven opened; around the Throne of Christ, four living

creatures filled with eyes, attended by seven angels with seven vials of the wrath of God, and above these seven Angels with the seven trumpets compose the cloud, which by its rolling away displays the opening seats of the Blessed, on the right and the left of which are seen the four-and-twenty Elders seated on thrones to judge the dead.

'Behind the seat and Throne of Christ appears the Tabernacle with its veil opened, the Candlestick on the right, the Table with Show-bread on the left, and in the midst, the Cross in place of the Ark, with the two Cherubim bowing over it.

'On the right hand of the Throne of Christ is Baptism, on his left is the Lord's Supper—the two introducers into Eternal Life. Women with infants approach the figure of an aged Apostle, which represents Baptism; and on the left hand the Lord's Supper is administered by Angels, from the hands of another aged Apostle; these kneel on each side of the Throne, which is surrounded by a glory: in the glory many infants appear, representing Eternal Creation flowing from the Divine Humanity in Jesus; who opens the Scroll of Judgment upon his knees before the living and the dead.

'Such is the design which you, my dear Sir, have been the cause of my producing, and which, but for you, might have slept till the Last Judgment.

'WILLIAM BLAKE.

'*January* 18, 1808.'

Blake and his wife were known to have lived so happily together, that they might unquestionably have been registered at Dunmow. 'Their hopes and fears were to each other known,' and their days and nights were passed in each other's company, for he always painted, drew, engraved, and studied, in the same room where they grilled, boiled, stewed, and slept; and so steadfastly attentive was he to his beloved tasks, that for the space of two years he had never once been out of his house; and his application was often so incessant, that in the middle of the night, he would, after thinking deeply upon a particular subject, leap from his bed and write for two hours or more; and for many years he made a constant practice of lighting the fire, and putting on the kettle for breakfast before his Kate awoke.

During his last illness, which was occasioned by the gall mixing with his blood, he was frequently bolstered-up in his bed to complete his drawings, for his intended illustration of Dante; an author so great a favourite with him, that though he agreed with Fuseli and Flaxman, in thinking Carey's translation superior to all others, yet, at the age of sixty-three years, he learned the Italian language purposely to enjoy Dante in the highest possible way. For this intended work, he produced seven engraved plates of an imperial quarto size, and nearly one hundred finished drawings of a size considerably larger; which will do equal justice to his wonderful mind, and the liberal heart of their possessor, who engaged him upon so delightful a task at a time when few persons would venture to give him employment, and whose kindness softened, for the remainder of his life, his lingering bodily sufferings, which he was seen to support with the most Christian fortitude.

On the day of his death, August 12,[1] 1827, he composed and uttered songs to his Maker so sweetly to the ear of his Catherine, that when she stood to hear him, he, looking upon her most affectionately, said, ' My beloved, they are not mine—no—they are not mine.' He expired at six in the evening, with the most cheerful serenity. Some short time before his death, Mrs. Blake asked him where he should like to be buried, and whether he would have the Dissenting Minister, or the Clergyman of the Church of England, to read the service: his answers were, that as far as his own feelings were concerned, they might bury him where she pleased, adding, that as his father, mother, aunt, and brother were buried in Bunhill Row, perhaps it would be better to lie there, but as to service, he should wish for that of the Church of England.

His hearse was followed by two mourning-coaches, attended by private friends: Calvert, Richmond, Tatham, and his brother, promising young artists, to whom he had given instructions in the Arts, were of the number. Tatham, ill as he was, travelled ninety miles to attend the funeral of one for whom, next to his own family, he held the highest esteem. Blake died in his sixty-ninth year, in the back-room of the first-floor of No. 3

[1] Not the 13th, as has been stated by several editors who have noticed his death.

Fountain Court, Strand, and was buried in Bunhill
Fields, on the 17th of August, at the distance of
about twenty-five feet from the north wall, numbered
eighty.

Limited as Blake was in his pecuniary circumstances, his beloved Kate survives him clear of
even a sixpenny debt; and in the fullest belief
that the remainder of her days will be rendered
tolerable by the sale of the few copies of her husband's works, which she will dispose of at the
original price of publication; in order to enable
the collector to add to the weight of his book-
shelves, without being solicited to purchase, out of
compassion, those specimens of her husband's talents
which they ought to possess.

Extract from 'A Book for a Rainy Day'

[1784].—This year Mr. Flaxman, who then lived
in Wardour Street, introduced me to one of his
early patrons, the Rev. Henry Mathew, of Percy
Chapel, Charlotte Street, which was built for him;
he was also afternoon preacher at Saint Martin's-
in-the-Fields. At that gentleman's house, in Rathbone Place, I became acquainted with Mrs. Mathew
and her son. At that lady's most agreeable con-
versaziones I first met the late William Blake, the
artist, to whom she and Mr. Flaxman had been
truly kind. There I have often heard him read
and sing several of his poems. He was listened

to by the company with profound silence, and allowed by most of the visitors to possess original and extraordinary merit.'[1]

[1] A time will come when the numerous, though now very rare works of Blake (in consequence of his taking very few impressions from the plates before they were rubbed out to enable him to use them for other subjects), will be sought after with the most intense avidity. He was considered by Stothard and Flaxman (and will be by those of congenial minds, if we can reasonably expect such again) with their highest admiration. These artists allowed him their utmost unqualified praise, and were ever anxious to recommend him and his productions to the patrons of the Arts; but, alas! they were not sufficiently appreciated as to enable Blake, as every one could wish, to provide an independence for his surviving partner, Kate, who adored his memory.

(VIII.) LIFE OF BLAKE
BY ALLAN CUNNINGHAM. 1830

[ALLAN CUNNINGHAM's Life of Blake occupies pp. 142-179 of the second volume of his *Lives of the most eminent British Painters, Sculptors, and Architects.* (London : John Murray, Albemarle Street, MDCCCXXX.) It is largely indebted to Smith, but contains a few anecdotes not found elsewhere, and probably derived from Varley and Linnell. In a letter to Linnell, printed in Mr. Story's Life, Cunningham says that 'much valuable information' has been received from Varley, and asks for more, adding, with characteristic impertinence : 'I know Blake's character, for I knew the man. I shall make a *judicious* use of my materials, and be merciful where sympathy is needed.' He reproduces the Phillips portrait of Blake, which had been engraved by Schiavonetti for Blair's *Grave*, in a less showy and more lifelike engraving by W. C. Edwards.]

WILLIAM BLAKE

PAINTING, like poetry, has followers, the body of
whose genius is light compared to the length of its
wings, and who, rising above the ordinary sympathies of our nature, are, like Napoleon, betrayed
by a star which no eye can see save their own.
To this rare class belonged William Blake.

He was the second son of James Blake and
Catherine his wife, and born on the 28th of
November, 1757, in 28 Broad Street, Carnaby
Market, London. His father, a respectable hosier,
caused him to be educated for his own business,
but the love of art came early upon the boy;
he neglected the figures of arithmetic for those of
Raphael and Reynolds; and his worthy parents often
wondered how a child of theirs should have conceived a love for such unsubstantial vanities. The
boy, it seems, was privately encouraged by his
mother. The love of designing and sketching grew
upon him, and he desired anxiously to be an artist.
His father began to be pleased with the notice
which his son obtained—and to fancy that a painter's
study might after all be a fitter place than a hosier's
shop for one who drew designs on the backs of all
the shop bills, and made sketches on the counter.

He consulted an eminent artist, who asked so large a sum for instruction, that the prudent shopkeeper hesitated, and young Blake declared he would prefer being an engraver—a profession which would bring bread at least, and through which he would be connected with painting. It was indeed time to dispose of him. In addition to his attachment to art, he had displayed poetic symptoms—scraps of paper and the blank leaves of books were found covered with groups and stanzas. When his father saw sketches at the top of the sheet and verses at the bottom, he took him away to Basire, the engraver, in Green Street, Lincoln's Inn Fields, and bound him apprentice for seven years. He was then fourteen years old.

It is told of Blake that at ten years of age he became an artist, and at twelve a poet. Of his boyish pencillings I can find no traces—but of his early intercourse with the Muse the proof lies before me in seventy pages of verse, written, he says, between his twelfth and his twentieth year, and published, by the advice of friends, when he was thirty. There are songs, ballads, and a dramatic poem; rude sometimes and melodious, but full of fine thought and deep and peculiar feeling. To those who love poetry for the music of its bells, these seventy pages will sound harsh and dissonant; but by others they will be more kindly looked upon. John Flaxman, a judge in all things of a poetic nature, was so touched with

many passages, that he not only counselled their
publication, but joined with a gentleman of the
name of Matthews in the expense, and presented
the printed sheets to the artist to dispose of for
his own advantage. One of these productions is
an address to the Muses—a common theme, but
sung in no common manner.

> ' Whether on Ida's shady brow,
>   Or in the chambers of the east,
> The chambers of the sun, that now
>   From ancient melody have ceas'd ;
>
> Whether in heaven ye wander fair,
>   Or the green corners of the earth,
> Or the blue regions of the air,
>   Where the melodious winds have birth ;
>
> Whether on crystal rocks ye rove,
>   Beneath the bosom of the sea,
> Wandering in many a coral grove,
>   Fair Nine ! forsaking poesie ;
>
> How have ye left the ancient love,
>   That Bards of old enjoyed in you ;--
> The languid strings now scarcely move,
>   The sound is forced—the notes are few.'

The little poem called ' The Tiger ' has been
admired for the force and vigour of its thoughts
by poets of high name. Many could weave smoother
lines—few could stamp such living images.

> ' Tiger ! Tiger ! burning bright
>   In the forest of the night,
> What immortal hand or eye
>   Framed thy fearful symmetry ?

In what distant deeps or skies
Burned the fervour of thine eyes ?
On what wings dare he aspire—
What the hand dare seize the fire ?

And what shoulder and what art
Could twist the sinews of thy heart ?
When thy heart began to beat,
What dread hand formed thy dread feet?

What the hammer ! what the chain !
Formed thy strength and forged thy brain ?
What the anvil ! What dread grasp
Dared thy deadly terrors clasp ?

When the stars threw down their spheres,
And sprinkled heaven with shining tears,
Did he smile, his work to see ?
Did he who made the lamb make thee ?'

In the dramatic poem of King Edward the Third
there are many nervous lines, and even whole passages of high merit.   The structure of the verse
is often defective, and the arrangement inharmo-
nious ; but before the ear is thoroughly offended,
it is soothed by some touch of deep melody and
poetic thought.   The princes and earls of England
are conferring together on the eve of the battle of
Cressy—the Black Prince takes Chandos aside,
and says—

' Now we 're alone, John Chandos, I 'll unburthen
And breathe my hopes into the burning air—
Where thousand Deaths are posting up and down,
Commissioned to this fatal field of Cressy :
Methinks I see them arm my gallant soldiers,

And gird the sword upon each thigh, and fit
The shining helm, and string each stubborn bow,
And dancing to the neighing of the steeds ;—
Methinks the shout begins—the battle burns ;—
Methinks I see them perch on English crests,
And breathe the wild flame of fierce war upon
The thronged enemy.'

In the same high poetic spirit Sir Walter Manny
converses with a genuine old English warrior, Sir
Thomas Dagworth.

' O, Dagworth !—France is sick !—the very sky,
Though sunshine light, it seems to me as pale
As is the fainting man on his death-bed,
Whose face is shown by light of one weak taper—
It makes me sad and sick unto the heart ;
Thousands must fall to-day.'

Sir Thomas answers.

' Thousands of souls must leave this prison-house
To be exalted to those heavenly fields
Where songs of triumph, psalms of victory,
Where peace, and joy, and love, and calm content
Sit singing on the azure clouds, and strew
The flowers of heaven upon the banquet table.
Bind ardent hope upon your feet, like shoes,
And put the robe of preparation on.
The table, it is spread in shining heaven.
Let those who fight, fight in good steadfastness ;
And those who fall shall rise in victory.'

I might transcribe from these modest and un-
noticed pages many such passages. It would be
unfair not to mention that the same volume contains some wild and incoherent prose, in which

we may trace more than the dawning of those strange, mystical, and mysterious fancies on which he subsequently misemployed his pencil. There is much that is weak, and something that is strong, and a great deal that is wild and mad, and all so strangely mingled, that no meaning can be assigned to it; it seems like a lamentation over the disasters which came on England during the reign of King John.

Though Blake lost himself a little in the enchanted region of song, he seems not to have neglected to make himself master of the graver, or to have forgotten his love of designs and sketches. He was a dutiful servant to Basire, and he studied occasionally under Flaxman and Fuseli; but it was his chief delight to retire to the solitude of his chamber, and there make drawings, and illustrate these with verses, to be hung up together in his mother's chamber. He was always at work; he called amusement idleness, sight-seeing vanity, and money-making the ruin of all high aspirations. 'Were I to love money,' he said, 'I should lose all power of thought! desire of gain deadens the genius of man. I might roll in wealth and ride in a golden chariot, were I to listen to the voice of parsimony. My business is not to gather gold, but to make glorious shapes, expressing godlike sentiments.' The day was given to the graver, by which he earned enough to maintain himself respectably; and he bestowed his evenings upon

painting and poetry, and intertwined these so
closely in his compositions, that they cannot well
be separated.

When he was six-and-twenty years old, he married Katharine Boutcher, a young woman of humble connections—the dark-eyed Kate of several of
his lyric poems. She lived near his father's house
and was noticed by Blake for the whiteness of her
hand, the brightness of her eyes, and a slim and
handsome shape, corresponding with his own notions of sylphs and naïads. As he was an original
in all things, it would have been out of character
to fall in love like an ordinary mortal; he was
describing one evening in company the pains he
had suffered from some capricious lady or another,
when Katharine Boutcher said, ' I pity you from
my heart.' ' Do you pity me ? ' said Blake, ' then
I love you for that.' ' And I love you,' said the
frank-hearted lass, and so the courtship began.
He tried how well she looked in a drawing, then
how her charms became verse ; and finding more-
over that she had good domestic qualities, he
married her. They lived together long and
happily.

She seemed to have been created on purpose for
Blake :—she believed him to be the finest genius
on earth ; she believed in his verse—she believed
in his designs ; and to the wildest flights of his
imagination she bowed the knee, and was a wor-
shipper. She set his house in good order, prepared

his frugal meal, learned to think as he thought, and, indulging him in his harmless absurdities, became, as it were, bone of his bone, and flesh of his flesh. She learned—what a young and handsome woman is seldom apt to learn—to despise gaudy dresses, costly meals, pleasant company, and agreeable invitations—she found out the way of being happy at home, living on the simplest of food, and contented in the homeliest of clothing. It was no ordinary mind which could do all this; and she whom Blake emphatically called his 'beloved,' was no ordinary woman. She wrought off in the press the impressions of his plates—she coloured them with a light and neat hand—made drawings much in the spirit of her husband's compositions, and almost rivalled him in all things save in the power which he possessed of seeing visions of any individual living or dead, whenever he chose to see them.

His marriage, I have heard, was not agreeable to his father; and he then left his roof and resided with his wife in Green Street, Leicester Fields. He returned to Broad Street, on the death of his father, a devout man, and an honest shopkeeper, of fifty years' standing, took a first-floor and a shop, and in company with one Parker, who had been his fellow-apprentice, commenced printseller. His wife attended to the business, and Blake continued to engrave, and took Robert, his favourite brother, for a pupil. This speculation did not

succeed—his brother too sickened and died; he
had a dispute with Parker—the shop was extinguished, and he removed to 28 Poland Street.
Here he commenced that series of works which
give him a right to be numbered among the men
of genius of his country. In sketching designs,
engraving plates, writing songs, and composing
music, he employed his time, with his wife sitting
at his side, encouraging him in all his undertakings.
As he drew the figure he meditated the song which
was to accompany it, and the music to which the
verse was to be sung, was the offspring too of the
same moment. Of his music there are no specimens—he wanted the art of noting it down—if it
equalled many of his drawings, and some of his
songs, we have lost melodies of real value.

The first fruits were the 'Songs of Innocence
and Experience,' a work original and natural, and
of high merit, both in poetry and in painting. It
consists of some sixty-five or seventy scenes, presenting images of youth and manhood—of domestic sadness, and fireside joy—of the gaiety and
innocence, and happiness of childhood. Every scene
has its poetical accompaniment, curiously inter-
woven with the group or the landscape, and
forming, from the beauty of the colour and the
prettiness of the pencilling, a very fair picture of
itself. Those designs are in general highly poetical ;
more allied, however, to heaven than to earth,—a
kind of spiritual abstractions, and indicating a

better world and fuller happiness than mortals enjoy. The picture of Innocence is introduced with the following sweet verses.

'Piping down the valleys wild,
  Piping songs of pleasant glee,
On a cloud I saw a child,
  And he laughing said to me—

Pipe a song about a lamb ;
  So I piped with merry cheer.
Piper, pipe that song again—
  So I piped—he wept to hear.

Drop thy pipe, thy happy pipe,
  Sing thy songs of happy cheer—
So I sung the same again,
  While he wept with joy to hear.

Piper, sit thee down and write
  In a book that all may read—
So he vanished from my sight :
  And I plucked a hollow reed,

And I made a rural pen,
  And I stained the water clear,
And I wrote my happy songs,
  Every child may joy to hear.'

In a higher and better spirit he wrought with his pencil. But then he imagined himself under spiritual influences ; he saw the forms and listened to the voices of the worthies of other days ; the past and the future were before him, and he heard, in imagination, even that awful voice which called on Adam amongst the trees of the garden. In this kind of dreaming abstraction, he lived much of his life ; all his works are stamped with it ; and though they owe much of their mysticism and obscurity to the circumstance, there can be no doubt that they also owe to it much of their singular loveliness and beauty. It was wonderful that he could thus, month after month, and year after year, lay down his graver after it had won him his daily wages, and retire from the battle for bread, to disport his fancy amid scenes of more than earthly splendour, and creatures pure as unfallen dew.

In this lay the weakness and the strength of Blake, and those who desire to feel the character of his compositions, must be familiar with his history and the peculiarities of his mind. He was by nature a poet, a dreamer, and an enthusiast. The eminence which it had been the first ambition of his youth to climb, was visible before him, and he saw on its ascent or on its summit those who had started earlier in the race of fame. He felt conscious of his own merit, but was not aware of the thousand obstacles which were ready to interpose. He thought that he had but to sing songs and draw designs, and become great and famous. The crosses which genius is heir to had been wholly unforeseen—and they befell him early ; he wanted the skill of hand, and fine tact of fancy and taste, to impress upon the offspring of his thoughts that popular shape, which gives such productions immediate circulation. His works were looked coldly on by the world, and were only esteemed by men of poetic minds, or those who were fond of things out of the common way. He earned a little fame, but no money by these speculations, and had to depend for bread on the labours of the graver.

All this neither crushed his spirit, nor induced him to work more in the way of the world ; but it had a visible influence upon his mind. He became more seriously thoughtful, avoided the company of men, and lived in the manner of a hermit, in that vast wilderness, London. Necessity made him frugal, and honesty and independence prescribed plain clothes, homely fare, and a cheap habitation. He was thus compelled more than ever to retire to worlds of his own creating, and seek solace in visions of paradise for the joys which the earth denied him. By frequent indulgence in these imaginings, he gradually began to believe in the reality of what dreaming fancy painted—the pictured forms which swarmed before his eyes, assumed, in his apprehension, the stability of positive revelations, and he mistook the vivid figures, which his professional imagination shaped, for the poets, and heroes, and princes of old. Amongst his friends, he at length ventured to intimate that the designs on which he was engaged were not from his own mind, but copied from grand works revealed to him in visions , and those who believed that, would readily lend an ear to the assurance that he was commanded to execute his performances by a celestial tongue !

Of these imaginary visitations he made good use, when he invented his truly original and beautiful mode of engraving and tinting his plates. He had made the sixty-five designs of his Days of Innocence, and was meditating, he said, on the best means of multiplying their resemblance in form and in hue ; he felt sorely perplexed. At last he was made aware that the spirit of his favourite brother Robert was in the room, and to this celestial visitor he applied for counsel. The spirit advised him at once : ' write,' he said, ' the poetry, and draw the designs upon the copper with a certain liquid (which he named, and which Blake ever kept a secret); then cut the plain parts of the plate down with aqua-fortis, and this will give the whole, both poetry and figures, in the manner of a stereotype.' The plan recommended by this gracious spirit was adopted ; the plates were engraved, and the work printed off. The artist then added a peculiar beauty of his own. He tinted both the figures and the verse with a variety of colours, amongst which, while yellow prevails, the whole has a rich and lustrous beauty, to which I know little that can be compared. The size of these prints is four inches and a half high by three inches wide. The original genius of Blake was always confined, through poverty, to small dimensions. Sixty-five plates of copper were an object to him who had little money. The Gates of Paradise, a work of sixteen designs, and those exceedingly small, was his next undertaking. The meaning of the artist is not a little obscure; it seems to have been his object to represent the innocence, the happiness, and the upward aspirations of man. They bespeak one intimately acquainted with the looks and the feelings of children. Over them there is shed a kind of mysterious halo which raises feelings of devotion. The Songs of Innocence, and the Gates of Paradise, became popular among the collectors of prints. To the sketch book and the cabinet the works of Blake are unfortunately confined.

If there be mystery in the meaning of the Gates of Paradise, his succeeding performance, by name URIZEN, has the merit or the fault of surpassing all human comprehension. The spirit which dictated this strange work was undoubtedly a dark one; nor does the strange kind of prose which is intermingled with the figures serve to enlighten us. There are in all twenty-seven designs representing beings human, demoniac, and divine, in situations of pain and sorrow and suffering. One character —evidently an evil spirit—appears in most of the plates; the horrors of hell, and the terrors of darkness and divine wrath, seem his sole portion. He swims in gulphs of fire—descends in cataracts of flame—holds combats with scaly serpents, or writhes in anguish without any visible cause. One of his exploits is to chase a female soul through a narrow gate and hurl her headlong down into a darksome pit. The wild verses which are scattered here and there, talk of the sons and the daughters of Urizen. He seems to have extracted these twenty-seven scenes out of many visions—what he meant by them even his wife declared she could not tell, though she was sure they had a meaning and a fine one. Something like the fall of Lucifer and the creation of Man is dimly visible in this extravagant work; it is not a little fearful to look upon; a powerful, dark, terrible though undefined and indescribable impression is left on the mind—and it is in no haste to be gone. The size of the designs is four inches by six; they bear date, 'Lambeth, 1794.' He had left Poland Street and was residing in Hercules Buildings.

The name of Blake began now to be known a little, and Edwards, the bookseller, employed him to illustrate Young's Night Thoughts. The reward in money was small, but the temptation in fame was great: the work was performed something in the manner of old books with illuminated margins. Along the ample margins which the poetry left on the page the artist sketched his fanciful creations; contracting or expanding them according to the space. Some of those designs were in keeping with the poems, but there were others which alarmed fastidious people: the serious and the pious were not prepared to admire shapes trembling in nudity round the verses of a grave divine. In the exuberance of Young there are many fine figures; but they are figures of speech only, on which art should waste none of its skill. This work was so much, in many parts, to the satisfaction of Flaxman, that he introduced Blake to Hayley the poet, who, in 1800, persuaded him to remove to Felpham in Sussex, to make engravings for the Life of Cowper. To that place he accordingly went with his wife and sister, and was welcomed by Hayley with much affection. Of his journey and his feelings he gives the following account to Flaxman, whom he usually addressed thus, 'Dear Sculptor of Eternity.'

'We are arrived safe at our cottage, which is more beautiful than I thought it, and more convenient. It is a perfect model for cottages, and I think for palaces of magnificence, only enlarging and not altering its proportions, and adding ornaments and not principals. Nothing can be more grand than its simplicity and usefulness. Felpham is a sweet place for study, because it is more spiritual than London. Heaven opens here on all sides her golden gates; her windows are not obstructed by vapours; voices of celestial inhabitants are more distinctly heard, and their forms more distinctly seen, and my cottage is also a shadow of their houses. My wife and sister are both well, and are courting Neptune for an embrace.'

Thus far had he written in the language and feelings of a person of upper air; though some of the expressions are tinctured with the peculiar

enthusiasm of the man, they might find shelter
under the licence of figurative speech, and pass
muster as the poetic language of new-found
happiness. Blake thus continues :—

'And now begins a new life, because another
covering of earth is shaken off. I am more famed
in heaven for my works than I could well conceive.
In my brain are studies and chambers filled with
books and pictures of old, which I wrote and
painted in ages of eternity before my mortal life,
and those works are the delight and study of archangels. Why then should I be anxious about the
riches or fame of mortality ? You, O dear Flaxman,
are a sublime archangel, my friend and companion
from eternity. Farewell, my dear friend, remember me and my wife in love and friendship to Mrs.
Flaxman, whom we ardently desire to entertain
beneath our thatched roof of russet gold.'

This letter, written in the year 1800, gives the
true twofold image of the author's mind. During
the day he was a man of sagacity and sense, who
handled his graver wisely, and conversed in a
wholesome and pleasant manner ; in the evening,
when he had done his prescribed task, he gave a
loose to his imagination. While employed on those
engravings which accompany the works of Cowper,
he saw such company as the country where he
resided afforded, and talked with Hayley about
poetry with a feeling to which the author of the
Triumphs of Temper was an utter stranger ; but at

the close of day away went Blake to the seashore
to indulge in his own thoughts and

'High converse with the dead to hold.'

Here he forgot the present moment and lived in
the past; he conceived, verily, that he had lived
in other days, and had formed friendships with
Homer and Moses; with Pindar and Virgil; with
Dante and Milton. These great men, he asserted,
appeared to him in visions, and even entered into
conversation. Milton, in a moment of confidence,
intrusted him with a whole poem of his, which the
world had never seen; but unfortunately the communication was oral, and the poetry seemed to
have lost much of its brightness in Blake's recita-
tion. When asked about the looks of those visions,
he answered, 'They are all majestic shadows, gray
but luminous, and superior to the common height
of men.' It was evident that the solitude of the
country gave him a larger swing in imaginary
matters. His wife often accompanied him to these
strange interviews; she saw nothing and heard as
little, but she was certain that her husband both
heard and saw.

Blake's mind at all times resembled that first
page in the magician's book of gramoury, which
made

'The cobweb on the dungeon wall,
Seem tapestry in lordly hall.'

His mind could convert the most ordinary occur-

rence into something mystical and supernatural.
He often saw less majestic shapes than those of the
poets of old. 'Did you ever see a fairy's funeral,
madam?' he once said to a lady, who happened to
sit by him in company. 'Never, sir!' was the
answer. 'I have,' said Blake, 'but not before
last night. I was walking alone in my garden,
there was great stillness among the branches and
flowers and more than common sweetness in the air;
I heard a low and pleasant sound, and I knew not
whence it came. At last I saw the broad leaf of a
flower move, and underneath I saw a procession of
creatures of the size and colour of green and gray
grasshoppers, bearing a body laid out on a rose
leaf, which they buried with songs, and then disappeared. It was a fairy funeral.' It would, perhaps, have been better for his fame had he
connected it more with the superstitious beliefs of
his country—amongst the elves and fairies his
fancy might have wandered at will—their popular
character would perhaps have kept him within the
bounds of traditionary belief, and the sea of his
imagination might have had a shore.

After a residence of three years in his cottage at
Felpham, he removed to 17 South Molton Street,
London, where he lived seventeen years. He came
back to town with a fancy not a little exalted by the
solitude of the country, and in this mood designed
and engraved an extensive and strange work which
he entitled 'Jerusalem.' A production so exclu-

sively wild was not allowed to make its appearance in an ordinary way : he thus announced it. 'After my three years' slumber on the banks of the ocean, I again display my giant forms to the public.' Of those designs there are no less than an hundred ; what their meaning is the artist has left unexplained. It seems of a religious, political, and spiritual kind, and wanders from hell to heaven and from heaven to earth ; now glancing into the distractions of our own days, and then making a transition to the antediluvians. The crowning defect is obscurity ; meaning seems now and then about to dawn ; you turn plate after plate and read motto after motto, in the hope of escaping from darkness into light. But the first might as well be looked at last ; the whole seems a riddle which no ingenuity can solve. Yet, if the work be looked at for form and effect rather than for meaning, many figures may be pronounced worthy of Michael Angelo. There is wonderful freedom of attitude and position ; men, spirits, gods, and angels, move with an ease which makes one lament that we know not wherefore they are put in motion. Well might Hayley call him his 'gentle visionary Blake.' He considered the Jerusalem to be his greatest work, and for a set of the tinted engravings he charged twenty-five guineas. Few joined the artist in his admiration. The Jerusalem, with all its giant forms, failed to force its way into circulation.

His next work was the Illustrations of Blair's
Grave, which came to the world with the following
commendation by Fuseli :   'The author of the
moral series before us has endeavoured to awaken
sensibility by touching our sympathies with nearer,
less ambiguous and less ludicrous imagery, than
what mythology, Gothic superstition, or symbols as
far fetched as inadequate could supply.   His
avocation has been chiefly employed to spread a
familiar and domestic atmosphere round the most
important of all subjects, to connect the visible and
the invisible world without provoking probability,
and to lead the eye from the milder light of time to
the radiations of eternity.'   For these twelve 'Inventions,' as he called them, Blake received twenty
guineas from Cromeck, the engraver—a man of
skill in art and taste in literature.   The price was
little, but nevertheless it was more than what he
usually received for such productions ; he also
undertook to engrave them.   But Blake's mode of
engraving was as peculiar as his style of designing ;
it had little of that grace of execution about it,
which attracts customers, and the Inventions, after
an experiment or two, were placed under the
fashionable graver of Louis Schiavonetti.   Blake
was deeply incensed—he complained that he was
deprived of the profit of engraving his own designs,
and, with even less justice, that Schiavonetti was
unfit for the task.

Some of these twelve 'Inventions' are natural and

poetic, others exhibit laborious attempts at the
terrific and the sublime.   The old Man at Death's
Door is one of the best——in the Last Day there are
fine groups and admirable single figures——the Wise
Ones of the Earth pleading before the inexorable
Throne, and the Descent of the Condemned, are
creations of a high order.   The Death of the
Strong Wicked Man is fearful and extravagant,
and the flames in which the soul departs from the
body have no warrant in the poem or in belief.
The Descent of Christ into the Grave is formal
and tame, and the hoary old Soul in the Death of
the Good Man, travelling heavenward between two
orderly Angels, required little outlay of fancy.
The frontispiece——a naked Angel descending headlong and rousing the Dead with the Sound of the
last Trumpet——alarmed the devout people of the
north, and made maids and matrons retire behind
their fans.

If the tranquillity of Blake's life was a little disturbed by the dispute about the twelve 'Inventions,' it was completely shaken by the controversy
which now arose between him and Cromeck
respecting his Canterbury Pilgrimage.   That two
artists at one and the same time should choose the
same subject for the pencil, seems scarcely credible
——especially when such subject was not of a
temporary interest.   The coincidence here was so
close, that Blake accused Stothard of obtaining
knowledge of his design through Cromeck, while

Stothard with equal warmth asserted that Blake
had commenced his picture in rivalry of himself.
Blake declared that Cromeck had actually commissioned him to paint the Pilgrimage before
Stothard thought of his ; to which Cromeck replied,
that the order had been given in a vision, for he
never gave it. Stothard, a man as little likely to
be led aside from truth by love of gain as by
visions, added to Cromeck's denial the startling
testimony that Blake visited him during the early
progress of his picture, and expressed his approbation of it in such terms, that he proposed to
introduce Blake's portrait in the procession, as a
mark of esteem. It is probable that Blake obeyed
some imaginary revelation in this matter, and
mistook it for the order of an earthly employer ;
but whether commissioned by a vision or by mortal
lips, his Canterbury Pilgrimage made its appearance in an exhibition of his principal works in the
house of his brother, in Broad Street, during the
summer of 1809.

Of original designs, this singular exhibition contained sixteen—they were announced as chiefly
' of a spiritual and political nature '—but then the
spiritual works and political feelings of Blake were
unlike those of any other man. One piece represented ' The Spiritual Form of Nelson guiding
Leviathan.' Another, ' The Spiritual Form of
Seth guiding Behemoth.' This, probably, confounded both divines and politicians ; there is no

doubt that plain men went wondering away. The
chief attraction was the Canterbury Pilgrimage,
not indeed from its excellence, but from the circumstance of its origin, which was well known about
town, and pointedly alluded to in the catalogue.
The picture is a failure. Blake was too great a
visionary for dealing with such literal wantons as
the Wife of Bath and her jolly companions. The
natural flesh and blood of Chaucer prevailed against
him. He gives grossness of body for grossness of
mind,—tries to be merry and wicked—and in
vain.

Those who missed instruction in his pictures,
found entertainment in his catalogue, a wild performance, overflowing with the oddities and dreams
of the author—which may be considered as a kind
of public declaration of his faith concerning art and
artists. His first anxiety is about his colours.
'Colouring,' says this new lecturer on the *Chiaro-
scuro*, 'does not depend on where the colours are
put, but on where the lights and darks are put, and
all depends on form or outline. Where that is
wrong the colouring never can be right, and it is
always wrong in Titian and Corregio, Rubens and
Rembrandt; till we get rid of them we shall never
equal Raphael and Albert Durer, Michael Angelo
and Julio Romano. Clearness and precision have
been my chief objects in painting these pictures—
clear colours and firm determinate lineaments, un-
broken by shadows—which ought to display and

not hide form, as in the practice of the later
schools of Italy and Flanders. The picture of the
Spiritual Form of Pitt is a proof of the power of
colours unsullied with oil or with any cloggy
vehicle. Oil has been falsely supposed to give
strength to colours, but a little consideration must
show the fallacy of this opinion. Oil will not
drink or absorb colour enough to stand the test of
any little time and of the air. Let the works of
artists since Rubens' time witness to the villainy of
those who first brought oil-painting into general
opinion and practice, since which we have never
had a picture painted that would show itself by the
side of an earlier composition. This is an awful
thing to say to oil-painters ; they may call it madness, but it is true. All the genuine old little
pictures are in fresco and not in oil.'

Having settled the true principles and proper
materials of colour, he proceeds to open up the
mystery of his own productions. Those who failed
to comprehend the pictures on looking at them, had
only to turn to the following account of the Pitt
and the Nelson. 'These two pictures,' he says,
' are compositions of a mythological cast, similar to
those Apotheoses of Persian, Hindoo, and Egyptian
antiquity, which are still preserved in rude monuments, being copies from some stupendous originals
now lost or perhaps buried to some happier age.
The artist having been taken, in vision, to the
ancient republics, monarchies, and patriarchates of

Asia, has seen those wonderful originals, called in
the sacred Scriptures the cherubim, which were
painted and sculptured on the walls of temples,
towns, cities, palaces, and erected in the highly
cultivated states of Egypt, Moab, and Edom, among
the rivers of Paradise, being originals from which
the Greeks and Hetrurians copied Hercules, Venus,
Apollo, and all the groundworks of ancient art.
They were executed in a very superior style to
those justly admired copies, being with their
accompaniments terrific and grand in the highest
degree. The artist has endeavoured to emulate the
grandeur of those seen in his vision, and to apply
it to modern times on a smaller scale. The Greek
Muses are daughters of Memory, and not of Inspiration or Imagination, and therefore not authors of
such sublime conceptions ; some of these wonderful
originals were one hundred feet in height; some
were painted as pictures, some were carved as bass-
relievos, and some as groups of statues, all containing mythological and recondite meaning. The
artist wishes it was now the fashion to make such
monuments, and then he should not doubt of
having a national commission to execute those
pictures of Nelson and Pitt on a scale suitable to
the grandeur of the nation who is the parent of his
heroes, in highly finished fresco, where the colours
would be as permanent as precious stones.'

The man who could not only write down, but
deliberately correct the printer's sheets which re-

corded, matter so utterly wild and mad, was at the same time perfectly sensible to the exquisite nature of Chaucer's delineations, and felt rightly what sort of skill his inimitable Pilgrims required at the hand of an artist. He who saw visions in Cœle-Syria and statues an hundred feet high, wrote thus concerning Chaucer: 'The characters of his pilgrims are the characters which compose all ages and nations: as one age falls another rises, different to mortal sight, but to immortals only the same: for we see the same characters repeated again and again, in animals, in vegetables, and in men; nothing new occurs in identical existence. Accident ever varies; substance can never suffer change nor decay. Of Chaucer's characters, some of the names or titles are altered by time, but the characters themselves for ever remain unaltered, and consequently they are the physiognomies of universal human life, beyond which nature never steps. Names alter—things never alter; I have known multitudes of those who would have been monks in the age of monkery, who in this deistical age are deists. As Linnæus numbered the plants, so Chaucer numbered the classes of men.'

His own notions and much of his peculiar practice in art are scattered at random over the pages of this curious production. His love of a distinct outline made him use close and clinging dresses; they are frequently very graceful—at other times they are constrained, and deform the figures which they so scantily cover. 'The great and golden rule of art (says he) is this :—that the more distinct and sharp and wiry the bounding line, the more perfect the work of art; and the less keen and sharp this external line, the greater is the evidence of weak imitative plagiarism and bungling : Protogenes and Apelles knew each other by this line. How do we distinguish the oak from the beech ; the horse from the ox, but by the bounding outline ? How do we distinguish one face or countenance from another, but by the bounding line and its infinite inflexions and movements ? Leave out this line and you leave out life itself: all is chaos again, and the line of the Almighty must be drawn out upon it before man or beast can exist.'

These abominations—concealed outline and tricks of colour—now bring on one of those visionary fits to which Blake was so liable, and he narrates with the most amusing wildness sundry revelations made to him concerning them. He informs us that certain painters were *demons*—let loose on earth to confound the 'sharp wiry outline,' and fill men's minds with fears and perturbations. He signifies that he himself was for some time a miserable instrument in the hands of Chiaro-Scuro demons, who employed him in making ' experiment pictures in oil.' 'These pictures,' says he, ' were the result of temptations and perturbations labouring to destroy imaginative power by means of that infernal machine called Chiaro-Scuro, in the hands

of Venetian and Flemish demons, who hate the
Roman and Venetian schools. They cause that
everything in art shall become a machine; they
cause that the execution shall be all blocked up
with brown shadows; they put the artist in fear
and doubt of his own original conception. The
spirit of Titian was particularly active in raising
doubts concerning the possibility of executing without a model. Rubens is a most outrageous demon,
and by infusing the remembrances of his pictures,
and style of execution, hinders all power of
individual thought. Corregio is a soft and effeminate, consequently a most cruel demon, whose
whole delight is to cause endless labour to whoever
suffers him to enter his mind.' When all this is
translated into the language of sublunary life, it
only means that Blake was haunted with the
excellences of other men's works, and, finding
himself unequal to the task of rivalling the soft and
glowing colours and singular effects of light and
shade of certain great masters, betook himself to
the study of others not less eminent, who happened
to have laid out their strength in outline.

To describe the conversations which Blake held
in prose with demons and in verse with angels
would fill volumes, and an ordinary gallery could
not contain all the heads which he drew of his
visionary visitants. That all this was real, he himself most sincerely believed; nay, so infectious
was his enthusiasm, that some acute and sensible

persons who heard him expatiate, shook their heads,
and hinted that he was an extraordinary man, and
that there might be something in the matter. One
of his brethren, an artist of some note, employed
him frequently in drawing the portraits of those
who appeared to him in visions. The most pro-
pitious time for those ' angel-visits ' was from nine
at night till five in the morning ; and so docile were
his spiritual sitters, that they appeared at the wish
of his friends.   Sometimes, however, the shape
which he desired to draw was long in appearing,
and he sat with his pencil and paper ready and
his eyes idly roaming in vacancy ; all at once the
vision came upon him, and he began to work like
one possest.

He was requested to draw the likeness of Sir
William Wallace—the eye of Blake sparkled, for
he admired heroes.   'William Wallace ! ' he exclaimed, ' I see him now—there, there, how noble
he looks—reach me my things ! '   Having drawn
for some time, with the same care of hand and
steadiness of eye, as if a living sitter had been
before him, Blake stopped suddenly, and said, ' I
cannot finish him—Edward the First has stept in
between him and me.'   ' That's lucky,' said his
friend, ' for I want the portrait of Edward too.'
Blake took another sheet of paper, and sketched
the features of Plantagenet ; upon which his
majesty politely vanished, and the artist finished
the head of Wallace.   'And pray, sir,' said a

gentleman, who heard Blake's friend tell his story
—'was Sir William Wallace an heroic-looking
man? And what sort of personage was Edward?'
The answer was: 'There they are, sir, both framed
and hanging on the wall behind you, judge for
yourself.' 'I looked (says my informant) and saw
two warlike heads of the size of common life.
That of Wallace was noble and heroic, that of
Edward stern and bloody. The first had the front
of a god, the latter the aspect of a demon.'

The friend who obliged me with these anecdotes,
on observing the interest which I took in the subject, said, 'I know much about Blake—I was his
companion for nine years. I have sat beside him
from ten at night till three in the morning, sometimes slumbering and sometimes waking, but Blake
never slept; he sat with a pencil and paper drawing portraits of those whom I most desired to see.
I will show you, sir, some of these works.' He
took out a large book filled with drawings, opened
it, and continued, 'Observe the poetic fervour of
that face—it is Pindar as he stood a conqueror in
the Olympic games. And this lovely creature is
Corinna, who conquered in poetry in the same
place. That lady is Lais, the courtesan—with the
impudence which is part of her profession, she
stept in between Blake and Corinna, and he was
obliged to paint her to get her away. There!
that is a face of a different stamp—can you con-
jecture who he is?' 'Some scoundrel, I should

think, sir.' 'There now—that is a strong proof of the accuracy of Blake—he is a scoundrel indeed! The very individual task-master whom Moses slew in Egypt. And who is this now—only imagine who this is?' 'Other than a good one, I doubt, sir.' 'You are right, it is the Devil—he resembles, and this is remarkable, two men who shall be nameless; one is a great lawyer, and the other—I wish I durst name him—is a suborner of false witnesses. This other head now?—this speaks for itself—it is the head of Herod; how like an eminent officer in the army!'

He closed the book, and taking out a small panel from a private drawer, said, 'This is the last which I shall show you; but it is the greatest curiosity of all. Only look at the splendour of the colouring and the original character of the thing!' 'I see,' said I, 'a naked figure with a strong body and a short neck—with burning eyes which long for moisture, and a face worthy of a murderer, holding a bloody cup in its clawed hands, out of which it seems eager to drink. I never saw any shape so strange, nor did I ever see any colouring so curiously splendid—a kind of glistening green and dusky gold, beautifully varnished. But what in the world is it?' 'It is a ghost, sir—the ghost of a flea—a spiritualisation of the thing!' 'He saw this in a vision then,' I said. 'I'll tell you all about it, sir. I called on him one evening, and found Blake more than usually excited. He told

me he had seen a wonderful thing—the ghost of a
flea! And did you make a drawing of him? I
inquired. No, indeed, said he, I wish I had, but I
shall, if he appears again! He looked earnestly
into a corner of the room, and then said, here he is
—reach me my things—I shall keep my eye on
him. There he comes! his eager tongue whisking
out of his mouth, a cup in his hand to hold blood
and covered with a scaly skin of gold and green ;—
as he described him so he drew him.'

These stories are scarcely credible, yet there
can be no doubt of their accuracy. Another friend,
on whose veracity I have the fullest dependence,
called one evening on Blake, and found him sitting
with a pencil and a panel, drawing a portrait with
all the seeming anxiety of a man who is conscious
that he has got a fastidious sitter; he looked and
drew, and drew and looked, yet no living soul was
visible. 'Disturb me not,' said he, in a whisper,
'I have one sitting to me.' 'Sitting to you!'
exclaimed his astonished visitor, ' where is he, and
what is he ?—I see no one.' 'But I see him, sir,'
answered Blake haughtily, 'there he is, his name
is Lot—you may read of him in the Scripture.
He is sitting for his portrait.'

Had he always thought so idly, and wrought on
such visionary matters, this memoir would have
been the story of a madman, instead of the life
of a man of genius, some of whose works are
worthy of any age or nation. Even while he was

indulging in these laughable fancies, and seeing
visions at the request of his friends, he conceived,
and drew, and engraved, one of the noblest of all
his productions—the Inventions for the Book of Job.
He accomplished this series in a small room, which
served him for kitchen, bedchamber, and study,
where he had no other companion but his faithful
Katherine, and no larger income than some seventeen or eighteen shillings a week. Of these
Inventions, as the artist loved to call them, there
are twenty-one, representing the Man of Uz sus-
taining his dignity amidst the inflictions of Satan,
the reproaches of his friends, and the insults of his
wife. It was in such things that Blake shone; the
Scripture overawed his imagination, and he was too
devout to attempt aught beyond a literal embody-
ing of the majestic scene. He goes step by step
with the narrative; always simple, and often sublime—never wandering from the subject, nor
overlaying the text with the weight of his own
exuberant fancy.

The passages, embodied, will show with what
lofty themes he presumed to grapple. 1. Thus
did Job continually. 2. The Almighty watches the
good man's household. 3. Satan receiving power
over Job. 4. The wind from the wilderness
destroying Job's children. 5. And I alone am
escaped to tell thee. 6. Satan smiting Job with
sore boils. 7. Job's friends comforting him.
8. Let the day perish wherein I was born. 9. Then

a spirit passed before my face. 10. Job laughed
to scorn by his friends. 11. With dreams upon
my bed thou scarest me—thou affrightest me
with visions. 12. I am young and ye are old,
wherefore I was afraid. 13. Then the Lord
answered Job out of the whirlwind. 14. When the
morning stars sang together, and the sons of God
shouted for joy. 15. Behold now Behemoth, which
I made with thee. 16. Thou hast fulfilled the
judgment of the wicked. 17. I have heard thee
with the hearing of my ear, but now my eye
rejoiceth in thee. 18. Also the Lord accepted Job.
19. Every one also gave him a piece of money.
20. There were not found women fairer than the
daughters of Job. 21. So the Lord blessed the
latter end of Job more than the beginning.

While employed on these remarkable productions, he was made sensible that the little approbation which the world had ever bestowed on him
was fast leaving him. The waywardness of his
fancy, and the peculiar execution of his compositions, were alike unadapted for popularity ; the
demand for his works lessened yearly from the
time that he exhibited his Canterbury Pilgrimage ;
and he could hardly procure sufficient to sustain
life, when old age was creeping upon him. Yet,
poverty-stricken as he was, his cheerfulness never
forsook him—he uttered no complaint—he con-
tracted no debt, and continued to the last manly
and independent. It is the fashion to praise genius

when it is gone to the grave—the fashion is cheap and convenient. Of the existence of Blake few men of taste could be ignorant—of his great merits multitudes knew, nor was his extreme poverty any secret. Yet he was reduced—one of the ornaments of the age—to a miserable garret and a crust of bread, and would have perished from want, had not some friends, neither wealthy nor powerful, averted this disgrace from coming upon our country. One of these gentlemen, Mr. Linnell, employed Blake to engrave his Inventions of the Book of Job; by this he earned money enough to keep him living—for the good old man still laboured with all the ardour of the days of his youth, and with skill equal to his enthusiasm. These engravings are very rare, very beautiful, and very peculiar. They are in the earlier fashion of workmanship, and bear no resemblance whatever to the polished and graceful style which now prevails. I have never seen a tinted copy, nor am I sure that tinting would accord with the extreme simplicity of the designs, and the mode in which they are handled. The Songs of Innocence, and these Inventions for Job, are the happiest of Blake's works, and ought to be in the portfolios of all who are lovers of nature and imagination.

Two extensive works, bearing the ominous names of Prophecies, one concerning America, the other Europe, next made their appearance from his pencil and graver. The first contains eighteen and the other seventeen plates, and both are plentifully seasoned with verse, without the incumbrance of rhyme. It is impossible to give a satisfactory description of these works; the frontispiece of the latter, representing the Ancient of Days, in an orb of light, stooping into chaos, to measure out the world, has been admired less for its meaning than for the grandeur of its outline. A head and a tail-piece in the other have been much noticed—one exhibits the bottom of the sea, with enormous fishes preying on a dead body—the other, the surface, with a dead body floating, on which an eagle with outstretched wings is feeding. The two angels pouring out the spotted plague upon Britain—an angel standing in the sun, attended by three furies —and several other Inventions in these wild works, exhibit wonderful strength of drawing and splendour of colouring. Of loose prints—but which were meant doubtless to form part of some extensive work—one of the most remarkable is the Great Sea Serpent; and a figure, sinking in a stormy sea at sunset—the glow of which, with the foam upon the dark waves, produces a magical effect.

After a residence of seventeen years in South Molton Street, Blake removed (not in consequence, alas! of any increase of fortune) to No. 3 Fountain Court, Strand. This was in the year 1823. Here he engraved by day and saw visions by night, and occasionally employed himself in making Inventions for Dante ; and such was his application that he designed in all one hundred and two, and engraved seven. It was publicly known that he was in a declining state of health; that old age had come upon him, and that he was in want. Several friends, and artists among the number, aided him a little, in a delicate way, by purchasing his works, of which he had many copies. He sold many of his Songs of Innocence, and also of Urizen, and he wrought incessantly upon what he counted his masterpiece, the Jerusalem, tinting and adorning it, with the hope that his favourite would find a purchaser. No one, however, was found ready to lay out twenty-five guineas on a work which no one could have any hope of comprehending, and this disappointment sank to the old man's heart.

He had now reached his seventy-first year, and the strength of nature was fast yielding. Yet he was to the last cheerful and contented. 'I glory,' he said, 'in dying, and have no grief but in leaving you, Katherine; we have lived happy, and we have lived long; we have been ever together, but we shall be divided soon. Why should I fear death? nor do I fear it. I have endeavoured to live as Christ commands, and have sought to worship God truly—in my own house, when I was not seen of men.' He grew weaker and weaker—he could no longer sit upright; and was laid in his bed, with no one to watch over him, save his wife, who, feeble and old herself, required help in such a touching duty.

The Ancient of Days was such a favourite with
Blake, that three days before his death, he sat
bolstered up in bed, and tinted it with his choicest
colours and in his happiest style. He touched
and retouched it—held it at arm's-length, and then
threw it from him, exclaiming, 'There! that will
do! I cannot mend it.' He saw his wife in tears
—she felt this was to be the last of his works—
'Stay, Kate! (cried Blake) keep just as you are—
I will draw your portrait—for you have ever been
an angel to me'—she obeyed, and the dying artist
made a fine likeness.

The very joyfulness with which this singular
man welcomed the coming of death, made his dying
moments intensely mournful. He lay chaunting
songs, and the verses and the music were both the
offspring of the moment. He lamented that he
could no longer commit those inspirations, as he
called them, to paper. 'Kate,' he said, 'I am
a changing man—I always rose and wrote down
my thoughts, whether it rained, snowed, or shone,
and you arose too and sat beside me—this can be
no longer.' He died on the 12th of August, 1828,
without any visible pain—his wife, who sat
watching him, did not perceive when he ceased
breathing.

William Blake was of low stature and slender
make, with a high pallid forehead, and eyes large,
dark, and expressive. His temper was touchy, and
when moved, he spoke with an indignant eloquence,

which commanded respect. His voice, in general, was low and musical, his manners gentle and unassuming, his conversation a singular mixture of knowledge and enthusiasm. His whole life was one of labour and privation,—he had never tasted the luxury of that independence, which comes from professional profit. This untoward fortune he endured with unshaken equanimity—offering himself, in imagination, as a martyr in the great cause of poetic art;—*pitying* some of his more fortunate brethren for their inordinate love of gain; and not doubting that whatever he might have won in gold by adopting other methods, would have been a poor compensation for the ultimate loss of fame. Under this agreeable delusion, he lived all his life—he was satisfied when his graver gained him a guinea a week—the greater the present denial, the surer the glory hereafter.

Though he was the companion of Flaxman and Fuseli, and sometimes their pupil, he never attained that professional skill, without which all genius is bestowed in vain. He was his own teacher chiefly; and self-instruction, the parent occasionally of great beauties, seldom fails to produce great deformities. He was a most splendid tinter, but no colourist, and his works were all of small dimensions, and therefore confined to the cabinet and the portfolio. His happiest flights, as well as his wildest, are thus likely to remain shut up from the world. If we look at the man through his best

and most intelligible works, we shall find that he
who could produce the Songs of Innocence and
Experience, the Gates of Paradise, and the Inventions for Job, was the possessor of very lofty
faculties, with no common skill in art, and more-
over that, both in thought and mode of treatment,
he was a decided original. But should we, shutting
our eyes to the merits of those works, determine to
weigh his worth by his Urizen, his Prophecies
of Europe and America, and his Jerusalem, our
conclusion would be very unfavourable; we would
say that, with much freedom of composition and
boldness of posture, he was unmeaning, mystical,
and extravagant, and that his original mode of
working out his conceptions was little better than
a brilliant way of animating absurdity. An
overflow of imagination is a failing uncommon in
this age, and has generally received of late little
quarter from the critical portion of mankind. Yet
imagination is the life and spirit of all great works
of genius and taste; and, indeed, without it, the
head thinks and the hand labours in vain. Ten
thousand authors and artists rise to the proper, the
graceful, and the beautiful, for ten who ascend into
'the heaven of invention.' A work—whether from
poet or painter—conceived in the fiery ecstasy of
imagination, lives through every limb; while one
elaborated out by skill and taste only will look, in
comparison, like a withered and sapless tree beside
one green and flourishing. Blake's misfortune

was that of possessing this precious gift in excess. His fancy overmastered him—until he at length confounded 'the mind's eye' with the corporeal organ, and dreamed himself out of the sympathies of actual life.

His method of colouring was a secret which he kept to himself, or confided only to his wife; he believed that it was revealed in a vision, and that he was bound in honour to conceal it from the world. 'His modes of preparing his grounds,' says Smith, in his Supplement to the Life of Nollekens, 'and laying them over his panels for painting, mixing his colours, and manner of working, were those which he considered to have been practised by the early fresco painters, whose productions still remain in many instances vividly and permanently fresh. His ground was a mixture of whiting and carpenters' glue, which he passed over several times in the coatings; his colours he ground himself, and also united with them the same sort of glue, but in a much weaker state. He would, in the course of painting a picture, pass a very thin transparent wash of glue-water over the whole of the parts he had worked upon, and then proceed with his finishing. He had many secret modes of working, both as a colourist and an engraver. His method of eating away the plain copper, and leaving the lines of his subjects and his words as stereotype, is, in my mind, perfectly original. Mrs. Blake is in possession of the secret, and she ought to receive something considerable for its communication, as I am quite certain it may be used to advantage, both to artists and literary characters in general. The affection and fortitude of this woman entitled her to much respect. She shared her husband's lot without a murmur, set her heart solely upon his fame, and soothed him in those hours of misgiving and despondency which are not unknown to the strongest intellects. She still lives to lament the loss of Blake—and *feel* it.'

Imperative 14